Imperialism
in the
Seventies

Imperialism in the Seventies

by Pierre Jalée

Translated by Raymond and Margaret Sokolov

FOREWORD BY HARRY MAGDOFF

THE THIRD PRESS

Joseph Okpaku Publishing Company, Inc.
444 Central Park West, New York, N.Y. 10025

A JOSEPH OKPAKU BOOK

Foreword

With this volume Pierre Jalée has capped his two previous books and has made, in my opinion, a major contribution to our knowledge of modern imperialism. This should come as no surprise to the readers of his earlier work in this field: *The Pillage of the Third World* (New York, Monthly Review Press, 1968) and *The Third World in World Economy* (New York, Monthly Review Press, 1969).

Most writers on imperialism can be classified as belonging to one of three types: apologists for the policies and practices of the metropolitan centers; agitators who detail the depredations of the metropolitan centers, often accompanying the bill of particulars with the cries of pain and outrage of the oppressed; and those who dig deeply to find the roots, and the modes of operation, of imperialism. Jalée clearly belongs to the last group. This does not mean that he is not as emotionally involved as the writers of the second group in his hatred of imperialism. But the task he sets himself is that of coldly examining reality. His underlying assumption is that such knowledge is necessary if the imperialist system is to be effectively destroyed and if the dependent countries enmeshed in the imperialist network are ever to attain true independence. Because of this perspective, Jalée digs into the cold facts without the usual inhibitions of the university professor.

As a rule, polite academic scholars prefer not to use the term "imperialism." They find it distasteful and unscientific. Thus, Professor Thornton of Toronto University writes, "Imperialism . . . is no word for scholars. It has been analyzed too often, given too many shades of meaning. In our time it has become a football, a war cry, a labelled card in a sociological laboratory." [1] Similarly, "exploitation" is not a nice word. One of today's leading academic specialists on colonialism, David K. Fieldhouse, Beit Lecturer in the History of the Commonwealth at Oxford University, in a paper on economic exploitation of Africa explains, "Exploitation, like imperialism, is no word for scholars because it had long been confused by ideological concepts." [2]

Scholars generally have had no trouble with emotionally-laden words—such, for example, as murder, rape, or syphilis—even when the existing mores frowned on such usage in polite society.[3] It is only a certain class of words, significantly enough, that over the years has raised the hackles of scholars. Thus, not only "imperialism" and "imperialist exploitation," but even such an important term in the socio-economic lexicon as "capitalism" is treated by academics with great circumspection.

To be sure, academics are becoming somewhat desensitized to the use of the term "capitalism." Among other things, the growth of socialist societies enforces some sort of taxonomy of social systems, although many, if not most, academics still prefer some such euphemism as "free" or "private" enterprise. However, even those bourgeois economists who bravely adopt the term "capitalism" still balk at the combination of "capitalist" and "exploitation," since their system of thought excludes the very possibility of capitalist exploitation, other than as a rare and temporary aberration.

Desensitization to the use of the word "imperialism" is also

---

1. A. P. Thornton, *The Imperial Idea and its Enemies*. London, Macmillan & Co., 1959, p. x.
2. David K. Fieldhouse, *The Economic Exploitation of Africa: Some British and French Comparisons*. Mimeographed, no date, p. 1.
3. As to social taboos, one need only recall how London's respectable mid-Victorian critics venomously attacked Ibsen's *Ghosts* because it dealt openly with venereal disease.

coming along, but at an exceptionally slow pace. On the whole, scholars as well as publicists find it easier to attach the label of imperialism to another country, not to one's own, or to a past period of history, not to the present. Thus, one may find in the United States considerable agreement that French occupation of Indo-China, and the French war against the revolutionary war of independence of the Indochinese people, should be identified as imperialism. Similarly, the Spanish-American War can today be labelled, even in polite U.S. society, as imperialism, although the nature of that war as one waged against the peoples of the Philippines, Cuba, and Puerto Rico is not as generally acknowledged. Nevertheless, the underlying continuity of U.S. imperialism—including the similarities between the U.S. attempt to reap the fruit of the final dissolution of Spain's empire in the Western Hemisphere and in the Pacific and the current attempt to fill the imperialist vacuum created by the dissolution of France's empire in Asia—is as yet barely recognized. But it is also true that the ferocity and tenacity of the U.S. war against the peoples of South Vietnam, Laos, and Cambodia is opening more and more eyes: an experience which is stimulating the more advanced and critical minds in the United States to learn more about the history and practices of imperialism, including that of the United States in the present epoch.

The major obstacle to such enlightenment is the pervasiveness of the ideological rationalization for imperialism. The extent of this pervasiveness is not easy to perceive because such rationalization is deep-seated. Its roots are intertwined with the accepted, conventional modes of thought and the consciousness of a people. Thus, they are located in the false patriotism and racism that sink deeply and imperceptibly into the individual's subconscious; in the traditions, values, and even aesthetics of the cultural environment—an environment evolved over centuries during which self-designated "superior" cultures assumed the right to penetrate and dominate "inferior" cultures. These roots are also buried in the sophisticated theorems of both liberal and conservative economics, sociology, political science, anthropology, and history. For these reasons, citizens of an imperialist country who wish to understand imperialism must first emancipate themselves from the seemingly endless web of threads that bind them emotionally and intellectually to the imperialist condition.

It is, of course, easier to identify the preconceptions of past generations than to recognize one's own blinders. For this reason it is instructive to look back at the way imperialist thinking has permeated the consciousness of even many socialists and advanced reformers. Such a retrospective view should alert us to the need for critical exploration of our own accepted doctrines. We cite here only one example from English history, though there are plenty of cases of "social imperialism" in other periods of English history and in other imperialist centers to choose from.

At the time of the Boer War an intense debate took place in Britain's Fabian Society over whether the Society should criticize Great Britain's militarism and imperialism.[4] The pro-imperialists won; and to consolidate the victory, George Bernard Shaw wrote a pamphlet called *Fabianism and the Empire*. In it that committed socialist and independent thinker, who so often dissected the hypocrisy of the existing culture with a sharp scalpel, explained:

> Great Power, consciously or unconsciously, must govern in the interests of civilization as a whole; and it is not in those interests that such mighty forces as gold-fields, and the formidable armaments that can be built upon them, should be wielded irresponsibly by small communities of frontiersmen. Theoretically they should be internationalized, not British-imperialized, but until the Federation of the World becomes an accomplished fact we must accept the most responsible Imperial Federation available as a substitute for it.[5]

By "the most responsible Imperial Federation" Shaw obviously meant Great Britain. What else would a typical Englishman

4. The background to this debate can be found in Bernard Semmel, *Imperialism and Social Reform*. London, George Allen & Unwin, 1960, pp. 66–72.
5. G. B. Shaw, *Fabianism and the Empire* (1900), as quoted in Annette T. Rubinstein, *The Great Tradition in English Literature: From Shakespeare to Shaw*. New York, Monthly Review Press, 1969, Vol. II, p. 908.

think, be he socialist, tory, or whig? But what is especially significant here is that Shaw's argument is but a variation of the dominant imperialist theme of his times and of his country: Great Britain's responsibility for empire arose from its obvious superiority in political administration; its manifest destiny was to civilize the heathens by teaching them the art of government. With the progress of formal decolonization, the manifest destiny of the imperialist centers has changed. The new manifest destiny—the manifest destiny of our times—is the responsibility to teach the heathens the art of economics, so that these poor people can also become healthy, wealthy, and wise. Accordingly, the rationalization of contemporary imperialism leans heavily on bourgeois economic theory. This is not meant to imply that the imperialist centers are aloof from the politics of the former colonial areas and current spheres of influence. Waging wars, fomenting counter-revolution, bribing officials—these and other means of direct and indirect intervention are very much part of the game. But the longer-run imperialist strategy for the Third World falls into two main categories: First, stabilization of those political arrangements which most reliably, under the given conditions, guarantee continuation of the capitalist property system. And second, control and influence over economic development with a view to assuring dependency upon, and integration with, the trade and investment network of the imperialist sector of the world.

The accepted ideas of the advanced capitalist societies provide a rich breeding ground for the ideology of this new phase of imperialism—imperialism without colonies. The equation of freedom of the individual with freedom of enterprise is a useful formula to justify the political programs of the imperialist centers. Over and above this is the implicit assumption that freedom of trade along with freedom of enterprise will inevitably foster the most advantageous path of economic development.

According to the conventional wisdom, all that is needed to get the underdeveloped countries moving is a healthy push; freedom of trade and investment will take care of the rest. Not unlike an inert mass in Newton's laws of motion, the underdeveloped countries will roll endlessly along, gaining momentum from an occasional further push, if only an initiating source of new energy is applied. Such an initial push, liberals and conservatives agree, can only come from an adequate injection of technically-advanced capital via private investment, and, if that is not enough, by public foreign aid.

Comforted by this universal dogma of the Western world, liberals and progressives with their humanitarian instincts can find themselves in substantial agreement with the programs devised in the imperialist centers for control and influence of the periphery. Liberals worry about the insufficiency of foreign aid, and they criticize the crass use of such aid to obtain special political privilege or to prop up reactionary governments. They therefore press for more and "purer" foreign aid, and they pray for honest and intelligent governments in the underprivileged nations which will use the aid to best advantage. Not unlike G. B. Shaw at the time of the Boer War, they are practical realists. Sensible enough to believe that reform must occur in the real world in which great and rich powers dominate the scene, they are thereby caught in today's imperialist ideological trap.

The more theoretically inclined of the liberals go so far as to speculate about the consistency of their policies with the true, long-term interests of the dominating monopoly corporations. They see a global harmony of interests in the rapid economic development of the underdeveloped countries. Since such economic development will presumably mean higher standards of living for the starving masses, it will also mean larger markets and higher profits for the international business community. All that remains, therefore, is for these corporations and foreign offices of the imperialist states to see the light.

Such liberals unfortunately do not understand that capitalists live in the actual present and not in the uncertain future. Of course capitalists want ever larger markets yielding ever larger profits. But these must be sought in the here and now, not in some hypothetical promised land. As a rule, corporations judge the feasibility of a foreign investment on its ability to return the initial outlay from the profits of the first three to five years.

The capitalist imperative to concentrate on the present reality at home and abroad does not stem from psychological weakness or physical shortsightedness, but from the practical necessity of operating in a world of giant rivals and under the restraint of inherent financial limitations. If history delivers to them larger markets, they will eagerly exploit their new-found opportunities. But their decisions and actions have to be decided in terms of the concrete alternatives confronting them, always keeping in mind the imperative need to protect their assets and to raise their profits to the greatest possible extent. Imperialist governments, it is true, can afford to base their practices on a somewhat longer perspective; but they too have to touch base from time to time with the practical necessities of their business community, in view of the ineluctable fact that under capitalism the economic health of the social body rests on the economic health of the large corporations.[6]

The distorted bourgeois vision of economic development possibilities in the underdeveloped nations is traceable in large part to a special kind of myopia: the inability to focus on the facts (a) that the lop-sided array of a few rich alongside many poor capitalist countries is the result of, and still influenced by, the history of colonialism and semi-colonialism; and (b) that the normal economics of free and equal trade continuously reproduces and perpetuates the international maldistribution of wealth. In short, the conscious and unconscious defenders of the imperialist world system have not yet grasped, or are simply unwilling or unable to grasp, the heart of the question, as summarized in Marx's observation, "If the freetraders cannot understand how one nation can grow rich at the expense of another, we need not wonder, since these same gentlemen also refuse to

6. To appreciate just some of the limitations in the real life of the corporate world, in contrast with the fantasies about the omnipotence and possible farsightedness of the corporation, observe the nature of the cash liquidity crisis of 1970. For this, see "The Long-run Decline in Liquidity," *Monthly Review*, September 1970. An example of the limitations of the potential far-sightedness of the imperialist state can be seen in its inflation and dollar crisis. For this, see "The End of U.S. Hegemony," *Monthly Review*, October 1971.

understand how in the same country one class can enrich itself at the expense of another." [7]

A major source of mystification about the causes of unequal income and wealth is faith in the efficacy of the market place. Left alone, markets will presumably iron out all artificial or unjustified inequities. They are the objective and impersonal regulators which achieve the most efficient allocation of resources: in the long run they make sure that every one gets what's coming to him. It follows, conversely, that everyone's "getting what's coming to him"—and the inequality of incomes implied in this formula of distribution—is the product of hard facts, of objective and necessary economic laws. (When efficiency and economic necessity enter the door, morality and social justice fly out the window.)

The reality is different. In practice the market is merely an instrument of existing institutions. And these institutions are as much, if not more, the products of politics and the way power is exercised as of economics. This becomes especially apparent when we examine the "law of markets" as it pertains to foreign trade.

The accepted doctrine here is that worked out by David Ricardo, a doctrine that is drummed into every student who takes an economics course in the United States. We are referring, of course, to what is known in the economics literature as the theory of comparative advantage. According to this theory, when the impersonal market place is the master, each country will concentrate on making those goods for which it is best suited and will buy from other countries products for which they are best suited. In this way, each country gets the maximum benefit from foreign trade.

To make his point, Ricardo used the following example: (a) Portugal and England as trading partners, and (b) wine and cloth as the items of trade. Since England produces cloth more efficiently than it could make wine, it pays for England to concentrate on the production of cloth and to exchange its cloth

7. Karl Marx, *On the Question of Free Trade,* an address delivered in 1848 and reprinted as an appendix to Marx, *The Poverty of Philosophy.* New York, International Publishers, 1969, p. 223.

surplus for foreign wine. Portugal, on the other hand, is a relatively more efficient producer of wine than cloth. Hence Portugal specializes in wine and exchanges its wine surplus for cloth. According to Ricardo's theory, Portugal ought to specialize in wine even if she were able to make cloth more efficiently than England. What is decisive is that each country should use its resources in such a way as to get the greatest possible amount of both wine and cloth. Thus, if Portugal could get more wine *and* more cloth by putting all its capital into wine and then importing cloth, the best course for Portugal's prosperity would be to concentrate on wine even if, hypothetically, Portugal could produce cloth more efficiently than England. It follows that each country is better off under the banner of free trade, for which free trade each country will make maximum use of its comparative advantages—comparative advantages arising from the quality of the soil, the skills of labor, the experience of capitalists, etc.

This comparative advantage doctrine has, as noted above, become almost universal dogma in Western culture, to the point of becoming accepted as the common sense of our times. Not only is the doctrine itself treated as absolute truth in economics textbooks, but Ricardo's very illustration is repeated over and over again.[8] The frequent recurrence of this illustration is easy to understand, since it is plausible, and the facts seem to be consistent with the theoretical model. Indeed, at the time Ricardo wrote, and perhaps up to this day, he was absolutely right: England did have a comparative advantage in making cloth and Portugal in making wine. But the rub is that he was equally wrong in thinking that this was the inevitable result of "pure" economics or that it proved the inevitable superiority of free trade.

Here, what is needed is not a knowledge of abstract economic laws but of history. And what a study of history reveals is that

8. It should be noted that in what Keynes would probably have included in his "underground of economics," some unorthodox liberal economists disturbed by the too-flagrant contradiction between facts and theory are questioning the validity of the comparative advantage doctrine as applied to the case of the underdeveloped nations.

the comparative advantages of England and Portugal had their origin not so much in *economics* as in *politics*. The comparative advantage that mattered was not rooted in soil or labor productivity, but in the superiority of British seapower and in Portugal's inability to hold on to its overseas empire without the protection of the British navy.

These remarks on Portugal and England, and what follows on this subject, are based on, and abstracted from, a recent, most illuminating and useful book by Sandro Sideri, *Trade and Power*.[9] The close ties between England and Portugal go back to the fourteenth century. In the early stages of the "friendly" relationship between the two countries, Portugal was the dominant power, due to her strong navy and the use of that navy to obtain vast and rich colonial possessions. But Portugal had a small population and was unable to stand alone against the inroads of neighboring Spain. Conquered by Spain in 1580, Portugal required sixty years to regain its independence.

The many years of foreign control and the struggle for independence greatly weakened Portugal. To maintain her independence and to keep control over her far-flung colonial empire, she needed English help—support that became increasingly meaningful as a result of the rising strength of the English fleet. England in turn could make good use of Portugese harbors in her own striving for empire and for command of the sealanes of the South Atlantic Ocean and the Mediterranean Sea. But a simple *quid pro quo* was not enough for England, given the great disparity of power between the two countries. In a series of four commercial treaties, beginning with the Treaty of 1642 and ending with the Methuen Treaty of 1703, England imposed the conditions which established and enforced the "ideal" international division of labor celebrated to this day as a prime example of the virtues of objective and independent economic laws. The terms of the several treaties increasingly fostered Portugal's economic dependence on England—a price Portugal had to pay for maintaining a colonial empire without adequate military resources.

9. S. Sideri, *Trade and Power, Informal Colonialism in Anglo-Portuguese Relations*. Rotterdam, Rotterdam University Press, 1970.

The earlier treaties (a) opened the door to English ships in Portugal and in Portugal's African and Indian territories, (b) gave special privileges to English traders in Portugal, and (c) required that Portugal buy all her ships from England. Each subsequent treaty broadened England's advantages, including the right to trade with all the Portugese colonies (except for some trade monopolies Portugal retained in Brazil), the setting of limits to duties on imported British goods, and the exclusive right to rent ships to Portugal. The privileges thus obtained by England gave it access to the profitable African slave trade and the trade with Portugal's American colonies, boosted the British shipbuilding industry, and opened up markets for British manufactures.

All this, however, was merely the setting for the definitive international division of labor imposed by the Methuen Treaty of 1703.[10] In barest outline, the background to this treaty can thus be summarized: (1) A series of economic problems in Portugal had led to the development of a protectionist policy. Since commercial treaties inhibited the raising of tariff barriers, Portugal practiced protection by forbidding its people to wear foreign cloth. In addition, she took various steps to stimulate successfully the domestic manufacture of cloth. A lucrative market for British manufacturers and merchants was thus cut off. (2) While the British people preferred the lighter French clarets to the heavier Portuguese wines, wars with France and France's own protectionist policies induced Britain to look for alternative sources of wine. (3) Gold had been discovered in Brazil, and over the years productive gold mines had been developed there.

Against this background, the provisions of the commercial Methuen Treaty were few, but they hit directly at the crux of Britain's problem: Portuguese restrictions on English woolen cloth and wool manufactures were lifted; in return, Britain lowered the duty on Portuguese wine relative to French wine. The

10. The treaty is named after John Methuen, who negotiated the treaty for England. The full text of the treaty is given in Adam Smith, *The Wealth of Nations*, Book IV, Chapter VI, "Of Treaties of Commerce." (Pages 512–3 in the 1937 New York, Modern Library edition.)

results were likewise clear and simple: Portuguese cloth manufacture was smothered in its infancy; instead of developing a
dynamic manufacturing industry, Portuguese capital flowed into
viticulture and wine-making—to such an extent that investment
in these fields replaced not only manufactures but even such
investment as was needed to expand production of corn and
other foodstuffs. As for England, the Methuen Treaty contributed
substantially to expansion of English cloth production and the
resulting larger-scale production helped reduce manufacturing
costs and thus aided in English ability to penetrate other foreign
markets.

On top of all this, the gold obtainable in Portugal's Brazilian
colony came to play a strategic role in these new trade arrangements, as well as in Britain's subsequent great economic development. Consequent to the treaty, Portugal's economy—with its
concentration on wine, and in the absence of a manufacturing
industry which would have given greater economic flexibility—
became increasingly dependent on the British economy. While
trade between the two countries flourished, Portugal's imports
of goods from England far exceeded exports to England.[11] A
large portion of the ocean trade between the two nations was
carried in English bottoms, thereby intensifying Portugal's unfavorable balance of payments. The solution: the gold mined
in Brazil was used to settle the bulk of Portugal's accounts with
England. Portugal thus became a transmission belt, actually
more like a sieve. Brazil's gold was shipped to Portugal and was
then in large measure trans-shipped to England. Thus, Christopher Hill observes, "Especially after the Methuen Treaty of
1703, Portuguese trade, and particularly the gold of Brazil, contributed to the establishment of London as the bullion market
of the world."[12] It would take us too far afield to explore the
significance of London's becoming the world's bullion market.

11. "According to the official figures, England achieved a surplus in her visible
    trade with Portugal in every year between 1700 and 1760." H. E. S. Fisher,
    The Portugal Trade, A Study of Anglo-Portugese Commerce 1700–1770.
    London, Methuen & Co., 1971, p. 19.
12. Christopher Hill, *Reformation to Industrial Revolution.* New York, Pan-
    theon Books, 1967, p. 187.

Suffice it to say, for the present, that this development was a valuable stimulus to England's evolution as world banker and foremost capitalist nation.

Those who are not economists, and perhaps some who are, may well wonder why so much space has been devoted here to the commercial treaties between Portugal and England. Our hope is that this will provide a beneficial illustration of the need to shake loose from the preconceptions of accepted "knowledge." For what is generally believed to have been natural and efficient when treated abstractly as a "pure" problem of international trade turns out to be historically created—created in the context of colonialism, war, nationalist rivalries, and military power. Moreover, this is but a mild example of the origins of the international division of labor: it occurred, after all, between two Christian, colonizing powers. This illustration barely touches upon the kind of international division of labor imposed by the practices of outright colonialism, including the changes in those countries where production ability previously had been superior to that of the colonizers. As the noted economic historian Carlo Cippola wryly comments, it was fortunate for England that India had had no Ricardo of her own:

> The story of the East India silks and calicoes that were imported into England and caused difficulty for the English textile industry is so well known that it does not need to be told here. It was fortunate for England that no Indian Ricardo arose to convince the English people that, according to the law of comparative costs, it would be advantageous for them to turn into shepherds and to import from India all the textiles that were needed. Instead, England passed a series of acts designed to prevent importation of Indian textiles and some "good results" were achieved.[13]

One of the chief hindrances to a full understanding of imperialism, and especially of imperialism without colonies, is the lack of appreciation of the extent to which international economic relations are the result of the social transformations imposed by colonialism and the whole complex history of imperial-

13. Carlo M. Cippola, *European Culture and European Expansion*, Baltimore, Penguin Books, 1970, p. 152.

ism. Such social transformations concern not only production and trade, but also the class structure, the politics, and (last but not least) the social psychology of peoples with a long history of subjugation under direct and indirect foreign rule.

The economic aspect of such social transformations is especially obscure because of what one might call, to use Marx's term, the fetishism of commodities. The dictionary defines a fetish as "a material, commonly an inanimate object regarded with awe as being the embodiment or habitation of a potent spirit, or as having magical potency because of the materials and methods used in compounding it." Conditioned as we are by living in a society operating with commodities and money prices, we endow the market with magical potency and regard the price system with equal awe. And in the process we forget, or never, realize, that markets and prices are not the ultimate controllers of our lives. To the extent that they do control our lives, it is only because we accept, and live under, our existing class structure and political system. The underlying reality is to be found in the social relations of our time, in the relations among people. It is this reality which is masked by the worship of the impersonal magical powers of the price system.

If one has the presumption to talk about, or even hint at, unequal exchange between industrially advanced and industrially backward nations, the professor of economics cries out in rage, or explains patiently: "That is a contradiction in terms. There can be no inequality of exchange, since the market adjusts all inequities. All prices must, under the force of economic laws, represent exchange between equivalents." Up to a certain point, the professor is absolutely right. For once the price system is in existence, the system cannot continue unless each price at the very least covers the cost of what is needed to produce the commodity. If the price of a given commodity does not cover these costs, the commodity cannot for very long continue to be produced. It is in this sense that prices govern the use of productive resources.

But what are costs? In the final analysis all costs are reduced to labor, mental and physical and the way labor is used. The other components of the production process—raw materials and machinery—are also the products of labor, and the way labor was used in the recent or distant past.

But where does this labor come from? How does it happen that there is a labor force available to work for wages and to shift from one job to another? What determines the cost of labor? These are far from easy questions, and we surely don't pretend to know all the answers. However, it is clear that any reliable set of answers must take into account two propositions: (1) The creation and maintenance of a labor force are far from "pure" economic phenomena. (2) There is no absolute "correct" or "equal" cost of labor, other than the rock-bottom biological minimum for keeping body and soul together. Labor as a cost in the production process varies from country to country, from region to region within country, and from occupation to occupation.

Entering into these differences are elements of force, politics, class struggle, and a long history of economic manipulation by those who hold the economic rains. Lurking behind, and incorporated into, today's wages and wage differentials is the history of slavery and semi-slavery, and the exploitation of ethnic, national, racial, and inter-regional disparities. This may not be easily discerned in the advanced capitalist nations where the creation of a wage-seeking labor force, along with its inner incongruities, evolved over centuries. But it should be more obvious as far as the areas of Western penetration are concerned, where a good deal of their capitalist history occurred in the last hundred years. Here, quite clearly, superior military power was the ultimate determining factor in obtaining the labor to dig the mines and harvest the plantation crops, as well as in creating the kind of money economy which prevails in these areas to this day. Whatever equality of exchange one may assume exists between the products of the metropoles and the periphery, one thing is obvious: it contains within it an inequality in wages that congeals a long and bitter history of force and oppression.

The costs that enter into prices are determined not only by the costs of living labor but also by the exertion of past, dead labor—the way labor was used to create harbors, canals, railroads, irrigation trenches, dams, factories, machinery, and equipment. On this score, striking disparities also obtain between, on the one hand, the kind of investments made in the imperialist centers, and, on the other hand, those made in the colonial periphery designed to serve the interests of the metropoles. The interests of the metropoles, it should be noted, included not only the means of transportation and communication needed to extract and export the resources of the periphery, but those needed to effectuate the military occupation by an alien power. Furthermore, these and other so-called external economies were created to meet the particular needs of countries whose boundaries were artificially created in the foreign offices of London, Paris, and Berlin. Notably in Africa, the setting of boundaries, and the resulting trade routes, were the product of secret trade-offs and deals by the great powers—resembling, if anything, a parlor game of Monopoly, with complete indifference to either economic efficiency or the well-being of the people of the colonies.

Prices, of course, include profits as well as the costs of past and present labor: the profits of industrialists, landowners, bankers, and merchants. Here, too, obviously, the power relations between, on the one hand, capital and labor in each country, and, on the other hand, capital in the metropole and in the periphery are of decisive significance. Thus from whichever angle we approach the cost-price relations, we find that prices and costs are themselves the products of the social system and the current as well as the congealed past power relations of that system. The technical parameters which economists study are those that at best condition the manner in which the arrived-at social system behaves. That is why, if one wants to come to grips with the essentials of capitalism and imperialism, the investigation must be able to penetrate the screen created by the fetishism of commodities and commodity exchange. In one sense, prices and wages undoubtedly do reflect exchange of equivalents. But these equivalents are the products of a specific historical process. They are far from God-given, eternal, and immutable; and by no means are they objectively necessary—except within the given historic and technological framework.

The equivalents of our time—created, as noted, by a social system and its particular history—are instruments which facilitate the efficient reproduction of the *existing* allocation of resources and of the *existing* property arrangements. In this context, prices and markets are impartial: they repeatedly reproduce the existing class structure of a society, the existing income distribution within a country, and the existing income differentials among countries. They are the impartial regulators of the attained capitalist institutions, and of the economic dependency of the periphery on the metropolis.

Tinkering with and reforming backward capitalisms will have little effect on basic social inequities, internal or external. For even honest provision of foreign aid, technical assistance, education for the elites, and peace-corps devices can—in the absence of a break-away from the imperialist network—at best only help make the imperialist system more efficient and perhaps extend its life somewhat. Reforms and "improvements" of this type cannot accomplish more, for the simple but profound reason that the historically arrived-at property, exchange, and wage system will continue relentlessly to reassert the imperialist relations of dependency. And this is why the primary task of the peoples of the Third World, as they struggle to throw off the shackles of imperialism and to achieve a humanitarian economic development, is the abolition of the capitalist system itself, with all that it implies with respect to price and wage relationships. This is an absolutely necessary condition—though in itself no guarantee of ultimate success—for entrance on the road to independence and development.

No wonder, then, that the academics have their troubles with such words as imperialism and capitalism, for it is around these concepts and the phenomena they define that the mass upheavals of our times are erupting. Bourgeois scholars naturally have difficulty facing up to either the fundamentals of revolutionary change or the processes whereby imperialism and capitalism will meet their doom. In this sense, Jalée's work, undertaken in the framework of a bold confrontation with the issues that involve the vast majority of the world people, assumes its true significance. While in his two previous volumes on the subject he concentrated on the impact of imperialism on the Third World, he now engages in an analysis of the imperialist system as a whole, taking into account the view from the metropolis as well as from the periphery. He has no illusions that he has said the last word on the subject, but he most definitely opens the door to the kind of rigorous study needed by those who wish not only to interpret the world, but also to change it.

HARRY MAGDOFF

January, 1972

Contents

Foreword *by Harry Magdoff*   v

Introduction   xxv

1. Going Back to the Sources   1
2. Imperialism and Raw Materials   17
3. Imperialism and International Trade   49
4. Capital Exports   67
5. The New Technological Revolution   96
6. Concentration of Production   106
7. The Financial and Industrial Oligarchy   121
8. Monopoly State Capitalism   136
9. Imperialism, the Third World and the Socialist World   150
10. Imperialist Contradictions and Integration. American Superimperialism   178
11. The Main Contradiction. Political Perspectives   211

Introduction

My two earlier works, *The Pillage of the Third World* and *The Third World in World Economy*, were a unified pair; the latter being essentially an extension and an elaboration of the former.

Though this volume is closely related to those books, it is also somewhat different in that it relates to them like the second panel of a diptych. Imperialism was present everywhere in my first two studies, but it was viewed, one might say, from the outside, as it manifested itself in the domination and exploitation of the Third World. Here it will be studied more or less from within, or, rather, in its totality.

I am in no way deceived about the extremely ambitious nature of such an enterprise. I would have much preferred to assemble a group of researchers, who would have been able to push the investigations and analyses farther and wider and would have been able to draw conclusions with greater certainty. That was not possible.

Should the project, therefore, have been dropped?

I think that, in all areas, daring pays so long as it is carried off reasonably and deliberately, which is not at all a paradoxical goal. It was a piece of audacity to publish *The Pillage of the Third World*. But it was amply rewarded, simply because it was a first step towards alleviating a particularly keen hunger for knowledge, notably among the students who make up the great mass of my readers.

In publishing *Imperialism in the Seventies,* I make no other claim than to bring still more preliminary relief to that hunger, but certainly not any final relief. In confronting head-on an immense and difficult subject, (which, I am really obliged to note, has forced many others to retreat who should be better armed than I to attack it) I wish, moreover, to reopen a path that has been, in my opinion, insufficiently cleared and to provoke controversies which will help Marxist analysis to progress. That is the best objective one can set for oneself.

Perfectly aware of my inadequacies, prepared for the fact that I will leave things out and make mistakes, totally rash and totally humble at the same time, I am throwing myself directly into the water without really knowing how to swim, in the hope that others will dive in too and help me reach the other bank, even if this will involve some splashing and ducking.

Must I still add that this new study, like the earlier ones, is entirely unacademic and that it basically aims to solidify political thought and political choice through economic analysis? I am convinced that the anti-imperialist struggle is more than ever a necessity of the first order, and, therefore, the deeply-rooted motivation of my work is to bring to this struggle, within the limits of my means but to their fullest limit, materials and weapons.

TERMINOLOGY

I will be employing certain expressions quite frequently, whose meaning, in my special usage, I should clarify.

The *Third World,* for me, encompasses the exploited and dominated countries (those still referred to as underdeveloped) dependent on the capitalist system, namely: Latin America, except Cuba; all of Africa; Asia, except the socialist countries on the one hand and Japan and Israel on the other; Oceania, except Australia and New Zealand.

Imperialism is the "system" which Lenin defined as the "highest stage of capitalism."

The *imperialist countries* are the industrialized capitalist countries which participate as beneficiaries in the imperialist international division of labor. They include: the United States and Canada; all of non-socialist Europe; Japan and Israel. They are thus identical with the countries that belong to OECD, with two exceptions: Turkey, a member of OECD, is excluded from the list (she is part of the Third World, in my view); whereas Israel, unaffiliated with OECD, is included among the imperialist countries.

The expression *imperialist zone* or *area* refers to all the countries, developed or not, that fall within the capitalist system, in other words, both the Third World and the imperialist countries, plus Australia and New Zealand, which are developed countries but principally exporters of simple products.

The term *monopolies* is used here, unless otherwise specified, in its current, imprecise sense, which lumps together monopolies and oligopolies.

ABBREVIATIONS

DAC   Development Assistance Committee (of OECD)
ECSC   European Coal and Steel Community
EEC   European Economic Community, the Common Market
EFTA   European Free Trade Association
GATT   General Agreement on Tariffs and Trade
GDP   Gross Domestic Product
GNP   Gross National Product
NATO   North Atlantic Treaty Organization
OECD   Organization for Economic Cooperation and Development
R and D   Research and Development
SEATO   Southeast Asia Treaty Organization
UNCTAD   United Nations Conference on Trade and Development

I

Going Back
to the Sources

FOR MOST authorities, if not all, imperialism came into being and developed at the end of the Nineteenth Century. By the early years of the Twentieth Century, it was already established as a world system. Hence it is appropriate for a Marxist study of contemporary imperialism to base itself on those fundamental works which defined imperialism a little over a half century ago as a new stage in the evolution of capitalism.

Lenin's *Imperialism, the Highest Stage of Capitalism* is generally regarded as the most authoritative of those books, but in addition it is a kind of critical summation of all that had been written on the subject. Lenin either praised or demolished his predecessors, but incorporated them all. "For this work," said P. Kerzhentsev, "he consulted hundreds of books in all languages, and made copious notes. His preparatory work and rough drafts comprised three volumes. He did not overlook a single book or article on the subject of imperialism . . ." [1]

Among the books that Lenin read, there is one that has been somewhat neglected, although it is very interesting from several points of view. Perhaps it has been neglected because Lenin himself makes only one brief allusion to it, and certainly another reason for its obscurity is that it has been overshadowed by a more outstanding work published at nearly the same time. In any event, it is interesting because it amounts to a forecast or rough outline of Lenin's book. I am referring to N. Bukharin's

Imperialism and World Economy,[2] a work which we ought to regard with feelings entirely separate from those we hold toward its author's historical role.

Lenin had not only read Bukharin's book, which was written in 1915, but he also wrote a preface to it in December of that year. "The scientific significance of N. I. Bukharin's work," he said, "consists particularly in this, that he examines the fundamental facts of world economy relating to imperialism as a whole, as a definite stage in the growth of a most highly developed form of capitalism." The fact that Lenin only mentions Bukharin once and then without any direct reference to his book seems to have only one explanation: one can only refer to something that is available to everyone; and so Bukharin's book had not yet appeared in book form before Lenin had written and published his own.

The similarity between the two books is striking: their objectives are the same and they both take some of the same approaches toward their subject. There are numerous common references, notably to Hilferding (however, Bukharin was not familiar with Hobson, whom Lenin makes use of frequently). There are the same criticisms of Kautsky, though Lenin's attack on him is sharper. Sometimes, they use the same quotations. Moreover, it is hardly a matter for doubt that Bukharin's work and his analyses were of significant assistance to Lenin. Thus it seems to me necessary to consider these two works more or less as a unit in this chapter, particularly since this chapter is meant only as an introduction. Its purpose is essential, but its scope has to be limited, and it will be more effective if it is firmly based on as small a group of basic books as possible.

Having stated how great I think Lenin's debt to Bukharin is, I can now concede that if Lenin does not entirely eclipse Bukharin, he certainly puts him in the shade. Lenin's analysis is more brilliant, more incisive and more powerful. His chapters are more rigorously interconnected, and, because of this logical structure, each individual chapter is more persuasive. And so, the theoretical and historical flashback I am about to make will essentially consist of a rapid review of Lenin's book. I shall bring in Bukharin's book only to note outstanding areas of agreement between the two or to point out Bukharin's personal contributions to the subject.[3]

Rather than simply summarize *Imperialism, the Highest Stage of Capitalism,* I would like to present an analysis which, though following the order of the chapters, will accentuate the principles and the essential features of Lenin's thought and will pass more rapidly over the sections that are mainly descriptions or proofs or that relate in minute detail certain examples that have no other purpose beyond illustrating ideas no Marxist of today would call into question.

Lenin's work seems to me to fall into two parts: while Chapters I through VI show how the constituent elements of imperialism evolved historically, Chapters VII through X are devoted to the elaboration of a synthesis and of a critique of imperialism viewed as a system and as a *fait accompli.*

Chapters I–VI

First of all, Lenin points out that "the enormous growth of industry and the remarkably rapid process of concentration of production in ever-larger enterprises represent one of the most characteristic features of capitalism." (16) He gives the United States as an example (even then!) of a country where nearly half the production is delivered by one per cent of the total number of businesses. In other words, three thousand giant companies hold sway over 268 branches of industry. And he adds, "From this it can be seen that, at a certain stage of its development, concentration itself, as it were, leads right to monopoly; for a score or so of giant enterprises can easily arrive at an agreement . . ." And he concludes, "This transformation of competition into monopoly is one of the most important—if not the most important—phenomena of modern capitalist economy." (17)

Lenin is anxious to ally himself with Marx who, in *Capital,* "by a theoretical and historical analysis of capitalism showed that free competition gives rise to the concentration of production, which, in turn, at a certain stage of development, leads to monop-

oly." (20) He argues that, "differences between capitalist countries, e.g., in the matter of protection or free trade, only give rise
to insignificant variations" in the form of monopolies or in the
date of their appearance. And he specifies once more that "the
rise of monopolies, as the result of the concentration of production, is a general and fundamental law of the present stage of
development of capitalism." (20)

For his part, Bukharin analyzed the same phenomenon in a
way strikingly similar to Lenin.[4] One finds that Bukharin even
uses the United States as his main example, not repeating but
completing Lenin.

For Lenin as well as Bukharin (though his analysis of this
point seems slighter[5]) the power and the role of monopolies can
not be understood except hand in hand with the role, which has
become pre-eminent, of the banks. Lenin studies in great detail
the consolidation of the banks and the rapidity with which it has
occurred, notably in Germany, in order to demonstrate "how the
concentration of capital and the growth of their turnover is
radically changing the significance of the banks." He shows that
the banks, when their operations "grow to enormous dimensions,"
reach the point of being able first to *ascertain* the position of
individual capitalists, then to *control* them, and finally to *determine* their fate. (35)

After observing that the replacement of the old capitalism of
competition by a new one where monopoly rule involves, among
other things, a diminution in the importance of the Stock Exchange, he stresses the idea that "the final word in the development of the banks is monopoly," and the result of that is that
"the industrial capitalist becomes more completely dependent
on the bank." (41) This means that "a very close personal union
is established between the banks and the biggest industrial and
commercial enterprises, the merging of one with another through
the acquisition of shares, through the appointment of bank directors to the Supervisory Boards (or Boards of Directors) of industrial and commercial enterprises, and *vice versa*." (41) At this
point occurs the only reference to Bukharin who, as Lenin puts
it, reveals, on the one hand, "the coalescence of bank and industrial capital" and on the other "a transformation of the banks

into institutions of a truly 'universal character.' " (44) And Lenin concludes Chapter II with these words: "Thus, the beginning of the twentieth century marks the turning point from the old capitalism to the new, from the domination of capital in general to the domination of finance capital." (46)

"This bank capital, *i.e.,* capital in money form which is thus really transformed into industrial capital, I call 'finance capital.' . . . Finance capital is capital controlled by banks and employed by industrialists." With this passage from Hilferding, also quoted by Bukharin,[6] Lenin begins his third chapter. (47)

Next Lenin undertakes to describe "how, under the general conditions of commodity production and private property, the 'domination' of capitalist monopolies inevitably becomes the domination of a financial oligarchy." (47)

As a foundation, he says, there is the "holding system" which permits the affairs of a company to be controlled by a shareholder possessing only 40% of the stock. Not only does this system infinitely increase the power of the monopolists, but it authorizes the worst kinds of "shady tricks," since the directors of the parent company are not, legally speaking, legally responsible for their officially autonomous subsidiaries.

To the profits drawn from subsidiaries active in industry and commerce, finance capital adds the enormous profits which it realizes from floating companies, from issuing stock, from state loans, etc., with everything conspiring to affirm the sovereignty of the financial oligarchies. Also, during periods of depression, when small or precarious enterprises perish, the big banks buy up their stock at cheap prices or take part in "schemes for their 'reconstruction' and 'reorganization,' " through which the power of the banks grows still greater.

Lenin remarks finally that it is characteristic of capitalism that "the ownership of capital is separated from the application of capital to production," money capital is separated from industrial capital, and the rentier who grows rich from money capital is separated from the industrialist who makes industrial capital grow. Imperialism, he says, is "that highest stage of capitalism" in which this separation "reaches vast proportions. The supremacy of finance capital over all other forms of capital means the predominance of the rentier and of the financial oligarchy; it means the crystallization of a small number of financially 'powerful' states from among all the rest." (59)

Lenin opens his crucial fourth chapter with this trenchant statement: "Under the old capitalism, when free competition prevailed, the export of *goods* was the most typical feature. Under modern capitalism, when monopolies prevail, the export of *capital* has become the typical feature." (62) Then he goes on to explain what he means and to prove it:

From the development of financial and monopolistic capitalism just outlined, there results an enormous "superabundance of capital" in the advanced countries. But because of unequal development, which is one of the laws of capitalism, because of the quest for profit maximization, this excess capital is not invested in its country of origin where agriculture is backward, but is exported by preference to backward nations where profits are high. "The necessity for exporting capital arises from the fact that in a few countries capitalism has become 'over-ripe' and (owing to the backward state of agriculture and the impoverished state of the masses) capital cannot find 'profitable' investment." (62)

Bukharin's analysis is the same.[7] He states in addition, ". . . the more developed the country, the lower is the rate of profit, the greater is the 'over-production' of capital and consequently the lower is the demand for capital and the stronger the expulsion process. Conversely, the higher the rate of profit, the lower the organic composition of capital, the greater is the demand for it and the stronger is the attraction." [8]

Supporting himself with figures, Lenin shows that the export of capital "reached formidable dimensions only in the beginning of the twentieth century." Moreover, neither Lenin nor Bukharin distinguishes very clearly between capital placements (loans) and capital investments. Lenin notes, however, that if English imperialism tends to be "colonial" French imperialism "might be termed usury capitalism." (65)

It seems that Lenin's theory about the export of capital is sometimes misunderstood to mean that the export of capital is a substitute for the export of commodities. This interpretation seems to me excessive if not erroneous. For Lenin, the export of capital is quite simply "extremely important." (89, Chap. VII) Far from seeing it as a substitute for the export of commodities, he shows that often "the export of capital abroad . . . becomes a means for encouraging the export of commodities," (66) which had been rendered more difficult since the spread of protective tariffs. If Bukharin, for his part, shows that because of heavy tariff burdens capital tends to go abroad in order to produce substitutes on the spot for certain blocked exports,[9] he also shows with the aid of examples that ". . . capital export creates favourable conditions also for the industry of its home country[10]," and not only for basic industries but for all sorts of producers.

The important thing to remember about Lenin's discussion of the export of capital is that it is the means by which "finance capital . . . spreads its net over all the countries of the world;" that "the capital exporting countries have divided the world among themselves in the figurative sense of the term." (67)

At the beginning of Chapter V, Lenin observes: "Capitalism long ago created a world market." Within the framework of this world market, things were progressing "naturally" towards an international agreement among the largest monopolist associations, "towards the formation of international cartels." (68) He bases his thesis primarily on the pact made in 1907 which divided the world between the German and American electricity trusts, whose previous development through mergers and shareholdings he had already traced. But for Lenin such agreements to divide the world are in no way final and do not exclude new divisions resulting from changes in the balance of power. The division of the world is the result of a permanent struggle. It can always be put in jeopardy by the vicissitudes of that struggle.

Another analysis, which also starts off from a concrete case, allows Lenin to demonstrate how "private monopolies and state monopolies are bound up together in the age of finance capital; how both are but separate links in the imperialist struggle . . . for the division of the world." (73) This remark played a more or less secondary part in Lenin's development, though its significance today is considerable.

Lenin ends Chapter V with an attack against Kautsky and

certain others holding the position that the development of international cartels offered a hope for peace among peoples living under capitalist regimes. But this is only a preliminary skirmish; the great offensive against Kautsky's super-imperialism is reserved for Chapters VII and IX. This opening thrust does, however, allow Lenin to emphasize the *object* of the struggle between capitalist groups. "The *forms* of the struggle may and do constantly change in accordance with varying, relatively particular, and temporary causes, but the *essence* of the struggle, its class *content, cannot* change while classes exist." He clarifies this point further: "The capitalists divide the world, not out of any particular malice, but because the degree of concentration which has been reached forces them to adopt this method in order to get profits. And they divide it in proportion to 'capital,' in proportion to 'strength.' " (75)

Alongside the economic division of the world among capitalist alliances, "certain relations are established between political alliances, between states, on the basis of the territorial division of the world, of the struggle for colonies, of the 'struggle for economic territory.' " (75)

Lenin observes in Chapter VI that by the turn of the century, the capitalist countries' colonial policy accomplished the division of the world, that is to say that in the future there could only be new divisions through which certain territories would pass from one "owner" to another. He makes a historical survey and a balance sheet of colonial conquests, on the basis of which it seems to him "beyond doubt . . . that capitalism's transition to the stage of monopoly capitalism, to finance capitalism, is *bound up* with the intensification of the struggle for the partition of the world." (77)

This is so because "these monopolies are most firmly established when *all* the sources of raw materials are controlled by the one group. . . . The more capitalism is developed, the more the need for raw materials is felt, the more bitter competition becomes, and the more feverishly the hunt for raw materials proceeds throughout the whole world, the more desperate becomes the struggle for the acquisition of colonies." (82) Noting that "present-day technical development is extremely rapid," Lenin observes that "finance capital is not only interested in the already known sources of raw materials; it is also interested in potential sources of raw materials." (83)

It should be mentioned here that if Lenin refers to iron and oil, he seems nevertheless to attach special importance to agricultural raw materials. Bukharin[11] does the same thing. I shall return to this point in Chapter II of this book.

Finally, having reached his own period, Lenin observes that "finance capital and its corresponding foreign policy, which reduces itself to the struggle of the Great Powers for the economic and political division of the world, give rise to a number of *transitional* forms of national dependence." He has in mind "a variety of forms of dependent countries; countries which, officially, are politically independent, but which are, in fact, enmeshed in the net of financial and diplomatic dependence." (85) There is the case of semi-colonies, there are other intermediary cases—Lenin refers to Argentina and Portugal—and all these cases become, during the period of capitalist imperialism "a general system" and form "part of the process of 'dividing the world.'" (86)

Chapters VII–X

"We must now try to sum up," declares Lenin at the outset of Chapter VII. (88) Then, after a quick resumé of the first six chapters, Lenin gives his famous definition of imperialism, which embraces the following five essential features:

1. The concentration of production and capital developed to such a high stage that it created monopolies which play a decisive role in economic life.
2. The merging of bank capital with industrial capital, and the creation, on the basis of this "finance capital," of a "financial oligarchy."
3. The export of capital, which has become extremely important, as distinguished from the export of commodities.
4. The formation of international capitalist monopolies which share the world among themselves.

5. The territorial division of the whole world among the greatest capitalist powers is completed.

Then Lenin recapitulates his definition and clarifies it still further:

> Imperialism is capitalism in that stage of development in which the dominance of monopolies and finance capital has established itself; in which the export of capital has acquired pronounced importance; in which the division of the world among the international trusts has begun; in which the division of all territories of the globe among the great capitalist powers has been completed . . . Imperialism, as interpreted above, undoubtedly represents a special stage in the development of capitalism. (90)

This last idea occurs again, in a very explicit form, in Bukharin.[12]

Lenin devotes the rest of Chapter VII and, indeed, the lion's share of it, to debating the definition of imperialism with Kautsky. Since this bitter controversy continues throughout the entire length of Chapter IX (entitled "The Critique of Imperialism"), I shall wait until that point to treat the matter as a whole.

In Chapter VIII, Lenin concentrates on an essential trait of imperialism which he feels is generally slighted, namely, "the parasitism of capitalism." This parasitism expresses itself in three principal forms:

a) Lenin notices two contradictory tendencies in monopoly capitalism. On the one hand, because of monopoly price-fixing, "the stimulus to technical . . . progress disappears to a certain extent." Patents are kept in drawers until their use becomes unavoidable. On the other hand, "the possibility of reducing cost of production and increasing profits by introducing technical improvements operates in the direction of change." But, he adds, "the tendency to stagnation and decay, which is the feature of monopoly, continues, and in certain branches of industry, in certain countries, for certain periods of time, it becomes predominant." (99)

b) "Imperialism is an immense accumulation of money capital in a few countries." (100) Lenin quotes figures, sometimes borrowed from other authorities, concerning Great Britain. In 1893, British capital invested abroad rose to around 15% of the wealth of the United Kingdom. The income of the rentiers was five times greater than the income from foreign trade. While the British national income doubled from 1865 to 1898, income coming from abroad increased ninefold during the same time. The result of this was an "extraordinary growth of a class, or rather a category, of *bondholders (rentiers), i.e.,* people who live by 'clipping coupons,' who take no part whatever in production, whose profession is idleness." (100) Lenin sees in this the essence of "imperialist parasitism," a characteristic not only of Great Britain, but of the other great imperialist countries which were becoming "rentier states" or usurer states. "The rentier state is a state of parasitic, decaying capitalism." (102) Lenin refers to Hobson's view, that such a situation could evolve to a point of complete degeneracy, and agrees that his hypothesis is a correct forecast, "unless the forces of imperialism are counteracted. . . . However, we must not lose sight of the forces which counteract imperialism in general, and opportunism in particular." (104)

c) Lenin quotes from Hobson again, where he maintains that the parasitical imperialist state dominates its colonies and dependencies "in order to enrich its ruling class and to bribe its lower classes into acquiescence." (102) He also quotes Engels who, as early as 1858, observed that the English proletariat was becoming more and more bourgeois, and who wrote in 1882: "There is no workers' party here, there are only Conservatives and Liberal-Radicals, and the workers merrily share the feast of England's monopoly of the colonies and the world market." (107)

Lenin also notes that in Germany, France and the United States, immigrants arrive in ever greater numbers to fill the worst paid jobs, while native-born workers become supervisors or perform the most remunerative work. "Imperialism," he writes, "has the tendency to create privileged sections even among the workers, and to detach them from the main proletarian masses." (106) And: "The imperialist ideology also penetrates the working class. There is no Chinese Wall between it and the other classes." (109)

As regards Chapter IX and the part of Chapter VII which I have held in reserve—both sections being devoted to an implacable indictment against Kautsky—I shall confine myself essentially to discussing the critique of Kautsky's theory of "super-imperialism" or "ultra-imperialism." Lenin quotes Kautsky:

> From the purely economic point of view it is not impossible that capitalism will yet go through a new phase, that of the extension of the policy of the cartels to foreign policy, the phase of ultra-imperialism,' i.e., of a super-imperialism, a union of world imperialisms and not struggles among imperialisms; a phase when wars shall cease under capitalism, a phase of 'the joint exploitation of the world by internationally combined finance capital. (93)

And later once again:

> Cannot the present imperialist policy be supplanted by a new, ultra-imperialist policy, which will introduce the common exploitation of the world by internationally united finance capital in place of the mutual rivalries of national finance capital? Such a new phase of capitalism is at any rate conceivable. (117)

For his part, Bukharin explains the Kautsky theory and summarizes it with this pointed conclusion: ". . . in this way rapacious imperialism is replaced by gentle ultra-imperialism." [13]
Lenin's critique concludes:

> Kautsky's utterly meaningless talk about ultra-imperialism encourages, among other things, that profoundly mistaken idea which only brings grist to the mill of the apologists of imperialism, viz., that the rule of finance capital lessens the unevenness and contradictions inherent in world economy, whereas in reality it increases them. (94)

Lenin develops a critique at length, the gist of which can only be given here. The essential thing for him is that under the capitalist system, it is possible to conceive of the use of force—economic, financial, military, etc.—only for the division of zones of influence, interests, colonies. As the relations of forces necessarily vary, redivisions by force are inevitable, and "inter-imperialist" or "ultra-imperialist" alliances are nothing but truces between wars.

Lenin, moreover, approves of Hilferding, who notes the correlation between imperialism and the strengthening of the oppression
of colonized or subordinate countries as nations, which leads to
"increasing resistance." "The result of these tendencies," Lenin
writes, "is reaction all along the line, whatever the political system, and an extreme intensification of existing antagonisms in
this domain also." (120–1)

Kautsky's theory, according to Lenin, is a "deception of the
masses; fundamentally opportunistic and reactionary, it is, therefore, absolutely irreconcilable with Marxism." (122)

Bukharin's critique is like Lenin's essentially.[14] It is also built
around the central idea that "the entire development of capitalism is nothing but a *process of a continuous reproduction of the
contradiction of capitalism on an ever wider scale.*" And it concludes that Kautsky's belief that trusts had become the representatives of a peaceful, expansionist policy was the worst kind of
utopian fantasy.

Lenin's tenth and last chapter justifies its title—"The Place
of Imperialism in History"—with its very first words. The single
fact that the economic essence of imperialism is the capitalism
of monopolies really is sufficient to place it in history, for monopoly, which arises out of free competition, "is the transition from
the capitalist system to a higher socio-economic order." (123)

Lenin recalls four manifestations of monopoly capitalism: 1.
Monopoly grew out of the concentration of production at a
very high degree of development. 2. Monopolies have increased
the rate at which the principal sources of raw materials have been
seized. 3. Monopoly sprang from the banks, for the union of industrial and bank capital have led to a financial oligarchy. 4.
Monopoly sprang from the colonial policy pursued to its limits.

"Monopolies, oligarchy, the striving for domination instead
of the striving for liberty, the exploitation of an increasing number of small or weak nations by an extremely small group of the
richest or most powerful nations—all these have given birth to
those distinctive characteristics of imperialism which compel us
to define it as parasitic or decaying capitalism." But, adds Lenin
immediately, and I take the liberty of putting it in italics, *"It
would be a mistake to believe that this tendency to decay pre-*

cludes the possibility of the rapid growth of capitalism." (125) However much its development may become more uneven in general, "on the whole, capitalism is growing far more rapidly than before." (125)

Lenin returns to the idea that high monopolistic profits permit capitalists "to corrupt certain sections of the working class, and for a time a fairly considerable minority," through which "is created that bond between imperialism and opportunism." (126) This analysis leads him to formulate what, from all evidence, amounts to a golden rule for him: "The most dangerous people of all in this respect are those who do not wish to understand that the fight against imperialism is a sham and humbug unless it is inseparably bound up with the fight against opportunism." (126)

The result of all this is that one must characterize imperialism "as capitalism in transition, or, more precisely, as moribund capitalism." (126) The social relations of production and private property in its monopolistic stage "constitute a shell which is no longer suitable for its contents, a shell which must inevitably begin to decay if its destruction be delayed by artificial means; a shell which may continue in a state of decay for a fairly long period (particularly if the cure of the opportunist abscess is protracted), but which will inevitably be removed." (127)

One of the principal points of the Leninist critique is that imperialism is expansionist by essence and by necessity. ("The capitalists divide the world . . . because the degree of concentration which has been reached *forces them*[16] to adopt this method.") Imperialism is thus dedicated—one could almost say condemned—to reign over the entire world, and, along the way, to conquer it, and divide it and redivide it.

But since 1917, and to a greater degree since the end of the Second World War, the imperialist world market has suffered the amputation of a part of its domain, which today represents a third of the population of the globe, because of the sudden appearance and consolidation of socialist states. Moreover, the wave of political decolonization that broke over the colonized world after the Second World War, if it has opened the way in most cases only to formal independence while leaving the imperialist system of exploitation intact, has nonetheless raised the consciousness of the peoples of what is called the Third World, and the opposition to imperialism there is infinitely more widespread and more vigorous than "the increasing resistance to the oppression of nations" which Lenin and Hilferding revealed in their day. The Third World has been shaken to its very depths. There is however no way of disregarding the fact that imperialism has not yet collapsed. Therefore, one must ask why and how this can be. And this is why it is interesting to study in what way and toward what ends its exchanges of goods, its movements of capital take place; what sources of supply its factories have for raw materials; how competition and monopolistic concentrations have evolved; in what way it tends to be organized under the direction of American super-imperialism and what rivalries result from it; what is the real impact of the new wave of scientific and technical progress; what is the nature of its relations with the socialist world and with the Third World; what possible modifications can be detected in the structures, the action, the strategy of imperialism, etc.

All these problems, which are extremely tangled up and interconnected, will be examined in the following chapters with the goal of simply stating them and clarifying them rather than, properly speaking, resolving them.

Notes to Chapter 1

1. P. Kerzhentsev, *Life of Lenin*, International (New York: 1937), p. 158.
2. International (New York: 1929).
3. In the French text, there follows a bibliographical paragraph discussing the various editions of *Imperialism, the Highest Stage of Capitalism.* I have made use, for this translation, of International's 1939 English edition, which is standard in English and easily available in paper in the Little Lenin Library.—Tr.
4. *Op. cit.*, especially pp. 65–67.
5. *Op. cit.*, pp. 71–2.
6. *Op. cit.*, p. 71.
7. *Op. cit.*, especially Chap. VII.
8. *Op. cit.*, pp. 45–46.
9. *Op. cit.*, p. 97.

10. *Op. cit.,* p. 100.
11. *Op. cit.,* pp. 20, 74, 92 especially.
12. *Op. cit.,* pp. 115 and 120 especially.
13. *Op. cit.,* p. 135.
14. *Op. cit.,* Chap. III and especially Chap. XII.
15. *Op. cit.,* p. 143.
16. My emphasis—P.J.

2

Imperialism and Raw Materials

LENIN (in Chapter VI) and Bukharin, as we have seen, have already emphasized the importance of external sources of raw materials for imperialism. The possession of these sources is one of the principal motivations, in their opinion, behind the imperialist division of the world.

But from all evidence, though they certainly do not neglect subterranean raw materials, they give pride of place to agricultural raw materials. Lenin takes note of the scarcity affecting lumber, copper and textiles. He discusses the possibility of extending the sources of raw materials in general by developing agriculture and by developing new lands, and he adds: "This also applies to prospecting for new minerals . . . ," (83) which shows clearly how he relegated minerals to a position of second-rate importance.

Bukharin's point of view follows almost exactly the same lines. For example: "International division of labour coincides here with the division of labour between . . . industry and agriculture." [1] He points out that ". . . the production of raw materials for the manufacturing industry is *in a great number of cases*[2] a by-product of the production of foodstuffs . . ." (a reference to leather, catgut, wool).[3] And elsewhere: "The increase in the economic territory opens agrarian regions to the national cartels and, consequently, markets for raw materials . . ." [4]

There is no doubt that Lenin and Bukharin perceived the

respective importance, for imperialism, of the diverse sources of raw materials with an eye conditioned by the situation which they were able to analyse more than a half century ago. But it is just as certain that, with industrial revolutions now complete in the most developed countries, the situation today has been reversed. The relative importance of agricultural raw materials for imperialism has decreased considerably, while the role of basic energy resources (oil, fissionable materials) and mineral raw materials for the processing industries (notably ores) has become startlingly crucial along with the importance of the countries of the Third World as suppliers of these materials to the imperialist countries.

This is what I shall attempt to throw some light on in the three sections of this chapter: 1. Agricultural raw materials. 2. Basic energy sources. 3. Metal-bearing ores.

A. Agricultural Raw Materials

From an economic perspective, the essential characteristic of these raw materials is that, in general (with the minor exception of rubber), they have no effect, or practically none, on the manufacture of industrial goods. For this reason their importance is limited, in this respect, to supplying the industrial sector of imperialist countries with food.

If one adds to this that none of the products derived from agricultural raw materials, which the imperialist countries obtain exclusively or largely from the countries they dominate and exploit, is not in any form at all really of vital importance (again with the exception of rubber and perhaps of fats), it is easy to see that the economic weight of such materials is, as a whole, relatively secondary. Secondary but not, however, negligible.

The Third World, which provides at least three-quarters of the logs (excepts conifers) produced in the world and which exports most of them to the developed capitalist countries, still only supplies factories of modest size and limited technological sophistication, factories that it is not possible to rank either among the leading sectors or the basic sectors of industry in the imperialist countries.

The same is true for basic animal products such as leather and skins. As for wool, its production has stagnated throughout the world for more than a dozen years. The Third World in any case is not a major producer and supplies a traditional industry whose activity has been declining before the growing competition of synthetic textiles.

Continuing on to the area of processed nutritional products, one approaches an industrial sector that produces consumer goods, among which some, like edible oils, are of great importance and originate as raw materials in the exploited countries of the Third World. These countries produce almost four-fifths of the peanuts and practically all the palm kernels harvested on this planet. And the fact that the Anglo-Dutch trust Unilever, the seventh largest company in the world, spreads its tentacles nearly everywhere in the Third World is significant here. Unilever owns plantations in Congo-Kinshasa, in Nigeria, in Cameroun, in Ghana, in Gabon, in Malaysia and in the Solomon Islands, covering a total area of 200,000 acres.[5] However, the production of palm kernels has been expanding for over a decade and that of peanuts is only progressing moderately. Still, in this sector, the industry of the imperialist countries is now, and looks as though it will remain, heavily dependent on the primary products of the Third World.

In the same area, the factories and companies of the industrialized countries that process cocoa are totally dependent on the underdeveloped countries of Latin America and especially of Africa. These countries supply the entire world production of cocoa beans, which has risen by a third over ten years. But the products derived from cocoa obviously cannot be considered of vital importance and their impact on industry is very slight.

The cotton industry of the developed capitalist countries represents a branch of activity that remains important, but which generally, and this includes the United States and Japan, has been tending toward stagnation for several years, although it is difficult to determine how much cotton and how much artificial and synthetic fiber goes into threads and fabrics that are very often mixtures of both. If world production of cotton fiber has risen about 25% for ten or twelve years, with a growing participation by the Third World, which today accounts for roughly 42% of the total, this is an exceptional instance, because the Third World itself processes 60% of the raw materials it produces. Since, moreover, American production could very easily be increased, one can say that although the cotton fiber of the Third World represents an important contribution to the factories of the imperialist countries as a whole, it does not hold them in a potential stranglehold.

The case of natural rubber, though it is also rivalled by a synthetic substitute, is quite different. In the first place, the Third World is the sole producer of rubber, and a still less than modest consumer of it. Besides, competition from synthetic rubber seems to have its limits, technological on the one hand, economic on the other. At the moment, natural rubber accounts for 38% of world consumption of the total output of natural and synthetic rubber combined, and world consumption of natural rubber grows in absolute figures quite regularly. It is therefore possible to say that, in this area, if there are no technological upheavals, the processing industry of the imperialist countries remains and will remain heavily dependent on the contributions of raw material from the Third World.

This rapid overflight is sufficient to show that, on the scale of the total industrial production of the imperialist countries, the contributions of agricultural raw materials from the Third World, although sizable and even crucial in certain areas, because they have no effect on dominant sectors capable of economic leadership, in a word, because they do not impinge on key sectors, are powerless to create bonds with imperialism that might truly bind imperialism to them. Should the Third World happen to default on its agricultural exports to the capitalist countries, this would only provoke difficulties in isolated sectors, and though these difficulties might be serious and without remedies in certain cases, they would have no repercussions in other sectors (this may not, however, apply to rubber).

B. Basic Energy Resources

Table I shows the evolution of overall energy requirements for the countries belonging to OECD, whose membership is practically a roster of the imperialist nations. It indicates what energy resources covered these needs and where they came from, between 1950 and 1980 (projected).

From this evidence it appears that there is and will be essentially no recourse to imports of coal and lignite for the entire length of the period under consideration. This is no surprise. It is well known that the Third World is very deficient in this area, while the imperialist countries remain abundantly provided for. In North America and Europe the reserves are considerable, and Japan possesses reserves capable of supplying sixty years of consumption at the current rate.[6]

TABLE I

HOW THE OECD COUNTRIES MEET THEIR ENERGY NEEDS

(expressed in millions of tons of oil equivalent)

	1950	1960	1964	1970	1980
TOTAL REQUIREMENTS	1,310	1,843	2,226	2,878	4,304
Supplied by indigenous resources—total	1,205	1,521	1,705	2,016	2,878
coal and lignite	712	676	701	715	861
oil	293	427	484	594	781
natural gas	165	355	445	598	821
hydroelectric power	35	62	70	83	114
nuclear power	—	1	5	26	301
NET IMPORTS—TOTAL	105	322	522	864	1,426
oil	99	281	432	*	*
natural gas	1	14	19	*	*
solid fuels	4	9	16	*	*

* depends in part on political decisions

SOURCE: Based on information in the table attached to: *"Problèmes et objectifs de politique énergétique,"* in *l'Observateur de l'OCDE*, no. 24, October, 1966.

But notice, however, the very rapidly decreasing role played by coal and lignite in fulfilling total energy needs. Although, together, they satisfied 55% of these needs in 1950, the rate fell to 32% in 1964 and should decline to about 20% in 1980.

Henceforth, I shall eliminate from consideration the case of hydroelectric power, which obviously can only be included among local resources, and which, after all, contributes only a small amount to total energy requirements (less than 3% in 1950 as well as in the projections for 1980).

Natural gas, which covered only 13% of total energy needs in 1950, rose to a little more than 20% in 1964. The projected percentage for 1980 cannot be calculated on the basis of Table I, since the quantities of gas to be imported are not given. But there is good reason to believe that they may be relatively modest: local resources of the OECD countries, as now estimated, represent by themselves 19% of the energy needs for 1980; North America, which today produces three-quarters of the world's gas, has reserves for at least twenty years at the current rate of use, Europe's reserves are equally large, but Japan's are quite small.[7] On the other hand, the imports which the OECD countries will use may not necessarily come from the Third World, and, in any case, whatever is exported from the Third World to the OECD countries will probably assume only a relatively marginal importance.

Therefore, the problem of imperialist dependence on the exploited countries of the Third World for energy resources does not seem to me significant except as regards oil. It also makes sense to look ahead for trouble over fissionable materials, which are the source of nuclear energy.

OIL

Table I shows us that net imports of oil by the OECD countries in 1964 surpassed their 1950 level by a factor of 4.3, while internal production for the same period advanced by a factor of only 1.65. This growing dependence on imports should continue, since internal production, as projected for 1980, will be 1.6 times the figure for 1964, while the need to import energy from all sources combined will be multiplied during the same period by 2.73. And without any doubt, oil will make up the lion's share of the increase. OECD estimates elsewhere in the same publication[8] that total imports will reach 1,173 million tons of oil in 1980. This tonnage will represent 27.3% of total energy needs, as against 19% in 1964 and 7.6% in 1950.

By country, or groups of countries, the outlook for imports is as follows: imports for 1964 reached:

115 million tons for North America
329 " " " Europe
68 " " " Japan

For a total of 512 million tons.[9]
This originated in:

the Middle East —269 million tons
the Caribbean —133 " "
Africa — 70 " "
the Far East — 14 " "
Socialist Countries 26 " "

In North America it is likely that oil imports will barely exceed its current proportion of total consumption in the future, namely one-fifth. By this hypothesis, imports should rise to 145 million tons in 1970, and to 185 in 1980.

In Europe, projected imports of crude oil are estimated at 370 tons in 1970 and 368 in 1980.

The character of these figures from OECD is somewhat tentative and it seems prudent to treat them merely as guidelines; nevertheless they do prophesy clearly that by 1980 dependence on imports, measured in reference to internal production, will hold steady for North America and increase for Europe and Japan.

We have seen in the discussion above, moreover, that 95% of the imports to the imperialist countries in 1964 came from the nations of the Third World and only 5% from the socialist countries (of Europe). It is possible to wonder if this relationship is susceptible to modification in the future. The distribution of proved world reserves as of January 1, 1967, is, on a percentage basis, as follows:[10]

United States	10.2
Canada	2.3
the Caribbean	5
Western Europe	0.8
Middle East	59.9
Africa	8.3
Socialist Countries	8.6
Others	4.9

It is worth noting, first of all, that the precentage of reserves in the United States and Canada (12.5%) is very much below their percentage of world production in 1966 (28%), which limits the force of the argument according to which the United States is holding in reserve unexploited deposits representing a high supplementary potential. The figures also show that the same is true for the socialist countries (reserves—8.6%, 1966 production—18.2% of the world total). If the Caribbean reserves appear equally modest in relative value, by contrast those of the Middle East are formidable, and all specialists agree in thinking the African reserves identified to date are only a foretaste of those that will be located in the future.

Even taking into account the imprecision of some of these figures (for example, the figure for the socialist countries as one entity) and the uncertainties of the future, it is still an inescapable fact that the position of the Third World, with nearly three-quarters of world reserves known today, is and will remain extremely special. It is difficult, therefore, not only to doubt the results of the work of OECD experts, but even to consider their conclusions as anything but a minimum hypothesis about the future dependence of the imperialist countries on oil exported by the Third World. In 1980, these exports should reach three to four times their 1964 tonnage and should fulfill 27 to 30% of the energy needs of all kinds in the imperialist countries, as against less than 20% in 1964. That amounts to dependence on a major scale, in a sector which is crucial for industry, without even mentioning the importance of oil as a raw material for petrochemistry.

The desperate efforts expended by the oil trusts as they rush headlong after prospecting concessions and scramble to control the exploitation and marketing of oil throughout the entire expanse of the imperialist system, should remove any doubts that linger on that score.

Without going into details that fill an abundant literature, let us recall simply that from the time of the Achna-carry Agreement (1928) between the big three companies of the era until around 1960—for thirty years—the international oil cartel made up of seven big companies (Standard Oil of New Jersey, Royal Dutch-Shell, British Petroleum, Gulf, Texas, Standard Oil of California, Socony-Mobil Oil) has reigned as lord and master over the world oil market through a variety of devices, not the least of which was the institution of a "world price" completely unrelated to the costs of production but which, besides guaranteeing huge profits, also allowed the cartel to finance 'reproduction', namely exploration and new drilling expeditions. As if it held a mandate from the imperialist system over the royal domain of oil, the cartel has been able, thanks to political support in its countries of origin and thanks to the weakness of the countries with the reserves, to make oil exploration and extraction, as well as its transportation and sale in all regions, conform to the interests of imperialism by playing a game of more or less official agreements of all kinds among its constituent companies. As for the "concessions," "conventions," or "treaties" imposed on the producing countries, notably on those of the Middle East, Nicolas Sarkis states that they "are the spit and image of colonial charters, instead of freely negotiated contracts," [11] while Daniel Durand says they have the effect of creating "veritable states within states." [12]

According to S. W. Landry, however, "the ideal market exists today only as a cracked façade that offers poor concealment for a reality of several foreign markets, each subject to the pressures of commercial rivalries and short term national antagonisms." [13] In the view of N. Sarkis as well, "for many reasons the role of the international companies as arbiters and intermediaries has been under attack for several years, by the Arab nations producing hydrocarbons and by the European consumers of hydrocarbons." [14] S. W. Landry emphasizes the part played by internal rivalries within the developed capitalist countries, "national oil policies," and the growth of "ever more vast participation by governments," while the companies known as "independents" (essentially American) "profit from the confusion by going after a piece of the market." He also conjectures that this current phase of history could produce an "atomization of the market," "which would reflect the sharp politico-economic contradictions among producers, among consumers and between both these categories."

Nicolas Sarkis sheds further light on the exploitation of the producing countries, in this case the Arab countries. On the one hand, the arrangement known as "profit-sharing on an equal basis," gives the corporations with concessions a rate of return that varies between 61 and 114% depending on the country, while in Western Europe this rate does not surpass 7.2%. On the other hand, he points out how all activities resulting from oil are centered abroad, since foreign companies rarely do their refining on the spot and petrochemical installations are non-existent. He also notes the desire of the Arab countries to "decolonize" their oil so that it can play the fundamental role which rightfully belongs to it in their own economic development. He recalls the Arab oil conferences, the creation of the Organization of Petroleum Exporting Countries (OPEC), the rapid development of national companies in the producing countries, all manifestations that "give testimony of the legitimate wish of the Arab countries to liquidate the after-effects of their colonial past." [15]

That this wish runs up against fierce hostility from the oil companies is demonstrated by the recent difficulties in Iran, which illustrate how imperialism intends to continue its domination of the Third World. I shall return to this in Chapter IX.

But one point in Nicolas Sarkis' article still seems to me to claim our attention.

After estimating, as we have seen, the enormous size of the profits realized by foreign companies in the Middle East, N. Sarkis notes that only 1.3% of these profits have been assigned to exploration in the countries of the Middle East. This amounts to 3.3% of the funds invested in oil exploration throughout the world (socialist countries excepted). During the same period, the expenditures for oil exploration in North America and Western Europe represented 80.6% of the world total. Of course, and rightly so, N. Sarkis sees in this "one of the most striking aspects of the mechanisms for transferring income from the poor countries to the rich countries. But one can also wonder why the imperialist countries are neglecting oil exploration in the Middle East today and intensifying it in their own territories. It is possible, certainly, to argue that with known Middle Eastern reserves making up 60% of today's world reserves, or some 70 years of production at the current rate, exploration in the Middle East could usefully pause for a bit, while exploratory energies were applied to the investigation of countries where only meager resources have so far been discovered. But if imperialism devotes 80.6% of the money it spends on research to North America and Western Europe alone (and 3.3% to the Middle East), very little remains (16%) for Latin America, Africa, and South and East Asia, whose known reserves equal altogether only 18% of the world total. Can't one argue also that imperialism is conscious of its dramatic dependence on the Third World in such a vital area and that, faced with more and more vigorous opposition not only in the Middle East but throughout the Third World, it is undertaking considerable efforts at home in the hope of discovering under its own roof that essential ingredient for industrial expansion which would protect it from all hazards? (The recent, large discoveries at Prudhoe Bay and on the Arctic archipelago cannot yet be seriously estimated, and the technical and financial problems of extraction and transportation are not resolved.)

URANIUM AND THORIUM

Table I shows us that in 1980 nuclear energy should fill only 7% of the energy needs of the OECD countries. But according to a report presented by M. Louis Saulgeot in the name of the Energy Committee of OECD and approved by the governments of the member countries,[16] the share of nuclear power plants in the production of electricity in Western Europe alone will go from 5.8% in 1970 to 30% in 1980 and to 41% in 1985. European energy production in 1980, estimated at the equivalent of 145 million tons of oil, would then be virtually equal to that of North America, in other words, 290 million tons for the two regions. My Table I, which gives as the total figure for the OECD countries' production of nuclear energy the equivalent of 301 million tons of oil, leaves Japan what seems too modest a share by comparison with the Saulgeot report, especially if recent indications are taken into account. By forcing these data a little, it is possible to estimate that, optimistically, nuclear energy in 1980 could cover up to 10% of the total needs, which is still relatively minimal and reduces the problem of the origin of basic nuclear materials to its true dimensions.

There is, moreover, very great uncertainty as to what the world's resources of fissionable materials will be in 1980. According to a third OECD document,[17] from which we have excerpted the figures for Table II, information is still unavailable "for countries whose territories are supposed to contain large uranium reserves." The estimates reproduced, therefore, must not be considered to be any more than a simple attempt to cast some light on an important new phase in uranium prospecting.

Since nuclear energy for peaceful purposes is in competition with energy produced from other sources, the resources and reserves have been classified according to their net cost. Only the lower scale seems to be worth taking into consideration for the moment, and, besides, the estimates for it have been made with greater precision. It would doubtless be hazardous, on the basis of such data, to attempt to judge how dependent all the imperialist countries are on the Third World for nuclear materials. I will limit myself to two indications:

1. France, though she has resources of her own, needs those of Gabon, of Niger and of the Central African Republic to cover all of her requirements.[18] For this reason, she created the SOMAIR company, at the beginning of 1968, to exploit the uranium mines of Niger. SOMAIR is controlled by the Atomic Energy Commissariat (40%), the Republic of Niger (20%), Mokta (20%), and the Compagnie Française des Mines d'Uranium (20%). Production capacity will reach 1000 tons per year starting in 1973.[19] Africa will then furnish France with a total of about 2000 tons of uranium, in addition to the 1200 tons produced domestically under a program purposely held back in order to preserve reserves. As a writer at *l'Express*

put it: "African production therefore insures relative autonomy for France." [20]

2. In 1966, the Common Market countries, all in short supply except for France, imported 5,637 tons of uranium extracts

TABLE II

ESTIMATE OF URANIUM RESOURCES
(based on data from October, 1967)

(expressed in units equal to 10,000 short tons of uraninite[1])

Price per Pound	Less than $10		$10 to $30	
COUNTRY	ASSURED RESOURCES	ESTIMATED SUPPL. RESERVES	ASSURED RESOURCES	ESTIMATED SUPPL. RESOURCES
Australia	11	3	4	1
Canada	200	290	230	470
Spain	11	—	19	280
United States	300	350	350	640
France	45	20	5	10
Portugal	10	7	—	22
Sweden	—	—	500	250
Other Imperialist Countries	1	—	39	—
TOTAL	578	670	1,147	1,673
South Africa	205	15	120	105
Argentina	9	21	26	105
Congo-Kinshasa	6	—	—	—
Gabon	4	4	—	—
India	—	—	27	62
Morocco	6	—	19	—
Niger	12	13	13	—
Angola	—	—	—	15
TOTAL	242	53	205	287
Others	5	20	6	—
GENERAL TOTAL	825	743	1,358	1,960

SOURCE: Uranium Resources—Revised Estimates, Dec. 1967, OECD, Table I.

[1] One short ton of uraninite = 1694 lb. of uranium metal.

altogether, of which 2,730 or 48% came from the Third World.

Thus, the least one can say is that partial dependence exists today, while the countries of the Third World as a whole have been much less explored by prospectors than the imperialist countries.

In conclusion, I shall speak only briefly, just in order not to omit the subject, about the extraction of uranium from sea water. The cost of extraction far exceeds feasible limits, and this is true too for thorium, for which assured resources of more than a half million short tons of uranium oxide exist. But at this time there is practically no commercial outlet for it as a nuclear combustible, and its future is uncertain.[21]

C. Metal-Bearing Ores

Altogether, according to the various authors who have expressed themselves on this point, the industrialized capitalist countries have seen their reserves of metal-bearing ores exhaust themselves more or less rapidly for a certain number of years, or else they have been left only with low-grade deposits or deposits that were difficult to extract. This has considerably raised net costs. As a result, the imperialist countries have increasingly turned to the abundant, rich and cheap ores of foreign countries and most especially of the countries of the Third World.

This situation is not, however, entirely universal, and the imperialist countries continue to enjoy a more or less privileged situation in regard to a small number of ores. These are, basically, nickel, molybdenum, and, to a lesser degree, vanadium, lead, and zinc. (I shall not discuss gold and silver, whose use is not predominantly industrial.)

The extraction of nickel within the imperialist world occurs almost exclusively in two countries, Canada and New Caledonia. In 1967, Canada produced 245,000 tons of pure metal,[22] while New Caledonia achieved a total of only 70,000 tons. But the reserves of the Third World (half of which are in Indonesia and the Philippines) equal 70% of the verified total in the imperialist world. The reserves of the socialist world are important, notably in Cuba. World demand is growing vigorously. The American-

Canadian combine, the International Nickel Corporation of Canada (INCO), controls almost all of Canadian production and has a 40% interest in a big new New Caledonian company (COFIMPAC).

The United States dominates the production of molybdenum ore in the imperialist world by a wide margin: 28,000 tons out of 30,000 in 1957, and 35,000 out of 45,000 in 1965. During this period, Canada's production went from 500 tons to 4,000, while Chile's rose from 1,300 to 3,700 tons.

The production of vanadium in the imperialist world more than doubled between 1957 and 1965, and the United States is still the preponderant producer, with five-sixths of the total in 1957, but only 57% in 1965, due especially to the great strides made in South Africa and South West Africa as well as in Finland.

While the production of these three ores is concentrated within a very small number of countries, the case of lead and zinc is quite different, for their extraction is much more widespread. World production of lead has advanced very moderately for a dozen years now, while the growth of zinc production has been much more rapid (up 53% between 1955 and 1966). In 1965, 71% of the lead tonnage mined in the imperialist world came from the industrialized countries and 29% from the Third World (as against 62% and 38% respectively in 1957). For zinc, the proportions are as follows:

	1957	1965
Imperialist Countries	70%	72%
Third World Countries	30%	28%

Now we shall examine in much greater depth the case of various metal-bearing ores for which the dependence of the imperialist countries on the Third World is either complete, or very great, or very rapidly growing. This includes iron and ores used in steel production (manganese, chromium, cobalt), aluminum, copper, and tin.

IRON

OECD itself sets the tone of this discussion: "World availability of iron ore, both at present and, it would seem, for many years to come, is ample to ensure the iron and steel industry's supply position with regard to high grade ores. The fall which is to be observed in the production of comparatively low grade ores in some Member countries is in fact caused by the large tonnages of higher-grade ores available at very competitive delivered prices." [23]

As confirmation of this point, here are the average percentages of iron in ore from various countries: United States 50%, Canada 55%, Japan 55%, Germany, Austria and Luxembourg 30%, France 35%, Spain 50%, Sweden 60%, Norway 65%, United Kingdom 30%, Sierra Leone 60%, Angola 63%, Gabon 64%, Mauritania 65%, South Africa 60–65%, Brazil and Venezuela 65%, Chile 60%, India 65%.[24] It is obvious, then, that North American and Japanese ore is medium grade, while in Europe, high grade Scandinavian ore contrasts with the low grade ore of the ECSC countries and the United Kingdom. As for Third World ore, it is of a remarkably high grade everywhere.

It is not surprising, therefore, to encounter the following outline of the evolution of the production of marketable iron ore in the OECD countries, by grade, during a brief period, for statistics only go back as far as 1963:[25]

		(in thousands of tons)				
		1963			*1966*	
	more than 58%	*42– 58%*	*less than 42%*	*more than 58%*	*42– 58%*	*less than 42%*
ECSC	33	4,392	71,062	50	3,650	66,025
Other OECD members in Europe	23,725	8,371	18,952	28,400	9,105	17,175
Canada	15,545	11,962	833	26,735	9,595	1,150
United States	74,012	—	—	—	91,595	—
Japan	2,358	—	24	2,375	—	—
TOTALS	115,673	24,725	90,871	57,560	113,945	84,350
		231,000 tons			256,000 tons	

These figures show a slight decline in the extraction of low grade ore, a moderate decline for high grade ore and a considerable increase for medium grade, which is mostly due to a basic shift in the United States from the mining of high grade ore to medium grade. In the aggregate, in gross tonnage of all grades, production between 1963 and 1966 moved ahead by 10.8%.

But at the same time and in the same group of countries, the production of cast iron and iron alloys increased by 25.6% and the production of unfinished steel by 23.3%. As the consumption of scrap iron by blast furnaces and steelworks increased only by 16%, it is quite natural to discover that the OECD countries heavily increased their use of iron ore imported from abroad in gross tonnage of all grades (same source as previously):

	(in thousands of tons)	
	1963 Net Imports	*1966* Net Imports
ECSC	18,000	30,975
Other OECD members in Europe	5,057	8,185
Canada	+ 1,657	440
United States	12,969	22,525
Japan	22,367	40,555
TOTALS	56,736	102,680

The increase of net imports between 1963 and 1966 amounted to a rise of 81%, which indicates the rapidity of the growth of the dependence of the OECD countries, as a group, on the countries of the Third World, also as a group, since the imports originating in other countries are slight (socialist countries: 2% of the total in 1966).

In gross tonnage for 1966, ore imported from the Third World represented 28% of the total ore produced in the OECD countries or imported by them. But since medium grade ore makes up an infinitely greater part of the imported ore than it does of the domestically produced ore, the proportion of the Third

World's contribution to the total, expressed in terms of iron content, is on the order of 33–34%. And there is no doubt that it can only continue to increase, despite the start of production in Australia equal to 3.5% of the world total in 1967 (of which 40% was used domestically).

The case of France, which alone mines four-fifths of the ECSC iron ore, is typical. Her mining activity has been diminishing for several years and it has been necessary to dismiss thousands of workers. Between 1959 and 1966, French imports have multiplied almost eightfold. In 1966, nine-tenths of them originated in the Third World (in order of prominence: Mauritania, Liberia, Brazil, Peru . . .) and 9% came from Sweden.

A report presented to the high authorities of ECSC in November, 1967, viewed without enthusiasm the prospects for European iron mine production. The steel industry would have to continue to supply itself more and more with rich ore imported at low prices from other countries.[26] The preceding table shows, moreover, that extra-OECD imports are actively increasing in the United States and Japan.

The problem of iron does not seem to be a problem of reserves. As far as one can judge in an area where evaluations are risky, if countries such as Japan and to a lesser degree the United Kingdom appear very poor, or poor, the United States, Scandinavia, and France possess large reserves, while African reserves are estimated to be of considerable size. But if these African reserves consist of very rich ore, the same is not true of the reserves of the imperialist countries, with the exception of the Scandinavian countries. The real problem, at the present moment at least, is a problem of costs versus yields. In a world where competition has not ceased to be the order of the day, the imperialist countries' need for the high-quality ore of the Third World—even when they have their own low or medium grade reserves—seems like an unavoidable and probably increasing necessity.

MANGANESE

Manganese is indispensable for the modern steel industry, which uses it in creating special steels. Since the Second World

War, in fact, its use has expanded more than that of any other metal except aluminum. World ore production, in thousands of tons, grew from 1780 in 1946, to 4700 in 1955, to 7700 in 1965.

The race for manganese, which is practically non-existent in the imperialist countries, has occasionally taken some spectacular turns. The rich Imini deposit in Morocco was exploited at a feverish pace during the years after the war. But because the ore was located beyond the Atlas Mountains, it was necessary to assemble a whole fleet of special trucks (Canadian Macks) which were deployed in veritable caravans to bring it across a 6600-foot pass. Then a cable conveyor system took over from the trucks. The transport costs, for the trip from the mine to Casablanca (250 miles), amounted to the equivalent of 19 dollars per ton (several times the cost of extraction), against a little more than three dollars for ore shipped from Bou-Arfa to Nemours (230 miles). But the Bou-Arfa ore contained only 25% metal, while the ore from Imini contained 56%.[27] From his vantage point, Raymond Furon tells the story of the Moanda mine in Gabon and concludes: "The history of manganese is a very good illustration of the big countries' desire for economic independence, for a 'strategic' independence. This desire is capable of driving them to the worst kinds of extremes." [28]

It is a fact that in 1965 world production (7.4 million tons) was divided almost exactly between the socialist countries (3.825 million tons, of which 3.4 were produced by the USSR) and the countries of the Third World (3.65 million tons). The imperialist countries only produced 230,000 tons (3% of world production).

Japan is the only imperialist country that produces a noteworthy amount: 104,000 tons. But production is stagnant and even a bit down compared with the peak of 120–124 thousand tons achieved in 1959–60. France, the leading producer in the world in 1885, no longer figures in the statistics. The ECSC countries all together have only an insignificant production (about 15,000 tons, almost exclusively Italian) and are therefore dependent on imports for virtually their entire supply. Indeed, their importation of manganese, in gross tonnage, rose from 1,380,000 tons in 1960 to 1,810,000 tons in 1966. Great Britain has no production and the United States itself, year in and year out, only extracts 47,000 tons of ore from its own soil. This amounts to 5% of U.S. requirements, so that, in 1960, 2,160,000 tons of manganese were imported and in 1966, 2,541,000 tons (gross tonnage).

The dependence of the imperialist countries on imports is therefore practically total as far as manganese is concerned. And the reason has nothing to do with economic conditions that work against these countries, but with the simple physical absence of ore. "This strategic ore," writes Raymond Furon, "has been actively sought after by the Bureau of Mines throughout the entire area of the United States, but without result. The USSR did not refuse to supply the USA, but this situation bothered the United States very much." [29]

It must, in fact, be noted that in the area of manganese the imperialist countries do not depend solely on the Third World —though the Third World remains by far predominant in this field—but also on the Soviet Union and some other socialist countries, which send small amounts of ore or metal to the European countries and Japan.

CHROMIUM

Production within the imperialist world has almost stagnated for the last dozen years at around 1200–1300 thousand tons. Its geographic spread is very much like that of manganese. With 30 or 35,000 tons produced annually (divided almost equally between Greece and Japan), the developed capitalist countries barely give evidence of any production at all, and even that is decreasing. Extraction in the Third World reached 1,260,000 tons in 1965. The principal producers are, in descending order, South Africa, Rhodesia, Turkey, the Philippines, and India. But to these 1200–1300 thousand tons should be added (still for 1965) 1,840,000 tons from the socialist countries (of which 1,420,000 were mined in the USSR and 350,000 in Albania). The imperialist countries are therefore all dependent on imports, with the exception of Japan, which is only partially dependent. But while ECSC imports decreased from 467,000 tons to 381,000 between 1960 and 1966, those of the United States rose during the same period from 496,000 to 604,000 tons (in gross tonnage). In this case too, the socialist countries and especially the USSR sell a certain amount to the imperialist countries, but the contributions of the Third World remain, nevertheless, overwhelmingly predominant.

As with manganese, the reason for the total dependence of the imperialist countries is the physical lack of resources. "The United States," wrote R. Fouet and C. Pomerol, "which has poor resources within its own national boundaries (Montana), promotes the extraction of chromite in the Philippines." [30] But since those words were written, poverty has apparently turned into total destitution, since any mention of U.S. production has been omitted from the statistics since 1962.

COBALT

World production (socialist countries excluded) has been hovering for a dozen years around 15,000 tons. There is also production in the socialist countries (USSR, Cuba, China, Bulgaria, Poland, East Germany, North Korea), which is untabulated but does not seem comparable in importance to their production of manganese and chromium. Moreover, I have been unable to discover any record of a sale of cobalt to the imperialist countries by these countries, and the discussion in this case seems to limit itself to the relations of the imperialist countries and the Third World.

The two big imperialist producers are Canada (1725 tons in 1965 and rising) and Finland (1500 tons and falling). As a whole, extraction in the imperialist countries seems to have reached a maximum of 3500 tons in 1965. In the Third World it came to 11,750 (8400 in Congo-Kinshasa, 1800 in Morocco, and 1550 in Zambia). The industrialized countries' share was thus 23% of the total extracted in the imperialist zone in 1965. But it was 35% in 1958 when the United States produced 2200 tons. This figure fell to 1360 the following year and to zero from then on.

While it is not total in this case, the dependence of the imperialist countries on the Third World is, however, considerable and growing. Despite the absence of definite data on the subject, it appears very likely that this dependence is based on a relative lack of physical resources.

ALUMINUM

World production of bauxite has been extraordinary; it doubled between 1956 and 1966. Thanks to its diverse qualities, its various uses and its comparatively low price, aluminum has rapidly become one of modern industry's most important metals, second only to iron.

The Third World accounted for 23,650,000 tons of bauxite in 1966, or 59% of world production (Jamaica 9,150,000, Surinam 4,850,000, Guyana 3,350,000, Guinea 1,650,000, Malaysia 1,100,000 . . .). The remainder was split almost equally between the socialist countries (8,450,000, of which the USSR produced 4,700,000) and the imperialist countries 8,100,000, or 20%, of which France produced 2,800,000, the United States and Australia 1,820,000 each, Greece 1,350,000).

But the imperialist countries as a group combined to produce 72% of the world's primary aluminum in 1966, which makes it obvious that their dependence on other countries for bauxite is substantial. The following table simultaneously illustrates the degree of this dependence and gives an exact idea of its development between 1956 and 1966. In order to make the table clearer, the figures for bauxite have been converted into metal content, using the most favorable yield ratio—25%—throughout:

(thousands of metric tons)

PRODUCTION OF

	Bauxite with 25% Metal Content		Primary Aluminum	
	1956	*1965*	*1956*	*1965*
Common Market	437	725	361	703
United States	525	505	1,523	2,499
Canada	—	—	563	762
United Kingdom	—	—	28	36
Sweden	—	—	12	30
Norway	—	—	93	276
Japan	—	—	66	294
TOTALS	962	1,230	2,646	4,600

SOURCES: Figures taken from the United Nations Statistical Annual, 1965 and 1966.

From these figures it is possible to calculate that the overall quantity of aluminum produced in 1956 was equal to the total metal content in the bauxite multiplied by 2.75, while in 1965 this coefficient increased to 3.74. That year, the countries in the table depended on foreign sources for 73% of their total aluminum production. But the situation varied considerably among the individual countries.

There is no problem interpreting the data for Canada, the United Kingdom, Sweden, Norway, and Japan, which have no bauxite resources at all. The production of bauxite in the Common Market is limited to France (90%) and Italy (10%). And it is clear that although the Common Market mined more bauxite in 1956 than it needed for aluminum production, by 1965 the gap had virtually closed, leaving only a thin margin of surplus bauxite. Italian bauxite production has declined for the past few years, and French production, which is growing, is still not growing fast enough to keep up with the aluminum needs of the Common Market.

As for U.S. bauxite production, it has been extremely stagnant for a dozen years, while metal production went up 64% between 1956 and 1965.

No data exists on the state of French bauxite reserves. As for U.S. reserves, R. Fouet and C. Pomerol wrote in 1961[32] that that country had been holding back the growth of production in order to conserve its reserves of this strategic raw material. Moreover, in 1967, Raymond Furon pointed out that there was a scarcity of bauxite in the United States.[33] Whatever the truth may be, it is certain that there is, relatively, a serious overall scarcity of bauxite within the borders of the imperialist countries. It is no less certain that the position of the Third World is extremely favorable in this area. Africa, which currently only accounts for 5% of world production, has reserves estimated to comprise 25% of the world's total.[34]

The Third World, however, is not the imperialist countries' only bauxite supplier. Australian production (large reserves) and Greek production have already been mentioned, and there is also bauxite exported from Yugoslavia. Taking into account the contributions of these countries, one can estimate that the industrialized countries, which according to the figures above depended on imports for 73% of their total bauxite requirements in 1965, depended specifically on the Third World for 64–65% of that total. It should also be noted that the USSR, Rumania, East Germany, and Hungary sell unfinished aluminum to various European members of OECD (100,000 tons in 1966).

COPPER

World production of copper ore increased by 48.5% between 1956 and 1966. It rose in 1966 to 5,620,000 tons (metal content), of which about 2,080,000 or 40% came from the imperialist countries (United States 1,290,000, Canada 460,000, Japan and Australia 110,000 each), 2,180,000 or 41% came from the Third World (Chile 660,000, Zambia 620,000, Congo-Kinshasa 315,000, Peru 185,000, etc.), and 1,000,000 or 19% came from the socialist countries (Soviet production: 750,000).

The imperialist countries' share of production is therefore significant, but they are still very far from being self-sufficient in this area, as the following table, which is based on the same sources as the table for aluminum, shows:

thausands of metric tons

PRODUCTION OF

	Ore (Metal Content)		Refined Copper[1]	
	1956	1965	1956	1965
Common Market	5	2	473	720
(Belgium)	—	—	(169)	(309)
United States	1,002	1,226	1,548	1,959
Canada	322	469	298	393
United Kingdom	—	—	220	256
Sweden	17	16	33	50
Japan	79	107	126	366
Australia	55	92	40	100
Other industrialized countries	48	75	76	135
TOTALS	1,528	1,987	2,184	3,979

Figures include secondary copper which, on the average, represents 17–18% of the total. If secondary copper is omitted from consideration, the following totals result:

			2,330	3,330

This table suggests several observations:

1. Refined copper (excluding secondary copper) was equal in 1956 to the metal content of domestic ore multiplied by 1.52. In 1965 the coefficient had increased to 1.65. Therefore the deficit of the countries under consideration had grown. In addition, while world production of ore rose 48.5% between 1956 and 1966, that of the countries in question only rose 36%. During the same time, their production of metal increased 41.5%.

2. All the countries or groups of countries considered, except Canada, and to a minor degree, Australia, produce an amount of metal greater than the metal content of their ore. The deficit is not, then, just an overall figure, but exists as a factor for most of the countries individually and for the Common Market. The United States itself, the world's foremost producer of ore, had a deficit of about 400,000 tons in 1965–66, even after deducting secondary metal.

3. The cases of the Common Market and the United Kingdom, namely, the essential producers of western Europe, are particularly characteristic in the sense that their production of copper metal—one-fourth of the world total—is integrally dependent on foreign supplies. I have also isolated the case of tiny Belgium, which by herself produces 43% of the Common Market total. This situation is quite evidently an inheritance from her colonial domination of the Congo, and it is a situation that not only continues but is becoming more blatant, since Belgium refines much more copper today than she did during the colonial period. And it is not surprising to observe that France, which imports no ore and therefore produces no primary copper, relies mostly on Belgium, or rather on Katanga, for her supplies of copper metal.

The dependence of the imperialist countries on ore imports, which amounted to an overall figure of 34% of their metal production in 1956 (apart from secondary metal), reached 40% in 1965, and this dependence is essentially dependence on the Third World. If the US-Canadian reserves, which are located where the basic portion of the production of the leading copper-producing nations is concentrated, still seem abundant, the re-

serves of the Andean Cordillera, of the African continental shelf
are even more abundant.

TIN

While world production of bauxite and copper ore has risen
rapidly in the last twelve years, the production of concentrated
tin ore fell after 1955–56, only to climb again and significantly
surpass the figures for ten years before, in 1965 and 1966. World
production for 1966, which equalled 215 million tons, originated
primarily in the Third World. Production in the imperialist
countries was very low (7 million tons), while that of the socialist countries was quite noteworthy, with 49 million tons (China
25, USSR 23) or 23% of the world total.

Third World production is therefore on the order of 160
million tons or 74% of the world total. It is heavily concentrated
in Southeast Asia (notably in Malaysia: 70 million, Thailand:
23, and Indonesia:13), while Latin America contributes 30
million tons, of which 26 come from Bolivia, and Africa produces 20, of which 9.5 come from Nigeria and 7 from Congo-
Kinshasa.

The industrialized countries account by themselves for 90%
of the industrial consumption of tin within the imperialist
zone. Their dependence on imports in this area is therefore
virtually complete. And in fact this dependence is almost exclusively a dependence on the Third World, although one can
point to certain Soviet shipments of smelted tin to various imperialist countries.

This review of the principal raw materials, which could usefully be extended to various minor but by no means negligible
ores such as antimony, beryllium, lithium, and tantalum, as well
as other mineral materials such as phosphates, supports the observation that a significant change has occurred since the time
when Lenin and Bukharin dealt with the problem.

World production of oil, which in 1966 reached 1,633 million
tons, had only risen to 191 million in 1929, with the United
States alone producing 72%, while the Middle East did not,
so to speak, enter into the picture at all. The value of world
mining production expressed in adjusted dollars, was only 5

billion dollars in 1920, but totalled 58 billion in 1963. And a list of the principal mining discoveries in Africa shows that more than three-quarters of them were made after 1915. World production of iron ore has almost quintupled since 1910. Aluminum production today is 22 times greater than it was in 1929. Such examples could be multiplied.[35]

My purpose therefore is no longer to repeat Lenin's remarks on this subject, but to try to analyze today's situation from his point of view. The following features are characteristic of imperialism now:

1. Relative decline in the importance of agricultural raw materials in general. The dependence of the imperialist countries on the Third World in this area is a matter for serious concern only for various oleaginous substances and, more so, for rubber.

2. In the area of energy resources, oil has not ceased to gain importance in comparison with other materials, and its supremacy should last for many more years. As the importance of oil has grown, so has that of the Third World as the major supplier to the imperialist countries, which, generally speaking, have to import most of their oil. Third World oil is, in fact, the basis of stable energy supply for the imperialist countries.

3. The enormous industrial expansion of the imperialist countries rests on a base of steel manufacture and metallurgy. In the case of steel manufacture, the imperialist countries today are not only dependent on the Third World for iron ore to meet at least one-third of their needs—and this dependence is increasing rapidly—but they are almost totally dependent upon foreign sources for those ever more indispensable materials, manganese and chromium, and they import more than three-quarters of their cobalt requirements. As for metallurgy, aluminum has become a basic metal and the imperialist countries can only satisfy their needs for it from the foreign countries that supply nearly three-quarters of these requirements. The imperialist countries also depend on foreign sources for two-fifths of their copper and virtually all their tin. In all

these areas, the countries of the Third World are either the exclusive source (cobalt, copper) or they predominate overwhelmingly (manganese, chromium, aluminum, tin) when competitive supplies of certain materials are traded to the imperialist countries by the socialist countries.

The reasons for the imperialist countries' deficiency in filling their own fundamental needs are either the lack of competitive resources with a high enough yield (iron) or the physical lack of resources, which may be either total or virtually total (manganese, chromium) or relative but very great (cobalt, aluminum, copper).

People sometimes make a big point of the stockpiles or certain deposits partially held in reserve or left totally unexploited by the United States. The stockpiles at best would only cover two to three years of domestic consumption, and, as for those deposits, they constitute—when they exist—a confession of middle-range or long-range weakness. Under the most favorable construction, they would act as an oxygen tent for the American economy, but they would not be able to correct an overall deficiency among the imperialist countries, which is an especially grave prospect for Europe and Japan.

4. The absolutely vital nature of numerous essential resources which imperialism procures from the Third World, explains its desperate eagerness to control those resources. Lenin and Bukharin long ago revealed the existence of this kind of control, but since their day it has undergone a quantitative growth in proportion to the increased importance of the dominated countries as suppliers of raw materials.

I have already touched on this problem as it affects oil. In the case of mining, it is well known that North American capital is in general control of South American interests. In this way Surinam's bauxite is under the control of ALCOA, the American giant, and Guyana's bauxite is dominated, partly by DEMBA, a subsidiary of the Canadian firm ALCAN, and partly by Reynolds Metal Co. of the United States. In Oceania, the nickel of New Caledonia is exploited on the one hand by the French company, Le Nickel and on the other, since quite recently, by a French-American-Canadian group.

Africa offers a particularly rich field for investigation into imperialist methods of seizing mining deposits. In Mauritania, the iron of MIFERMA is exploited by capital from a variety of sources (English, German, Italian . . .), the majority interest being French, while the copper of Akjoujt will be exploited by a company whose majority interest is vested in an Anglo-American group working in concert with a French combine. The government of Mauritania will play a captive role in this enterprise with its minority 25% interest. The bauxite lode at Boké, Guinea, one of the largest in the world, is under the 51% domination of capital from the USA, Canada, France, Germany and Italy, while the government of Guinea controls the other 49%. As for the lode and the mining complex at Fria, they are controlled by the French group Ugine-Kuhlmann. The iron of Liberia is under the control of German, Italian, Swedish and especially American capital. 56% of the copper of Zambia is controlled by the Anglo-American Corporation. COMILOG, which exploits Gabon's manganese, is a Franco-American company with 49% of the shares owned by U.S. Steel. SOMIFER, which will extract the iron, is a joint U.S., French and German venture.

5. Those are only examples. I have given them to create awareness of this new and characteristic fact of imperialist control of the sources of raw materials in the Third World. The phenomenon is becoming more and more international. This is the case in particular for virtually all recently instituted systems of control. While in former days the division of the world between monopolies was almost always geographic—a certain colonial country going to a certain imperialist nation —today imperialist control takes the form of combines set up for individual operations, often between competitors. The company holding the concession for the bauxite deposits at Boké is quite typical in this respect. I shall content myself for the moment with putting this fact on record and waiting to interpret it in Chapter X.

6. Sometimes, however, imperialist control is broken, and is no longer rigorously absolute. This is a perfectly obvious development in the area of oil (cf. above), notably in the Middle East and Algeria. But other facts should be put on record.

In 1969, Zambia announced its decision to take over 51% of the shares of Anglo-American and the Roan Selection Trust, the two groups that exploit her copper. In Congo-Kinshasa, the Mobutu government has "congolized" the former Union Minière of the Haut-Katanga under the name of Générale Congolaise des Minerais (GECOMIN), a Congolese company with 60% of the shares in the hands of Congolese investors. In Chile, in December, 1964, the North American companies became jointly controlled mining companies in which the state took on a 25% participation in most cases, but this went as high as 51% for the famous mine known as El Teniente, which up till then had been totally controlled by the Kennecott group from the United States.[37]

These partial nationalizations are hardly good cause for euphoria. Forty per cent of the shares of the congolese GECOMIN remain open to private foreign capital and could thus become an international consortium in which there would be no way of preventing the reappearance of Union Minière. In fact, GECOMIN made certain technological agreements in 1967 with the Société Générale des Minerais, a subsidiary of the powerful Société Générale de Belgique, for the exploitation of copper and other ores. It is no secret that control of capital can be exercised through the control of technology. Finally, Belgian interests have retained a monopoly over the commercialization of the ores, which leaves an equally essential means of control in their hands.[38]

The same conclusions apply to the partial "chileanization" of Chile's copper mines, which had to leave technological and commercial control in other hands. According to Geoffrey Owen, "It was not clear how permanent the arrangement would be." [He refers to the concessions made by the American companies.] "Chile's capacity to negotiate has been weakened," and if extraction "became too risky or unprofitable, copper production in other countries could be stepped up." [39]

Even so, these facts are indications of a trend as are the even stricter nationalizations in Mauritania, Guinea, Congo-Brazzaville and elsewhere. These reorganizations are sometimes the expression of a truly anti-imperialist policy (oil), despite their uncertainties and inconsistencies. For the most part, they are only gestures of defiance. But they bear witness at least to the need felt by servile rulers to make such gestures of defiance. And when one sees the Shah of Iran himself enter into conflict with the international oil consortium (cf. Chap. IX), one is forced to agree that something new is happening and that, whatever the weaknesses of the resistance may be and whatever the deceptions they so often conceal, a basic fact emerges: we are entering an era of general opposition to the imperialist control of the sources of raw materials in the countries which imperialism dominates and exploits.

NOTES TO CHAPTER 2

1. *Op. cit.,* p. 21.
2. My emphasis.
3. *Op. cit.,* p. 92.
4. *Op. cit.,* p. 107.
5. H. Peyret, *La Strategie des trusts, "Que sais-je?"* collection, P.U.F., (Paris: 1966).
6. According to *Energy Policy—Problems and Objectives,* OECD, 1966.
7. OECD, *op. cit.*
8. *Op. cit.*
9. This figure is different from the one in Table I, but the source in both cases is OECD.
10. *"L'industrie du pétrole et du gaz en Afrique,"* by Nicolas Sarkis, *Afrique* 68, Jeune Afrique.
11. *Le Monde,* 4-16-68, *"Les pays arabes veulent 'décoloniser' le pétrole."*
12. *La Politique petrolière internationale,* P.U.F., *"Que sais-je?"* Collection (Paris: 1962).
13. *"Le Pétrole, produit stratégique,"* Trois Continents, no. 3, 1967.
14. *Op. cit.*
15. *Op. cit.*
16. *Le Monde,* 8-4-66.
17. *"Uranium Resources—Revised Estimates, Dec. 1967,"* OECD.
18. France also has an interest in the resources of Madagascar, Iran, South Africa, and Senegal. Italy has an interest in the resources of Kenya and Somalia, while other countries have an interest in the resources of Nigeria, Zambia, and Mozambique.
19. *L'Express,* 19–25 February 1968.
20. 7-29-68, 8-4-68.

21. *Op. cit.*, "Uranium Resources," OECD.

22. Unless otherwise noted, all figures for ores are expressed in metal content.

23. *The Iron and Steel Industry in 1965*. OECD (Paris: 1966).

24. Beaujeu-Garnier, Gamblin and Delobez, *Images économiques du monde*, SEDES (Paris: 1967).

25. *The Iron and Steel Industry* (various years), OECD.

26. *Le Monde*, 12–13 No. 1967.

27. A. André and J. Le Coz, *Économie minière du Maroc* (Rabat: 1961).

28. *La terre est-elle une mine inepuisable?* Hachette (Paris: 1967).

29. *Op. cit.*, p. 47.

30. *Minerais et terres rares*, "Que sais-je" collection, P.U.F. (Paris: 1961).

31. These figures are not expressed in metal content but in gross tonnage. Of course, on the average, bauxite yields up 20 to 25 per cent of its weight as aluminum.

32. *Op. cit.*, p. 76.

33. *Op. cit.*, p. 92.

34. *Afrique* 69, Jeune Afrique.

35. According to Raymond Furon, *op. cit.*

36. *Le Monde*, 8-12-69.

37. *Images économiques du monde*, 1965, p. 108.

38. Claude Roire, *"Deux pays, deux produits,"* Trois Continents, no. 3, 1967.

39. *Industry in the U.S.A.*, Penguin, 1968.

3

Imperialism
and International Trade

FOR LENIN, as we have seen, "under the old capitalism . . . the
export of goods was the most typical feature. Under modern
capitalism . . . the export of capital has become the typical feature." (62) (Chap. IV). And he considered one of imperialism's
fundamental traits to be the fact that "the export of capital . . .
has become extremely important, as distinguished from the export of commodities." (Chap. VII) (89)

It should be worthwhile, then, to examine to what degree and
in what way the export of commodities and of capital are developing today, and to try to discover if either one or the other
is important in our time or possesses features of special interest.
I cannot give a complete answer to this question until the next
chapter.

As a first step, in this chapter, it is appropriate to point out
that since the Second World War the export of goods from the
imperialist countries has developed at a very brisk pace (cf. Table
III). Between 1952 and 1967, as everyone knows, they tripled in
(unadjusted) value. For the socialist countries, the growth of
export activity has been comparable and even more important
as a component of the total economic picture, although on an
infinitely more modest scale. But by contrast, the growth of exports has been much less rapid in the countries of the Third
World. Far from tripling, they less than doubled between 1952
and 1967 and the percentage increase from 1958 to 1967 was

only a little more than half that for exports from the imperialist countries.

But these statistics for exports (Col. 1) are expressed in unadjusted dollars and therefore reflect variations in price. The

TABLE III

GROWTH OF EXPORTS, 1952–1967

		TOTAL EXPORTS FOB (in millions of unadjusted dollars)		INDEX OF EXPORT VOLUME (1963 = 100)		ZONES OF DESTINATION FOR EXPORTS IN % OF THE TOTAL (ROUNDED OFF) DEVELOPED SOCIALIST WORLD	THIRD CAPITALIST COUNTRIES	
A. Imperialist								
countries	1952	48,770		70		66%	32%	2%
	1958	67,710	+ 111%		+ 94%	67%	30%	3%
	1967	143,090		136		75%	21%	4%
United								
States	1952	15,050		78		56%	44%	0%
	1958	17,760	+ 76%		+ 65%[1]	58%	41%	1%
	1967	31,250		129		68%	31%	1%
Common								
Market	1952	13,770		63		65%	33%	2%
	1958	23,440	+ 139%		+ 130%	68%	28%	4%
	1967	56,130		145		80%	16%	4%
EFTA	1952	12,020		75		65%	32%	3%
	1958	15,980	+ 79%		+ 59%	70%	26%	4%
	1967	28,670		119		77%	18%	5%
Japan	1952	1,270		51		40%	60%	0%
	1958	2,880	+ 262%		+ 273%	41%	56%	3%
	1967	10,440		190		51%	44%	5%
B. Third								
World	1952	20,970		75		73%	25%	2%
	1958	24,790	+ 61%		+ 65%	73%	24%	3%
	1967	39,960		124		74%	21%	5%
C. Socialist								
Countries	1952	7,020				17%	7%	76%
	1958	12,080				17%	11%	72%
	1967	24,820				24%	14%	62%

SOURCES: United Nations Statistical Yearbook, 1962 and 1967, several tables. United Nations Monthly Bulletin of Statistics, June 1968, Tables B and C.

N.B. The developed capitalist countries (column 3) include the imperialist countries (cf. introduction) plus Australia, New Zealand and South Africa. The Third World as I have defined it has thus had South Africa amputated from it. However, Cuba remains in the Third World statistics for 1967.

[1] This index applies to the United States and Canada.

growth of the volume of exports (Col. 2) for the imperialist countries as a whole was distinctly lower than the growth of their value, while the growth of export volume for the Third World was conspicuously greater. This regressive trend is merely the statistical notation of a process of "unequal exchange" or rather of a change in the terms of exchange, a change which is favorable to the advanced countries and unfavorable to the countries of the Third World. I shall return to this.

Continuing for the moment with general observations, it is clear that the socialist countries have increased the amount of their trade with the other two groups of countries, but that they still have only achieved a very low level of activity. Sales to the socialist countries represented only about 4% of total exports from the imperialist countries in 1967 and 5% (nearly 5.5%) of those from the Third World. East-West trade still amounts to a very small portion of world trade.

And trade between the imperialist countries and the Third World amounts to a less and less important factor, in dollar value at least. While sales by the developed countries to the Third World in 1952 represented 32% of their total exports, they did not reach 21% (rounded off on the high side) of these exports in 1967. The Third World is therefore becoming a less and less important client of the countries which dominate and exploit it, while those countries remain a very high priority outlet for the Third World: 73% of total Third World exports in 1952 and 74% in 1967 were sold to the imperialist countries.

The decline in relative value of the imperialist countries' exports to the Third World is compensated to a slight degree by the growth of sales to the socialist countries, but the rest of the slack, which amounts to more than four-fifths of the trade lost by the Third World, has been taken up by sales which the imperialist countries make with each other. These mutual transactions have gone up from 66% to 75% of their total export trade between 1952 and 1967.

In short, the Third World trades less and less with itself, and the imperialist countries, on the contrary, trade more and more among themselves. The vigorous development of trade among the industrialized capitalist countries is the essential explanation of the increased growth of world trade.

But all this is a matter of crude observation based on figures expressed in unadjusted dollars. This data calls for further analysis and investigation. I shall conduct this more detailed discussion in two parts: one dealing with trade between the imperialist countries and the Third World, the other with trade between the imperialist countries.

A. Trade Between the Imperialist Countries and the Third World

Structurally, commerce between the imperialist countries and the Third World is a very accurate reflection of the imperialist international division of labor. When the underindustrialized Third World sells products to the imperialist countries, manufactured articles account for only about 10% of total sales, while the whole range of primary products account for roughly 90%. This last figure can be broken down into about 32% for combustibles (oil) and lubricants, 30% for raw materials and semi-manufactured products (notably unfinished virgin metals), and 28% for foodstuffs. These percentages, which are actually the figures for 1965, will vary a bit from year to year, depending, for example, on the tonnage of foodstuffs offered for sale, which goes up and down along with harvest fluctuations. In addition, the general trend that is making itself felt involves an increase in the percentage for oil and a slow decline for foodstuffs as well as raw materials. But these percentages have once again been calculated in terms of value, and prices do not change in a comparable way from one sector to another. The figures given should therefore only be considered approximations.

As for exports from the industrialized countries to the Third World, nearly four-fifths of them now consist of manufactured products. The portion of these products in total sales by the imperialist countries to the Third World has varied as follows:[1]

1952	73.9%
1958	78.4%
1965	78.8%

The imperialist international division of labor therefore remains what it has always been, and the statistics for trade point this up so clearly that they almost seem like a caricature. "International exchange of commodities is based on the international division of labour," wrote Bukharin.[2] This is still true, completely true, at least in terms of trade between imperialism and the countries which it dominates so as to confine them to an economic state which is as purely complementary as possible to the economies of the dominant countries.

These exchanges between dominating and dominated countries within the imperialist zone obey, moreover, the rule of unequal exchange. The primary products of the Third World countries are exchanged for prices unequal to the prices of the industrialized products of the imperialist countries. In general, the prices of Third World products show a tendency to decline, while the prices of products from imperialist countries tend to rise—hence the deterioration of the "terms of exchange" in commerce between the Third World and imperialism. I shall pursue this problem in greater depth in Chapter IX. For the moment, I shall limit myself to setting forth the terms of exchange (relationship between the average unit value of exports and the average unit value of imports) between 1954 and 1965, based on 1958 = 100:[3]

	1954	1958	1965
Developed capitalist countries, total commerce	97	100	102
Third World, total commerce	109	100	95
Third World, commerce with the developed capitalist countries	112	100	93

In its exchanges with the developed capitalist countries, the Third World, therefore, lost ground to the extent of about 19%. In other words, to obtain the same manufactured product in 1965 as in 1954, the Third World had to sell a 19% greater volume of primary products. And it had to increase production by more than 19% in order to make any commercial headway at all. As I have dealt at length in my earlier books with the catastrophic consequences of this state of affairs for the Third

World, I shall not cover the same ground again. Instead, I shall pause a moment to look at the effect this situation has on imperialism.

I noted in the previous chapter the ever growing and ever more crucial importance that numerous raw materials extracted from the soil of the Third World have for the industry of the imperialist countries, and especially the importance of metal-bearing ores. But various factors combine to make this increasing and often absolute dependence for materials transform itself during the process of exchange into figures that decline in relative value and whose absolute level is finally very low. Among the explanations most often advanced for the declining role played by raw materials in world trade, are:

——technological progress, which brings with it lighter wear and tear on materials and the "miniaturization" of certain machines (a debatable argument in my opinion);

——higher yields obtained from raw materials (less ore to produce the same amount of metal);

——the importance assumed, in certain cases, of substitutes.

I shall add another element: because of scientific and technological progress, modern industry is ceaselessly creating new appliances and materials that are more and more complex and elaborate. Unfinished or half-finished raw materials make up less and less of their production costs.

I shall definitely not neglect giving the fullest importance to the almost constant decline, absolute or relative, in the price of raw materials from the Third World at the same time that the price of industrial products rises constantly in both relative and absolute value.

In any event, the conclusion that many authors draw, by taking into consideration only the statistics of exchange expressed as value, that imperialism depends less and less on the Third World in this respect, runs into the stumbling block I discussed earlier: for most mineral raw materials, including the ones most crucial to imperialist factories, the portion of total tonnage appropriated from the Third World is constantly growing. Most often the Third World is the major supplier and sometimes it provides the entire amount. Whatever future progress can be expected from science and technology, it is doubtful that one day it will be possible to manufacture steam shovels or harvester-threshers or computers out of plastic, or to transform low grade iron ore into high grade ore.

Out of this difference between the crucial and growing importance of Third World mineral raw materials for imperialism, and their declining relative role in the composition of world trade, imperialism makes a profit, derived by obtaining commodities which are the flesh and blood of its most essential manufactures at a price below their value.

But, by the same token, it also suffers from the same process. For as the Third World's export receipts continue to decline, its import capacity becomes more and more limited, which constantly cuts back the role of these countries as outlets for the manufactured products of imperialist products. At the moment, it is possible to estimate that the countries of the Third World still absorb between 5 and 6% (probably 5.5%) of the total production of goods manufactured by all the imperialist factories. This contraction of the Third World market tends to expose the excess productive capacity of the industries of the developed countries, and it confronts the imperialist system with the following contradiction: exploiting the Third World helped imperialism when its factories were on the upgrade, but it is a disservice today when they are on the downgrade, and it aggravates considerably the risk of a generalized recession for the imperialist countries.

And so the imperialist countries rival each other in their efforts to maintain their exports to the Third World. Export credits and the various kinds of insurance that accompany them, are offered more and more generously for sales in the Third World, and, despite all the hostility it arouses, foreign aid "with strings attached" has practically become the rule in these transactions. Moreover, numerous factories that produce consumer goods, and especially assembly plants, are being built by the imperialist countries in the Third World, not as components of a development plan, but quite simply because they are substitutes for exportation, which is hampered by the meager import capacities of the customer nations. I shall return to this problem.

Finally, as I already have pointed out in my previous books, trade between the imperialist countries and the Third World tends more and more to escape from the bilateral channels inherited from an earlier period. The imperialist world market is shrinking, in size, on the one hand, because of the appearance of new socialist states after the Second World War, and in volume, on the other hand, because of the increasingly smaller capacity of the Third World to absorb imported products. It is, therefore, no longer feasible for the dominating countries to content themselves with the outlets offered by the countries that each of them dominates. The old bilateral relationships, of course, still survive and remain the most important. Aided by the integration of the imperialist countries into multinational trade blocs, these onetime special relationships are crumbling and giving way to multilateral relationships that are developing or being created. This tendency is particularly clear in the case of exports from super-imperialist America:

	(in millions of dollars)			
	1955		1966	
UNITED STATES EXPORTS TO:	Amount	%	Amount	%
Latin America	3,300	59	4,170	44
Africa except South Africa	365	7	920	10
Third World Asia	1,895	34	4,340	46
	5,560	100	9,430	100

SOURCE: United Nations Statistical Yearbook, 1967 (World exports by Provenance and Destination, Table 149).

This is the way that the American superimperialism, which is, by a wide margin, the major supplier of manufactured goods to Latin America, can limit the relative value of its sales in that area in order to increase its commercial influence in Africa where it competes with European imperialisms, and in Asia where it is making heavy inroads on British trade. Britain and especially the other European industrial nations, by contrast, are gaining a foothold in Latin American markets, grousing all the while, but only grousing, over the unopposed supremacy of merchandise "made in USA." More and more, the American colossus is expanding its commercial influence throughout the entire Third World.

The result of all this is a greater internationalization of trade, which is not, however, limited to commerce between the imperialist countries and the Third World, as we shall see further on.

B. Trade Among the Imperialist Countries

At the beginning of this chapter, I set forth the details of the spectacular development of sales which the imperialist countries arranged among themselves between 1952 and 1967 and which today constitute more than half of the world's trade. This characteristic feature of international commerce in the postwar period is very often explained, exclusively or principally, by the growth of productive capacities, which, in the countries under consideration, tend to expand to an international level. Certain authorities go so far as to establish a sort of automatic link between growth of productive capacities and expansion of international trade.

It would obviously be hard to imagine this kind of expansion during a period of stagnant production, and no one would attack the notion that the growth of productive capacities encourages the development of trade. But Table IV shows that no parallel relationship, and consequently no automatic connection exists between the two in the sector of greatest importance: industrial production and manufacture.

The table, in fact, leads to the conclusion that between 1958 and 1966 the development of productive capacities in industry, to the extent that it is reflected by the indices for industrial production or manufacture, has been less brisk in the United Kingdom and the Common Market than in the United States. Indeed,

TABLE IV

COMPARISON BETWEEN THE GROWTH OF INDUSTRIAL PRODUCTION
(OR MANUFACTURING) AND THE DEVELOPMENT OF THE EXPORTATION
OF MANUFACTURED PRODUCTS

BASED ON FIGURES FOR 1958–1966	*(1)* % OF GROWTH OF INDUSTRIAL PRODUCTION (*except construction*)	*(2)* % OF GROWTH OF MANUFACTURES	*(3)* % OF GROWTH OF EXPORT OF MANUFACTURED PRODUCTS (*by volume*)
United States/Canada		69	
United States alone	67		52
Western Europe		57	
United Kingdom	32		36.5
Common Market	64	62	
West Germany	61		101
France	49		110
Italy	201		300
Japan	191		296

SOURCES: Col. 1: Basic Statistics of the Community [EEC], 1967, Table 44.
Col. 2: UN Monthly Bulletin of Statistics, May 1968, special Table A.
Col. 3: UN Monthly Bulletin of Statistics, June 1968, special Table D.

N.B. Column 1 includes manufacturing in the pure sense (Col. 2) plus mining, electricity and gas, all three of which, in the countries referred to, only constitute 11–12% of industrial production, omitting construction.

during the same period, exports of manufactured products has grown faster than industrial production or manufacturing in the United Kingdom and especially in the Common Market countries, while in the United States exports grew at a distinctly lower pace than production. Moreover, while the growth of production was much more vigorous in Japan than it was overall for the Common Market countries, the rise of exports compared with production in Japan was, with Italy excepted, altogether less rapid. The existence of any automatic link between the development of productive capacities and that of corresponding exports is therefore denied by the facts.

The experts at OECD, for their part, compared the average annual rate of growth in their countries between 1960 and 1965 of both foreign trade conceived in the broadest sense (imports and exports of merchandise, plus profit and loss from transport) and the GNP. While the growth rate of the GNP increased by an overall amount of 4.8% annually for the industrialized OECD countries, the growth rate for foreign trade went up 7.2% for the large industrialized countries and 8% for the small ones. These experts are obliged to observe that "the growth of foreign trade has been far superior to that of the gross national product." Among the causes of this sharp increase in foreign trade, they cite "general expansion," while elsewhere the expansion of trade itself seems to them "to contribute to economic growth." This dialectical explanation is certainly not groundless.

But they especially do not neglect to observe:

1. that intra-OECD trade has advanced more rapidly than trade as a whole, which "certainly is explained in part by the fact that the goal of free trade has been achieved more fully within the zone";
2. that intra-Common Market trade has developed even more rapidly than intra-OECD trade.[4]

And so we are now confronted with a very important fact: trade among industrialized capitalist countries develops, roughly speaking, in proportion to the degree of integration among the various groups of countries. The Common Market, which is by far the most integrated trade group, has also recorded the most active growth by far, in its internal as well as its external commerce.

It is general knowledge, in fact, that the integration of the Six has allowed them to develop their internal commerce so vigorously that the percentage of "intra" trade for the Six grew from around 33% to 43% of their total trade between 1959 and 1966. But that has not prevented the Six from increasing their trade with the rest of the capitalist world more rapidly than all other countries, as the following table shows:[5]

SHARE IN THE INCREASE OF WORLD TRADE, 1958–1965

(excluding intra-Common Market, intra-EFTA and intra-socialist trade)

	COMMON MARKET (external)	EFTA (external)	USA	JAPAN
IMPORTS	22%	19%	14%	9%
EXPORTS	21.5%	14%	18%	11%

If the extra-Common Market trade of the Six developed in this way, it did so, undoubtedly, because of the growth of productive forces encouraged by the Common Market, and especially because of the tendency for trade to concentrate itself among the industrialized countries, as has been previously shown. But the development of extra-Common Market trade is also related, and significantly so, as the authors of the document from which we borrowed the preceding data have written, to the "measures of tariff policy and free trade which have been taken by the Community" with regard to other countries. For, on the basis of these measures, the Common Market emerges not only as an internally integrated region, but also as an instrument for global imperialist integration.

But let's return for a moment to Bukharin. We have already seen that, in his view, "international exchange of commodities is based on the international division of labour," an observation which seemed to remain a totally accurate description of trade between the imperialist countries and the Third World. However, Bukharin immediately adds: "We must not think, however, that it takes place only within the limits set by the latter. Countries mutually exchange not only different products, but even products of the same kind. A, for instance, may export into B not only such products as are not produced in B, or produced in a very small quantity; it may export its products into B *to compete* with local production. In such cases, international exchange has its basis, not in division of labour . . . , but solely in different levels of production-costs, in values having various scales in the various countries, but reduced, through international exchange, to socially indispensable labour on a world scale." [6]

More than fifty years ago, therefore, a Marxist writer uncovered a fact which, since the Second World War, has broadened in importance considerably. In the total trade of the Common Market (intra plus extra), machinery and transport equipment rose from 14.4% to 18.6% of all imports between 1960 and 1966, while it rose from 30% to 33.5% of total exports during the same period. For other manufactured products, the percentage rose from 32% of imports in 1960 to 36.8% in 1966, while it retreated slightly for exports, from 48.6% to 47.4%, which marked a tendency toward a better import-export balance for this group of products. For the EFTA countries, imports and exports of both groups of products rose simultaneously.[7]

Of course, the situation noted above in the total trade figures for the Common Market and EFTA is an even more clearcut feature of the internal trade of the two zones, as is well known. But it is remarkable that it should also show up in their external commerce, that is to say, in the commerce of all the imperialist countries with each other. Between 1958 and 1965, industrial products increased their share of total external Common Market trade from 79 to 83% of all exports and from 28 to 36% of all imports.[8] Geoffrey Owen shows that European and Japanese industrial companies have been making aggressive inroads in the United States, which has become an importer of steel and automobiles in a period of a few short years. The role played by finished manufactured products in the American trade balance has doubled since the beginning of the Fifties.[9] And to complete the picture, Philippe Simonnot stated more recently that the growth of imports to the United States is due especially to imports of finished industrial products. He noted that between 1960 and 1966 imports of medical appliances, plumbing, heating and lighting, furniture, clothing and shoes, professional and scientific instruments, etc. doubled, and imports of machinery and transport equipment more than tripled.[10]

It is the same phenomenon I have already discussed:[11] the development of trade between the industrialized capitalist countries is essentially based on the exchange of products of one and the same category and very often even of similar products. The most startling examples of this process are products such as clothing, domestic electrical appliances, and automobiles. Of

course, in the case of products which are not similar but belong
to the same category, the expansion of trade can arise from a new
international division of labor: because of its technological head
start, the United States, for example, holds unopposed dominion
over the electronics field. There are other specialties that persist
(Swiss watches) or arise. But, generally speaking, what Bukharin
said can still be maintained—that the development of trade between industrialized capitalist countries is based on competition,
which is itself based less on the division of labor than on differences in production costs and individual national values.

But since all that was true a half century ago, while trade
between imperialist countries is growing much more quickly today than then, some other element has intervened that favors
such trade and permits international competition to function
better than before. That element is, once again, integration. The
diverse barriers, notably tariffs, about which Lenin and especially
Bukharin speak at length, have disappeared within groupings
such as the Common Market and EFTA. And they are on the
way out elsewhere. We have seen that these groupings, far from
cloistering themselves within regional integration, open themselves to worldwide integration. The Kennedy Round is the
most obvious example of this. Worldwide capitalist integration,
based on international agreements, was born with éclat at the
end of the Second World War. Its first concrete appearance on
a planetary scale was the General Agreement on Tariffs and
Trade (GATT), which virtually all developed capitalist countries have joined, and which advertises itself as a sort of international charter for world trade. Its basic tenets: general acceptance of the most favored nation arrangement, the general
elimination of quantitative restrictions, the sacrosanct principle
of non-discrimination, the struggle against dumping, etc. constitute a code for worldwide integration. The OECD Convention
(1960) fits into the same framework, since it aims at contributing
"to the expansion of world trade on a multilateral, non-discrimi-
natory basis, in accordance with international obligations."

Of course, these treaties are inspired by imperialist motives.
Under the capitalist system, freedom and non-discrimination *de
jure* serve in all cases to insure *de facto* discrimination favoring
the stronger parties. The heavyweight championship of the world

is theoretically open to boxers of all weights. Boxing admits the principles of liberty and non-discrimination. But neither a featherweight nor even a middleweight has ever been heavyweight champion of the world.

Worldwide imperialist integration, in all its guises, aims at insuring both the aggregate supremacy and, to a degree, the cohesion (without going so far as to exclude rivalries) of the principal imperialist powers in their confrontation with the socialist countries, on the one hand, and, increasingly, with the Third World on the other. It is no accident that the OECD agreement groups together in a Development Assistance Committee (DAC) "all the major capital-exporting countries of the free world" to coordinate "aid" to the underdeveloped countries, an essential instrument of imperialist policy in the Third World.

In any case, worldwide integration and regional integrations (the regional organizations are part of the worldwide effort even though they are advancing more quickly) tend generally to further the internationalization of the capitalist countries' trade throughout the world. One odd fact, however, deserves mention: on the one hand, if one compares the number of countries with which each of the major imperialist countries had commercial dealings worth noting in 1952 and then does the same thing for 1965, it is obvious that for all the major countries in question, the number was distinctly higher in 1965 than in 1952. A significant dispersion of trade among a greater number of foreign partners occurred. But on the other hand, if one calculates the overall percentage of total exports made by the principal imperialist countries that were absorbed by their three major clients, one obtains the following results:

SHARE OF THE LEADING THREE CUSTOMER COUNTRIES
IN TOTAL EXPORTS

	1952	1965
United States	27%	34%
United Kingdom	20%	22%
West Germany	23%	29%
France	28%	36%
Italy	29%	40%
Japan	33%	38%

Thus in every case, there was a growing concentration of exports among the three most important customers. This concentration already existed in 1952 and increased markedly by 1965. It is therefore possible to say that the imperialist countries' exports during the Fifties and Sixties moved in two directions: toward the atomization of sales among a greater and greater number of smaller buyers; and, conversely, toward the concentration of shipments among a reduced number of ever more important customers.

The overall expansion of exportation by the imperialist countries has as its basic condition, without any doubt, the development of their productive capacities. The concentration of an increasingly greater portion of their exports among a reduced number of big customers is the principal consequence of integration and, especially, of integrationist agreements, which cause the great markets of the rich, industrialized countries to make themselves more fully available to each other, and which, notably, permit competition over similar products. As for the atomization of sales toward a very great number of countries with weak absorption capacities, this process seems to me to be the special result, on the one hand, of the shrinking world market, which does not allow even the smallest and most distant market to remain unexplored, and on the other hand, it is the result of integration which encourages the penetration of the small but relatively advanced capitalist countries as well as the numerous countries of the Third World. Many of the Third World countries have indeed been practically forced to join GATT, and for, first 18, then 22 African and Malagasy nations, their association with the Common Market constitutes a very strict integration of the neo-colonialist type.

Let's try to summarize.

World trade, which had only increased by around 15% between the two world wars, has grown with extreme vigor since the end of the Second World War. This is especially true of trade between the imperialist countries. The increase of trade in the Third World has been much less rapid.

Trade between the imperialist countries and the countries of the Third World continues to give a faithful reflection, structurally, of the imperialist type of international division of labor: nine-tenths of Third World sales consist of unfinished or semi-finished primary products, while four-fifths of the imperialist countries' sales involve manufactured products.

Unequal exchange dominates the commercial relations of the two groups of countries. The main results of this are: the economic suffocation of the Third World countries; the camouflaging of the crucial importance of their shipments of raw materials behind a smokescreen of figures whose value is diminished; the contracting capacity of their markets for the industrial products of imperialism, which accentuates the importance of the excess production capacity of factories in the imperialist countries.

The heavy expansion of trade between imperialist countries, rendered possible by the development of their productive capacities, has been powerfully encouraged by the regional and worldwide integration of imperialism, which is one of the most important facts of the postwar era. Among the many results of this is that trade is based to a lesser degree on the complementarity of products, and more and more on competition, on the difference between national production costs for comparable or similar products.

This process of integration is particularly profitable to the great powers, for it stimulates a certain concentration of trade between them. This, combined with the shrinking or contraction of the world market, leads, moreover, to a greater internationalization of trade throughout the world.

Some of these conclusions have, however, a relatively provisional character, for commodity exports and capital exports seem to affect and clash with each other more often and with greater complexity today than formerly. I shall devote a special discussion to this problem in my next chapter.

NOTES TO CHAPTER 3

1. U.N. Statistical Yearbook, 1965 (table 151, sec. 4), 1966 (table 151, sec. 4).
2. *Op. cit.,* p. 24.

3. U.N. Statistical Yearbook, 1966 (table 151, sec. 3).
4. Economic Growth 1960–1970, OECD (Paris: 1966).
5. Notes et études documentaires, no. 3,405: "Le Commerce extérieur de la CEE, 1958–1965," table V, La Documentation française, Paris.
6. Op. cit., pp. 24–25.
7. Basic Statistics of the Community, 1961 and 1967.
8. "Notes et études documentaires," op. cit., p. 13.
9. Op. cit., p. 23.
10. Le Monde, 9-3-68.
11. "The Third World in World Economy," Monthly Review, 1969, Chap. V.

4

Capital Exports

ACCORDING to Lenin, who borrows his figures from various authorities and documents, foreign capital placements and investments made by the three principal capital-exporting countries of that day, the United Kingdom, France, and Germany, had increased considerably at the end of the previous century and at the beginning of this one. English and French capital exports had at least quadrupled between 1880 and 1914, and those of Germany did the same between 1900 and 1914. As Lenin observed: "the export of capital reached formidable dimensions only in the beginning of the twentieth century." [1]

This is confirmed today by Gilles-Y. Bertin,[2] who calls the period from 1800 to 1913, "the golden age of private investment," while specifying that Great Britain, which was the only exporter of capital until around 1860, then saw itself imitated by France and later Germany. This is especially noticeable after 1870. He arrives at the following relative figures for the countries that led the world in foreign investment in 1914 (in rounded-off percentages):

Great Britain	42%
France	19%
Germany	14%
United States	8%
Others (Belgium, Netherlands, Switzerland)	17%

The flow of capital abroad, he adds, sometimes represented a significant fraction of total savings: according to the year, it varied in amount from 30 to 90% in Great Britain and from 15 to 75% in France.

It is obvious, then, that at that time the capital-exporting countries were almost exclusively European and that the United States was only beginning to take its place among them. The other aspects of these exports which Bertin uncovers are:

——In the beginning, they were essentially private. Governments very rarely took part in them.

——They took the form of portfolio investments (purchases of, or subscriptions to, stock or bonds), which is a fact that also comes out in Lenin's analysis, as well as in Bukharin's, though less clearly—which is not surprising—because the dividing line is sometimes vague between what Bukharin calls the export of capital as interest capital and its export as profit capital.

——They were directed overwhelmingly toward the newer countries (United States, "white" territories) and the colonialized countries. According to Lenin, around 1910, the accumulated external investments of England, France, and Germany were divided up approximately as follows:

In Europe	32%
In America	36.5%
In Asia, Africa, Australia	31.5%

The period between the two wars was, in the eyes of Bertin, one of "recession in international investment." Indeed, the level falls from 44 billion dollars in 1914 to 33 in 1919, then climbs back to 47.5 in 1929 and to 53 in 1938. But this last figure is expressed in devalued dollars: the 53 billion in 1938 represent only around 30 in 1914 dollars.

The First World War, moreover, reversed the traditional roles. The European countries fighting the war were obliged to sell a large part of their foreign assets—almost all of them in the case of Germany—and as a result they yielded first place among capital-exporting countries to the United States, which has held on to it ever since.

Finally, among other things, G.-Y. Bertin notes that during the course of this period there was "a palpable increase in the role of direct investment," while capital was directed even more heavily toward the rich countries. Those who continued to invest in what would become the Third World were attracted to it especially because of its oil and minerals.

Everyone knows that after the Second World War capital exports of all kinds increased again at an accelerated rate. Bertin, who observes that during the peak period between the wars, namely 1925–1929, the world's annual flow of investment did not surpass three billion dollars, estimates that this statistic reached 3.3 billion per year from 1951 to 1955, then 6 billion between 1956 and 1959 and finally 14 billion in 1965. From another source, one learns that long term capital exports between 1951 and 1961, inclusive, rose to 71 billion dollars (for an annual average of about 6.5 billion, which breaks down into the following categories (in round numbers):[3]

governmental grants	23 billion
long term capital of public origin	17 "
long term capital of private origin	31 "

Since, with certain variations, this general trend continued in the years after 1961, we can conclude that there has been an overall similarity between the growth of commodity exports and that of capital exports since the First World War: first came a phase of approximate stagnation for both categories between the wars; then a phase of recovery and soaring activity for both after 1945.

But in this last period, to which I shall henceforth confine myself, capital exports exhibit certain characteristic features. The two most important, which are mutually explanatory, are: 1. the predominance of public capital: 40 billion of the 71 billion dollars recorded for 1951–1961; 2. the predominant flow of capital toward the under-developed countries: out of the same 71 billion dollars, 45.5 went to those countries, which are almost identical with those we now refer to collectively as the Third World.

This last point is, however, very far from being generally applicable on an equal basis across the entire spectrum of capital exports. While 22 of the 23 billion dollars recorded for governmental grants have been exported to the Third World, 12 out of 17 went to the Third World in the category of long term public capital (loans), but only 11.5 out of the 31 in private placements and investments went there. It is therefore official capital which, in the great majority of cases, finds its way to the Third World, while private capital in the imperialist countries, up to almost two-thirds of the total invested, is invested inside the developed capitalist countries. This tendency has increased since 1961.

Finally, it is not too soon to underline the enormous preponderance of the United States in the export of capital. According to figures drawn from the United Nations document already cited, of the total long term capital exports made by all capital-exporting countries during the period 1951–1961, the United States accounts for 70% of all capital, official and private, and for nearly 80% of all private capital. The prodigious growth of private foreign investments by the United States in the postwar era can be seen from the figures that follow[4] (in millions of dollars):

	1945	1950	1955	1960	1965
Direct investments	8,369	11,788	19,395	32,778	49,217
Portfolio investments	5,289	5,700	7,355	12,632	21,584

These American capital exports grew about twice as rapidly as exports of American merchandise.

According to Bertin, the estimated value (in billions of dollars) of investments of all kinds held abroad in 1964 was as follows:

United States	65
Great Britain	30
France	15(?)
West Germany	2
Others	5(?)

U.S. capital by itself therefore constitutes more than half of the total.

Bertin, moreover, distinguishes two periods in the postwar era: a) Until around 1955, moderate expansion of capital exports, with Europe absorbing 68.3% of American foreign aid while it rebuilt itself: b) after 1955, with European recovery complete, expansion became more vigorous, more widespread and took on the features which still distinguish it today.

My analyses will deal with this more recent and more characteristic period. I shall begin by discussing the export of capital to the Third World, go on to investigate capital exports between developed capitalist countries, and conclude by looking at the relation and conflict between commodity exports and capital exports.

A. The Export of Capital to the Third World

Between 1956 and 1966, the net movement (that is, with depreciations and disinvestment deducted) of long term official and private capital into the underdeveloped countries from the DAC countries, which include virtually all the developed capitalist countries, has been as follows (in millions of dollars):[5]

	1956	1959	1963	1966
PUBLIC BILATERAL CAPITAL	3,046	4,001	5,712	5,919
including: grants and grant-like flows	2,696	3,263	4,040	3,761
loans	(350)	(738)	1,672	2,158
PUBLIC MULTILATERAL CAPITAL	224	348	411	513
TOTAL PUBLIC CAPITAL	3,270	4,349	6,123	6,432
PRIVATE CAPITAL	2,578	2,435	1,838	2,300
including: new direct investments			1,011	1,039
reinvested earnings			620	916
total direct investments	(2,450)	(2,100)	1,631	1,955
portfolio investments			206	346

This chart calls for certain explanations: a) the underdeveloped countries it refers to include some Mediterranean countries (notably Spain, Greece, Yugoslavia); b) the heading "grants and grantlike flows" incorporates activities that do not cor-

respond, or not entirely, to real capital flows.[6] Therefore, the
preceding data must not be considered more than a broad ap-
proximation, and I shall not draw on it except where it is
sufficiently clear and indisputable.

The data is usable in the area of private capital, for this category is essentially made up of direct private investments. The
portfolio investments are slight and consist mainly of subscriptions to international organizations (World Bank and others).
Between 1956 and 1966, the annual amount of new direct private
investments went through relative highs and lows but dipped in
overall absolute value, and the 1968 Report of the IMF shows
that the low rate of 1966 was improved on only slightly in 1967.
The Third World, therefore, as we have already seen, attracts
much less private capital than the industrialized capitalist world.
And the reinvested earnings from these new direct private investments vary by a wide amount depending on the year. For the
five-year period 1962–66, these reinvested earnings rose to a
total of 3,816 million dollars, while the influx of external capital
reached 5,109 million (yearly average: 1,022). Consequently,
43% of the direct investment for those five years consisted of reinvested earnings and only 57% was due to the influx of new
capital.[7]

But despite the fact that a portion of the earnings were reinvested on the spot, the transfer of earnings back to the countries
where the capital had originated increased rapidly by a large
amount, which says a great deal about the profitability of the
investments and, consequently, about the extent of the surplus
value appropriated in the Third World. In the case of direct
private American investments alone, the annual income officially
repatriated represented a rate of 15.7% in 1964 and 14.6% in
1965.[8] If one adds reinvestments made on the spot to transferred
earnings, the result is an average profitability for those two
years of more than 18%. And that rate does not take into account
either rents and royalties or earnings transferred clandestinely,
which are significant but obviously impossible to calculate.

Whatever this figure may be, and confining ourselves to official
data, the World Bank evaluated income transferred from the
developing countries in 1964 at more than four billion dollars

for 1964 and at about five billion for 1965, southern Europe excluded. Since in the course of those two years, the influx of fresh capital in the form of direct private investments equalled only 970 and 1,360 million dollars, respectively, there was a net deficit of 3½ billion dollars annually for the countries in question, namely the Third World. This deficit was certainly higher in 1966, since the influx of fresh capital in the form of direct private investments reached only 1,040 million dollars, and the amount of profits transferred out grows every year. I have shown, moreover, in my previous book, that the figures released by the World Bank for the transfer of earnings were on the low side, since, on the basis of the figures for balances of payments published by the IMF, one arrives at a total of 4,900 million dollars instead of "more than four billion." And so we can estimate that at the least, the countries of the Third World recorded a minimum deficit of five billion dollars in direct private imperialist investment.

In addition, the overall trade deficit of the Third World countries for the individual years of 1964, 1965, and 1966 varies between 1.2 and 1.8 billion dollars.[9] This gaping hole of six to seven billion dollars which imperialist dealings in commodities and capital make each year in the external accounts of the Third World naturally has to be filled. This is essentially accomplished through imperialist foreign aid. And that suggests two conclusions: a) foreign aid is not a matter of choice or an option, and "Cartierism" [10] is economic idiocy. Official grants are a necessity without which the imperialist order would collapse; b) from another point of view, these grants, since they are public, amount to a form of assistance which the taxpayers of the imperialist countries bring, not to the Third World as a certain kind of propaganda claims, but to imperialism and particularly to the monopolies that trade and invest in the Third World. Since taxpayers are basically salaried workers, foreign aid, in its role as a handmaiden of monopolist state capitalism, is really a transfer of income within each imperialist country from the salaried classes to the imperialist bourgeoisie.

But imperialism would no longer be imperialism if foreign aid did not bear its trademark. Its need to balance the external accounts of the Third World, hugger-mugger, in no way prevents the imperialist system from using financial assistance to further its fundamental objectives. Foreign aid has become one of the instruments—and far from the least—of imperialist policy and exploitation in the Third World. The discussions I have devoted to this subject in my earlier books make it unnecessary for us to linger over it any further.

Confining ourselves, then, to the more strictly financial side of foreign aid, a glance at the first few lines of the table at the beginning of this section suggests certain observations:

1. Multilateral aid increased more than bilateral aid over the eleven years under consideration, but multilateral aid still only totalled one-tenth of the amount spent on bilateral aid, keeping in mind the qualifications that must be applied to the bilateral figures. The fact that there is so little multilateral aid in absolute figures undermines the importance of its greater relative growth.

2. The total amount of official aid barely doubled in absolute figures during eleven years. But it fell in relative value, or, more precisely, it fell percentage-wise with respect to the aggregate national income of the donor countries (DAC countries):[11]

1962	1963	1964	1965	1966
0.72%	0.69%	0.61%	0.60%	0.57%

Imperialism is therefore keeping its aid down to the minimum necessary for the system to continue functioning. This has nothing to do with aid for development; it is aid designed to maintain things the way they are.

3. Within the general category of bilateral aid, loans increased in relation to grants and grant-like flows.

The result of this last point is that, financially speaking, the public debt of the Third World countries, which had been increased anyway by the cost of secured export credits, grew rapidly (by 56% between 1962 and 1965). In 1966, payments for debt-servicing rose to 3.96 billion dollars for 95 countries including southern Europe, which equals roughly three-and-a-half billion dollars for the Third World.[12]

The cost of that debt is rapidly becoming insupportable, in the strict sense of the word, for numerous countries. For the Third World as a whole today, this expense consumes two-thirds of all new official aid. And so, as the former president of the World Bank put it, foreign aid is approaching closer and closer to the point when it will "eat itself up." [13] Imperialism is always confining itself more tightly within its own contradictions. In the most serious cases, it has no other recourse to fall back on than agreeing to moratoriums.

In this regard, it is important to note that if, on the one hand, the imperialist states take a dark view of multilateral aid administered by such organizations as the World Bank, no doubt because such aid is too depersonalized, they do not, on the other hand, hesitate to set themselves up in consortiums of eight or ten members when one or another of the large countries of the Third World has trouble meeting its various bilateral obligations: consortiums for aid to India, Pakistan, and Indonesia, for example, were even established on the recommendation of UNCTAD and under the aegis of the World Bank. Now there is an undeniable type of integration that, in various forms, has taken hold impressively during recent years.

Another example of integration that has sprung up within the aid structure is that of the Common Market with its African and Malagasy associate members, through the medium of the European Development Fund.

Finally, getting back to private capital, it can be established that the same tendency toward increasing dispersion and internationalization that affects commodity exports operates in this area as well. The old colonial powers are confining themselves less and less to investing their private capital only in their former colonies and dependencies. France, which is not, however, a model of initiative in foreign investment, has been investing its private capital more and more in Latin America and in Southeast Asia, in countries once colonized by others. In Argentina as of 1968, capital invested in the fifty largest companies included 22% originating in the United States and 29% from Europe (representing, in descending order of importance, England, Italy, France, Germany).[14] But in this area again, the case of U.S. private capital is significant. Between 1960 and 1965, the level of

American private investment went up only 16.6% in Latin America, where it nevertheless remains heavily predominant, but it rose by 57% in Asia and by 106% in Africa.[15] I can only paraphrase what I wrote in the previous chapter: more and more as times goes on, the American colossus is turning the entire Third World into a field of action for its capital.

Despite this trend, there has still been relatively little investment of private capital in the Third World during the postwar period, as was noted above. There are two main reasons for this:

a) An orientation toward specialized investment in certain sectors. U.S. private investors, who are typical, have 44% of their capital in oil and 12% in mines, that is, well over half of their funds are invested in mining industries. Imperialist private capital is generally only invested in manufacturing industries when there is no feasible alternative, as we shall see later. And, since mineral deposits are already known and reserved, imperialism only exploits them as its needs expand.

b) Political uncertainty and the risk of nationalization. The emancipation movements that have sprung up nearly everywhere in the dominated countries worry powerful capital investors a great deal. They decide to invest only when they must or when they see an opportunity for an extremely quick depreciation. It does not seem as if an international agreement worked out in 1965 for regulating disputes related to investments and signed by the principal imperialist countries and numerous Third World states has done much to allay the fears of the men with capital in Europe and North America.

B. Capital Exports Between Developed Capitalist Countries

We have already seen that this kind of capital export involves a relatively small amount of official capital, but that, worldwide, it is the predominant mode of investment for private capital. The industrialized capitalist countries increasingly export private capital to each other. And so, in 1964 U.S. long term private investment in Europe totalled 17.5 billion dollars, while long term private European investment in the United States equalled 17.7 billion. But, although direct American investments in Europe (12.1 billion dollars) represented almost 70% of private American investment there, direct European investment in the United States (5.8 billion dollars) was less than 33% of total European investment in the United States, since the bulk of European investments (10.8 billion dollars) consisted of portfolio placements.[16] In other words, exports of American private capital to Europe reflect an entrepreneurial capitalism, one that is active, whereas exports of European capital to the United States are to a large degree the result of a passive capitalism of placement.

Within the sphere of private direct investment, which is by far the most significant area for a study of imperialism, there are still other parallel examples worth noting. For example, direct private investment by the United States in Canada as of 1964 rose to 13,820 million dollars, but direct private Canadian investment in the United States totalled 2,284 million dollars (a ratio of six to one). And direct American investments in Europe reached 12,067 million dollars, while those of Europe in the United States amounted to 5,819 million dollars (a ratio of two to one, which had changed to 2.6 to one by the end of 1966).

But by looking more closely at this situation, one notices that Great Britain invested only 60% in the United States of the amount the United States invested in Great Britain; that the balance of direct investment between the United States and Switzerland was almost even; that the direct investments of the Netherlands in the United States were more than double the amount invested by the United States in the Netherlands.

We should, however, grant less importance to this snapshot of 1964 than to the enlargement available for the period 1950–1964. In 1950, the balance of reciprocal private investment was infinitely more favorable for Great Britain, Switzerland and the Netherlands. Rather than go into too much detail, let's look at the figures for Europe as a whole. Between 1950 and 1964, the amount of direct European investments in the United States went up by a factor of 2.6, while U.S. investment in Europe rose sevenfold (average annual increase: 13.8%). In 1950 the balance was very favorable to Europe; in 1964 it had become unfavorable by a ratio of 2.1 to one (and in 1966 by 2.6 to one), as we have seen. The same change took place between the United States and Canada.[17]

It is therefore possible to say that during the postwar era the interrelationship of capital exports between imperialist countries is overwhelmingly characterized, in the case of direct investments which are the most decisive indicator, by the substantial advances made by American capital in all the other countries.

No doubt this change, which continued through 1967, found little to stand in its way at the time. On the one hand, the measures taken by the American government to correct the imbalance of external payments slowed the expatriation of U.S. capital, and on the other hand, the rate of investment of foreign capital in the United States quickened considerably at the same time. It is too soon at the time I am writing to determine whether this is meant to be a long-lasting trend or an accidental and short-lived break in the overall rhythm of investment. If forced to decide, I would lean toward the second hypothesis.[18]

In any case, the constraints brought to bear against taking capital out of the United States have resulted in heavily increased demands on the European money market by American subsidiaries in Europe in need of capital to finance their investments: 1.5 billion dollars during the first half of 1968 as against 0.3 for the same period during 1967.[19] American investors learned to find capital inside Europe when they were no longer able to take it out of the United States.

In Great Britain private American investments loom very large among total private foreign investments (72% in 1962). In West Germany they represented about 34% of foreign capital invested as of 1964. And in France, in 1962, they had risen as high as 45% of the total amount of private foreign capital in the country.[20] This last figure is hard to reconcile with the figure for the portion of total gross private foreign investment made in France between 1962 and 1966 that was due to *new* American investment: 26%.[21] It is true that the official document from which I have taken this figure takes note of the fact that new investments financed from Switzerland (32% of the total between 1962 and 1966) include a great proportion of investments which "stopped off" in Switzerland, as it were, on their way from America. If this is the case for only half of the "Swiss" investments, we end up with the more realistic percentage of 42% for direct American investments in France, which is still probably below the real amount.

Christopher Layton states,[22] indeed, and with arguments to support his case, that the figures currently advanced for evaluating private American investment abroad are shaved severely, to roughly 60% of their true value. He estimates that in 1964 "American direct investors were responsible for between 5 and 6 per cent of fixed capital formation in the industry of Western Europe." That figure is, of course, quite a modest amount, but it is a percentage of total investment in all areas of industry, and, as such, it is difficult to interpret without doing an analysis of American investment sector by sector.

At the end of 1965, direct private American investment in Europe was distributed as follows among the major economic sectors:[23]

manufacturing industries	about	55%
oil	"	25%
commerce	"	12%
others	"	8%

Since oil investment in Europe has mainly to do with refining, 80% of direct private American investments were directed toward industrial activities.

The processing industries are also the sector toward which the principal European countries direct the lion's share of their private capital when they invest in advanced capitalist countries. France, with 52% of its exports of private capital within OECD committed to industrial investments, is the industrialized country with the lowest percentage of investment recorded in this area. The service industries absorbed 35%, and other sectors took up 13% (notably real estate placements in Spain) of the total private capital exported between 1962 and 1966.

Thus it is remarkable to observe that, in general, as with commodity exports, the growth of private capital exports from one imperialist country to another is principally and increasingly the result of investments in the industrial sector.

The United States sets the tone for this by devoting a relatively large proportion of its capital formation to foreign industrial investments. According to Christopher Layton, in fact, "roughly a fifth of United States investment in manufacturing industry goes abroad, with the most advanced industries taking the lead":

21.9% of the total electrical industry investment
24.6%   "   "   chemical   "   "
27.4%   "   "   rubber   "   "
29.5%   "   "   transport   "   "

The result of this is that, in numerous sectors of European industry especially, a high proportion of the total turnover of business is due to American companies:

30% for the European automotive industry[24]
25–30% for the oil industry in Great Britain and the EEC
75% for computers and adding machines in France
95% for carbon black in France and 75% in England
35% for farm machinery in France and more than 40% in Great Britain
and so on.

The same author points out that the large American companies which gained a foothold in Europe long ago dominate American activities there. Esso, General Motors, and Ford account for 40% of the direct American investments in France, West Germany and Great Britain, and two-thirds of the direct American investments in Europe are managed by only twenty companies.[25]

He puts emphasis, however, on a new tendency which has cropped up since 1960: medium-sized American companies are investing more and more in Europe. If American investment in Europe is still mainly engaged in by the great international enterprises, he concludes, "it has now become an accepted part of the operations of most large American corporations and many medium-sized companies as well." For his part, Geoffrey Owen notes that American companies have the "international habit" and regard the absence of foreign interests as "a sign of backwardness." [26] Thus the number of American companies with interests in Europe grows incessantly, while their influence appears in new sectors: food products, service industries and hotels.

It is far from the case, however, that the vigorous growth of private American assets in Europe results exclusively or principally from capital exports. According to Christopher Layton, private American investments are financed only to a slight degree by fresh American money. The influx of new capital, in his view, only covers about 30% of investment costs, while reinvested European earnings account for 46%, and 24% is borrowed in the host country.[27] According to others, direct American financing does not exceed 25% of the total, while the European money market supplies roughly 40%.[28] J.-J. Servan-Schreiber goes still further. He states that only 10% of the cost of these investments is met through the transfer of dollars and that 90% comes from money already earned in Europe or from various European resources.[29]

Whatever the differences between these figures, they all militate toward the same conclusion: direct private American investments in Europe are only marginally supported with capital originating in the United States. The substantial part of their financing is done on the spot.

Between 1960 and 1965, the amount of profits officially repatriated to the United States from direct private investments in Europe averaged out annually at 6.5% of the capital invested.[30] This relatively low percentage is a reflection of the large amount of earnings (from about 30 to 45% according to the authors cited above) reinvested locally in new American investments. It seems, moreover, on the basis of calculations and crosschecks that I have been able to make, that the proportion of earnings reinvested locally does not exceed 15% in the Third World, but is on the order of 50% in Europe. All this confirms the fact that American capital in Europe is not placement or speculative capital in the strict sense, but entrepreneurial capital intended to multiply itself on the spot, to snowball as it develops or creates subsidiary enterprises, capital invested with a view toward long-term growth. This is certainly one of the characteristic features of American capitalism in Europe.

Among all the countries of Western Europe, those of the Common Market have been especially successful in attracting private American capital during recent years, even more so than Great Britain. Nearly 70% of current American investment in the EEC has been made since 1960, as against 56% for Great Britain.[31]

If the EEC agrees, in effect, to lower its common external tariffs within the framework of negotiations (the Kennedy Round), external tariffs will still exist and goods will still be affected by them. But tariffs do not affect capital. Once it is transferred, a vast local market is open to it. It brings with it technology and "know how." And it has the use of cheaper labor than in the United States. It can establish itself on a European scale and create different subsidiaries with specialized functions. And so, between 1958 and 1966, among 2,820 different enterprises, American assets in the EEC rose from 1,680 to more than 7000 million dollars.[32] Objectively, therefore, and paradoxically for some people, the Common Market has encouraged worldwide monopolistic integration with regard to capital.

G.-Y. Bertin notes, moreover, that although the American enterprises have introduced practically no new kinds of business activity in the EEC, they have had, on the contrary, a remarkable consolidating effect on the sectors where they have been able to compete. "Their activities have brought about," he adds, "a certain movement away from *independence* and toward a profound economic *interdependence* among industrialized countries." I shall return to this.

Speaking of American private capital exports in general, Christopher Layton observes that "slowly, the organization of American corporations is changing to make international operations an integral part of their business instead of a haphazard appendage of the domestic firm." These international operations form a part today, as we have already seen, of the "operations" of the American companies. As Layton puts it, "if one wishes to isolate a single significant factor in American direct investment in Europe, it is expansion-mindedness . . . a new awareness by American firms that their market is the world." Moreover, he devotes a persuasive discussion to the idea that foreign investment is at least as much of an element of competition among the American firms themselves as it is part of the competition they are engaged in with foreign companies.[33]

One of the many results of the powerful rise of American investments in the other industrialized countries during recent years has been that American industry abroad, with production estimated at 120 billion dollars in 1967, has become the world's third-ranking industrial power, after the United States and the Soviet Union. There are now two powerful Americas: one inside the United States and one outside. These two Americas are, of course, both only part of the same phenomenon, and that's why the "invasion" of American capital sometimes raises problems for the other imperialist countries and why the newspapers during recent years have made a great fuss about the "anxieties" which the influx of transatlantic capital were provoking here and there.

Among the main criticisms levelled at American capital in Europe were: their "strategic" placement in key sectors; the location of decisionmaking centers outside the host countries; the American firms' ignorance of politics or national economic imperatives in their host countries. In return, others point out the benefits that Europe receives through the influx of American companies that bring along with them the most advanced technology and also stimulate domestic development. For the moment, I do not propose to enter into this discussion. What I want to do is merely emphasize that criticisms and anxieties have not prevented nor even slowed the rapid growth of private American investments anywhere in Europe.

It is no secret that the French government more than any other has openly expressed its reticence toward American investment within its borders. But it is sufficient to recall that, according to the French minister of industry at the time, only four American requests for permission to invest were refused, out of a total of 198 presented during 1965, and that none were refused during the first half of 1966, in order to judge how wide the gap is that separates feelings and inclinations from concrete acts. And to put heavy emphasis, as certain Marxist economists, whom I shall characterize as traditionalists (but the two terms clash when they're put together, don't they?), have done, on the contradictions and rivalries at the heart of the capitalist system which the rapid increase in the exportation of American capital has caused or worsened, is to give too much importance to a phenomenon that certainly exists but which loses significance as the predominance of imperialist integration grows. The rapid expansion of commerce and of capital flows between the industrialized capitalist countries indicates a greater internationalization of productive capacities and of production, a fact which, believe me, nobody disputes. That this growing internationalization should be brought about, within the capitalist system, through the action, and for the profit of, that strain of capitalism which is by far the most powerful, the American, is absolutely inevitable. The American superimperialism which results from the process does, on the one hand, undoubtedly generate or accentuate certain contradictions. But on the other hand, in the same way that the so-called "national" bourgeoisies of the dominated countries of the Third World can prosper *only* by trailing along after imperialism, so too the native capitalists of the industrialized countries know that the relationship of forces has evolved in such a way that henceforth they can hope to prosper *only* if they remain in relative harmony with the American giant. American domination is accepted, in fact sought after, from the moment it appears that it is the galley in which no one can avoid rowing who wishes to be assured of industrial growth and the continued growth of profits. It contributes to what Bertin calls "a certain movement away from *independence* and toward a profound *interdependence* among industrialized countries." Imperialist integration, a subject which I shall treat at greater length in Chapter X, seems to me to have become the most important fact of our time. And the supremacy acquired by the American monopolies over almost the entire imperialist zone, within the interlocking network of capital exports after the Second World War, is at once a cause of integration and one of its essential effects.

C. COMMODITY EXPORTS AND CAPITAL EXPORTS

We have seen (Chap. I) that Lenin long ago established a connection between commodity exports and capital exports—that the latter were a means of encouraging the former—and that Bukharin was a firm supporter of this view and maintained, moreover, that there was a tendency for capital to be expatriated in order to provide a substitute for blocked commodity exports.

Since the Second World War, as international trade and capital flow have both grown significantly in conjunction with each other, their interrelations have also developed considerably and become infinitely more complex. "Exports and direct investment," writes Christopher Layton, "mingle inextricably today in the strategy of the international corporation." [34]

I stated above that the EEC had, in effect, encouraged the investment of American capital within the borders of its members, which was, of course, a means of substituting American production within Europe for the importation of American-made products that would face tariff barriers on their entry into the Common Market. But it is certainly far from true to say that this process was a simple case of mechanical substitution.

On the one hand, indeed, according to Christopher Layton once again, "large companies have found that manufacture in Europe, designed at first to replace direct exports, has carried an even larger load of new exports on its back." In 1963, exports outside the host country by American industrial subsidiaries were equal to 23% of what they sold within their host countries, and a part of those exports went to the United States. The American subsidiaries export a larger part of their production than their local competitors.[35]

But on the other hand, these subsidiaries also requisition imports from the United States: semi-finished products, machine-finished parts, etc., and they import so heavily that in 1963, 23% of all U.S. exports went to American companies abroad. "The period of soaring United States capital exports has also been a period when United States direct exports have been rising fast." [36]

According to Geoffrey Owen, finding a substitute for exports was not the sole motive behind the creation of American subsidiaries in Europe in general or in the EEC in particular:

"In some cases," he observes, "competition from imports forced American producers to switch part of their production for the U.S. market to overseas factories. Manufacturers of shoes, apparel, and watches, for example, having lost part of their home market to Swiss, Italian and other foreign-made goods, began to produce in the United States only those items where they had an advantage over the foreigner, and to use their foreign plants for the rest. Because of the disparity in labour costs, conventional typewriters could be produced more cheaply in Europe than in the United States; instead of simply abandoning the U.S. typewriter market to foreign companies, American firms could establish or acquire their own plants in Europe. Burroughs Corporation could make adding machines in Scotland at a cost that was 40 per cent less than in Detroit. Hence it decided to close its Detroit plant and supply the U.S. adding-machine market from Scotland. At the same time Burroughs continued to manufacture computers in the U.S. and export them to Europe. Products with a high 'labour' content could often be produced economically overseas, where wages were lower than in the U.S. More advanced products with a high 'technological' content could still be produced in the U.S. and exported." [37]

The result of these trends and countertrends, which are, in fact, "inextricable" components of a single process, is, in the final analysis, the importance that American industry has assumed abroad. Between 1950 and 1962, when the volume of U.S. exports increased by a factor of 2.7, the production of American factories abroad had gone up by a factor of 4.2. And "most of the firms made more profit on their foreign production than on their domestic sales or on their exports." [38]

In another remarkable study, Harry Magdoff analyzes the phenomena we have just surveyed.[39] I shall return to this study for a longer discussion in Chapter X, but at this point I would like to extract certain data from it which is important for our present discussion.

H. Magdoff, in the table reproduced below (with percentages rounded off), shows the growth of the respective shares of the principal imperialist countries of total world exports of manufactured products between 1913 and 1967:

	1913	1929	1937	1950	1967
United States	13	20	19	27	21
United Kingdom	30	22	21	25	12
West Germany	27	21	22	7	20
France	12	11	6	10	8
Italy	3	4	3	4	7
Japan	2	4	7	3	10
Others	13	18	22	25	22

But we agree with H. Magdoff that the data in this table can not be appreciated unless they are combined with those in the following table, which shows, again in rounded-off percentages, the distribution of foreign investments of all kinds among the major capital-exporting countries:

	1914	1930	1960
United Kingdom	50	44	25
France	22	8	5
West Germany	17	3	1
United States	6	35	59
Netherlands	3	6	4
Sweden	1	1	1
Canada	1	3	5
TOTAL	100	100	100

The first thing to notice is that the first table records much smaller upheavals than the second. In other words, the development of imperialism and of the balance of forces among the imperialist countries reveals itself with particular sharpness in the area of capital exports.

Secondly, note the relatively large decline of imperialism in Great Britain, and to a lesser degree in Germany and France, which shows up both in the figures for exports of manufactured goods and those for exports of private capital. But the figures for Germany are undoubtedly a bit misleading since they do not refer to the same Germany before and after the Second World War.

Finally, though the first table indicates a more equal and uniform division of exports of manufactured goods today than in years past (the leading three countries accounted for 70% of the total in 1913, but only 53% in 1967), the second table, on the contrary, shows not only a very different polarization of private foreign investment in 1960 than in 1914, but a polarization which is also much more dramatic. Thus the internationalization of trade appears to be a much more real event than the internationalization of capital. I say "appears to be" advisedly. For H. Magdoff does not neglect to mention that since the First World War, and even more after the Second, the struggle for the conquest of markets has mainly been waged through the establishment of factories abroad and the purchase of foreign companies, that is, through capital investments in other countries.

On the one hand, a not at all negligible proportion of exports to foreign countries made by American companies is included in the national export statistics of most of the other countries (22% of the total sales of American companies in Europe), but on the other hand, and more to the point, the local sales of American companies abroad are much, much greater than corresponding exports from the United States. Thanks to H. Magdoff's data, I have been able to calculate direct U.S. exports as a percentage of the sales of the same products made by American foreign subsidiaries in 1965: paper and cardboard, 21%;

chemical products, 35%; rubber, 10%; metals, 52%; non-electrical equipment, 98%; electrical equipment, 42%; transport equipment, 30%. Overall, for these seven sectors, direct U.S. exports amounted to only 43% of the sales of foreign subsidiaries. And between 1957 and 1965, sales by subsidiaries grew two-and-a-half times faster than direct exports.

The principal result of this is that, in the first of the two tables above, the figure that stands for the relative amount of American exports compared to total world exports of manufactured products in 1967 (21%), and the downward movement of that figure between 1950 and 1967 have no great significance. But the figure in the second table that stands for the American share of the total of private foreign investments made by the principal capital-exporting countries in 1960 (59%) is all the more significant since, as H. Magdoff points out, it would be markedly higher if the table was limited to direct investments alone instead of including all private investment (direct and portfolio). And the figure is undoubtedly higher today.

And so it would be erroneous to draw any firm conclusions, especially about the imperialist countries, only on the basis of the figures for their external trade. Commodity exports and capital exports overlap so much that only a comparative analysis of them both offers any hope of sorting out the real economic lines of force that are at work. And the examination I have just performed leads me to affirm with greater conviction than ever that the growing internationalization of commodity exports and of capital exports from the imperialist countries in the postwar period, however widespread it may be, does not negate the fact that important modifications in the relationships of economic forces have taken place that work to the detriment of the old imperialisms and for the benefit of American superimperialism, which increasingly dominates the entire capitalist world.

But if capital exports serve as a corrective to certain data based on the figures for commodity exports alone, the same should be true in the special case of the relationship of the imperialist countries and the Third World. I noted in the previous chapter that especially because of the existence of unequal exchange, the import capacity of the countries of the Third World was going down almost constantly and that as a result the market which these countries represent for the manufactured products of imperialist factories is shrinking. But in this area too, capital exports tend, to a degree that can not be neglected, to fill the gap. Industrial investments in the Third World set up local production as a substitute for imports. In particular, the proliferation of assembly plants in the Third World can only be explained in this way. Between 1960, the year an automobile assembly plant was built in Morocco, and 1966, the year when the internal production of automobiles was sufficient to cover about half of a market that had remained almost the same, Moroccan automobile imports went down more than 50%. Imports of assembly parts only made up a small amount of the difference, since many sources for parts and materials were found locally. The foreign promoters of the assembly line acquired a solid position for themselves and even expanded a market which no longer depends on variations in Morocco's import capacity and which is no longer measured by a certain number of commodity exchanges.

Such operations and others that achieve the same result are becoming more and more the order of the day nearly everywhere and especially in Latin America. They act as a corrective to the figure I arrived at before: that the manufactured goods sold in the Third World represented 5.5% of the industrialized capitalist countries' total manufactured production. This figure minimizes the real importance of the markets of the Third World to imperialist industry.

At the end of a series of investigations and analyses that have dealt with a subject of particular complexity, an attempt at a synthesis of both this chapter and the previous one strikes me as indispensable.

1. Commodity exports and capital exports, which were both highly developed before the First World War, were both virtually stagnant between the two wars, but after 1945, and especially after 1955, they once again achieved an extremely

high growth rate, higher still in the case of capital exports.

This growth, of both commodity and capital exports, was made possible by the development of productive forces and the relatively large and continuous economic expansion of the advanced capitalist countries. It went up faster than the average increase of the GNP in those countries.

2. The special growth pattern of commodity and capital exports was helped along a great deal by worldwide and regional imperialist integration, which aims at an ever greater internationalization of productive forces and of production, and at their result: the growth of monopolies which become international in scope and achieve actual integration, which push for the creation of integrationist agreements and institutions: GATT, OECD, EEC, EFTA, the Kennedy Round, etc., which in turn offer the monopolies new opportunities to dominate the entire capitalist world market.

3. Integration gives an advantage to the most powerful countries. Imperialist America emerged from the Second World War stronger than ever and turned itself into a worldwide superimperialism while the older imperialist nations were still weak from the war. America's industrial strength (its GNP all by itself is greater than the combined GNP of all the other capitalist countries put together), its financial supremacy and the role of the dollar as an international reserve currency permit its goods and especially its capital to circulate with ease nearly everywhere. The United States is the capitalist world's leading industrial power; foreign-based American firms, as a group, are in second place.

4. The dominance of American capital provokes or aggravates contradictions and rivalries between industrialized capitalist countries and their respective monopolies. But these monopolies generally submit to the U.S. monopolies as soon as resistance appears vain or a common danger arises. And from then on the quest for a constant maximal profit is led by American capital. To be absorbed or controlled by it is no longer a somewhat shameful defeat, but an assurance of

survival. Absorption, control or cooperative agreements are accepted; sometimes they are requested.

The internationalization of production and the parallel internationalization of commodity and capital exports proceed at a particularly rapid pace, among developed capitalist countries, in the area of manufacturing. Integration encourages competition, and competition, in turn, reinforces the tendency toward monopolistic concentration.

5. The exchange of goods between the imperialist countries and the Third World continues, on the contrary, to reflect the complementary nature of production in the two groups of countries, and it is carried on according to the rule of unequal exchange. The result is a reduction in the dominated countries' capacity to import, and as a consequence of this, the market in these countries for the industrial products of imperialism contracts. Imperialism often reacts to this by investing in the production of goods locally as substitutes for imports. Because imperialist investments in the Third World are endangered by "political risk," they remain primarily oriented, however, toward the extraction of oil and raw materials, which are still the items of highest priority.

6. The annual repatriation of earnings from these private investments, added to the annual trade deficit, leaves a hole six to seven billion dollars wide in the combined external accounts of the Third World. The only substantial way this gap can be filled is through official "aid," which is itself the basis for unending imperialist exploitation in the dominated countries.

This official aid, which more and more frequently takes the form of interest-bearing loans, brings with it rapidly swelling national debts whose costs are becoming impossible for the Third World to support. More than two-thirds of all new funds received from foreign aid have to be devoted to amortizing the old grants. Thus aid tends to consume itself, and imperialism, as a result, finds itself imprisoned in its own contradictions.

7. Faced with the difficulties which many countries of the Third World have in paying off their debts, the imperialist countries unite in multinational action. They agree to moratoriums, which place the defaulting countries under collective protection. At the same time, internationalization is on the increase, and commodity exchange and capital flow are spread more and more thinly over the Third World. American imperialism, meanwhile, extends its tentacles ever more widely over the dominated countries of Asia, Africa and Latin America.

8. To ask the question inspired by Lenin: whether capital exports have assumed particular importance in the current phase of imperialism, now seems a rather pointless venture, since it is becoming more and more difficult all the time to treat foreign trade and capital flow as distinct categories. The monopolies, and especially the American monopolies, use one or the other, and most often both at the same time, as they seek to dominate the capitalist world through a complex game whose purpose is always supremacy.

It seems to me far more relevant to note that imperialism today wants to export only its goods to the Third World, while it prefers to reserve its private capital for the industrialized world. Confidence reigns here and not there. Here one can invest without fear. There one does it only when one has to and, then, within limits which give these investments an increasingly marginal character. In its relations with the Third World, where the contradictions are least soluble and most explosive, imperialism, which is just as piratical and greedy as ever, is from now on condemned to live in expectation, if not on the defensive.

Notes to Chapter 4

1. *Op. cit.*, p. 64.
2. *L'Investissement international*, *"Que sais-je?"* collection, P.U.F., Chap. I.

3. *International Flow of Long-term Capital and Official Donations,* 1951–1959 and 1959–1961, United Nations.

4. *Statistical Abstract of the U.S.,* 1967.

5. Sources: various OECD publications. The figures in parentheses are estimates.

6. Cf. Pierre Jalée, *The Third World in World Economy,* Chap. VI.

7. *Development Assistance, Efforts and Policies of the Members of the Development Assistance Committee,* OECD, 1966 and 1967.

8. *Statistical Abstract of the U.S.,* 1966 and 1967.

9. *World Bank Annual Report* 1968, Table 5.

10. Cartier, Raymond (1904–), author of celebrated series of three articles attacking the monetary aspects of foreign aid in *"Paris-Match"* (of which he is now *co-directeur general*), nos. 777–779 (Feb. 28, March 7, March 14, 1964): *"Attention: La France Dilapide Son Argent."*—Tr.

11. *Development Assistance,* 1967, OECD, p. 58.

12. *World Bank Annual Report* 1966–1967, p. 34.

13. Woods, George D., in a speech delivered at the Rio de Janeiro Monetary Conference, Sept. 26, 1967.

14. *Le Monde,* Sept. 15 and 16, 1968.

15. *Statistical Abstract of the U.S.,* 1966 and 1967.

16. Layton, Christopher, *Trans-Atlantic Investments,* The Atlantic Institute (Boulogne-sur-Seine: 1966), p. 21.

17. Figures taken from Layton, *op. cit.*

18. At the beginning of April, 1969, President Nixon significantly relaxed restrictions on capital exports.

19. IMF, Annual Report, 1968, p. 57.

20. Layton, *op. cit.,* p. 13.

21. Problèmes économiques, no. 1,044, study made by the French Finance Ministry.

22. *Op. cit.,* p. 15.

23. *Statistical Abstract of the U.S.,* 1967.

24. 40% in 1966, according to G.-Y. Bertin, *op. cit.,* p. 76.

25. *Op. cit.,* pp. 17–19.

26. Owen, *op. cit.,* p. 134.

27. *Op. cit.,* p. 15.

28. *Revue Politique et Parlementaire,* Feb. 1967, article by J. Ferronière.

29. *The American Challenge,* Atheneum, 1968.

30. *Statistical Abstract of the U.S.,* 1966 and 1967.

31. *Le Patronat français,* journal of the national organization of French employers, Feb., 1968.

32. Bertin, *op. cit.,* pp. 75–77.

33. *Op. cit.,* pp. 24–26.

34. *Op. cit.,* p. 77.

35. *Op. cit.,* p. 24, Table VIII.

36. *Op. cit.,* p. 125.
37. *Op. cit.,* pp. 133–134.
38. *Op. cit.,* p. 134.
39. "The Age of Imperialism," *Monthly Review,* June, 1968.

5

The New
Technological Revolution

Though I am devoting a special chapter to this subject—albeit the shortest in the book—I do not attach special importance to the new postwar technological revolution. On the contrary, I want to try to reduce it to its true proportions and do something to counteract the flood of literature which waxes lyrical about technology far too readily. Statements such as "scientific progress has been more important in the last forty years than it was in the preceding forty centuries" are a dime a dozen these days. They roll out of typewriters belonging to writers of every variety, including Marxists. And the economic and political conclusions which these panegyrists produce are in the same fanciful vein as their views on technology.

It seems to me that the sober approach to all this is to recall that today's scientific and technological revolution is not the first, and I cannot advise people too much to reread the long passage, also on the lyrical side, that Bukharin devoted to the previous scientific and technological revolution more than a half-century ago. He enumerated all the discoveries and inventions which made up "the general picture of a feverishly rapid technical progress," and concluded: "Never has the union of science with industry achieved greater victories." [1]

Charles Bettelheim judges wisely that "in the final analysis, economic growth has always depended on the progress of scientific and technological knowledge. If mankind had only been able to invest in the tools known during the stone age, there would have been no economic progress even if there had been a relatively high rate of investment." [2] As for Geoffrey Owen, he heavily discounts the effects of technological progress, even in the United States: "Recent studies suggest that the most important single factor in economic growth is the rise in the educational level of the labour force; it seems to be even more important than improved technology or increased capital investment per worker." [3]

The common failing of those, whoever they may be, who get excited too easily by the new technological revolution, is to substitute a superficial, technician's explanation for rigorous economic and political analysis. When J. K. Galbraith argues: "There is a broad convergence between industrial systems. The imperatives of technology and organization, not the images of ideology, are what determine the shape of economic society," [4] his method is the same—though I hardly dare say so—as those two Marxist authors, J. P. Vigier and G. Waysand [Révolution Scientifique et Impérialisme", a Report to the Havana Cultural Congress, 1968], who declare their "conviction that, in the last few decades, scientific and technological advances have brought important modifications to the process of production, modifications that *explain* [the emphasis is theirs] the present functioning of the imperialist system." But what can be pardoned in Galbraith cannot be condoned in these men, for to do so is to forget Marxism.

Let's try to look clearly at this and ask ourselves, first of all, the question: How do scientific and technical progress affect the economy? J. Thibaut attacks this problem and resolves it in a way that I support. [5] He observes, first, that more and more often Marxist literature contains the idea that "science is becoming a direct productive force." And his analysis leads him to believe that a distinction has to be made between basic research, on the one hand, and, on the other, the two other types of research included in what is called research and development (R and D), that is, technological or applied research and developmental research. Though he thinks that it is a mistake to attempt to make "a *direct* connection between basic research and industrial production," it seems to him, nevertheless, that technological and developmental research "must be considered as constituting direct productive forces." Let's take this opportunity to mention also that in the investments earmarked for R and D in the large industrialized capitalist countries, the portion allotted to basic research is quite small: 12 to 18%, and the lowest rate prevails in the United States and the United Kingdom.[6]

But from another point of view, investment in R and D can be divided up into funds budgeted 1) for nuclear, aerospace and military research; 2) for economic objectives; 3) or for social and miscellaneous purposes. Generally speaking, it is acknowledged that aerospace and military research, as Geoffrey Owen puts it,[7] produces only scattered "fallout" that benefits the productive sector of the economy. I shall concede that such fallout and the research done on nuclear power as an energy source balance out the basic research included in categories 2) and 3) above, which is a fairly rough and ready calculation but close to the truth all the same. And I shall limit the following discussion to the gross amounts earmarked for R and D with economic, social and miscellaneous objectives, of which economic objectives take up between four-fifths and nine-tenths of the total.

Thus defined, R and D in 1964 absorbed funds equal to about 1.36% of the GNP (figured at 1964 price levels) in the United States and 1.40% in the United Kingdom as against 0.95% in France, 1.15% in Germany, and 0.48% in Italy. The effort made in this area by the two Anglo-Saxon countries is clearly superior to that of the three others, and everyone knows that they are technologically far more advanced as well. The gap between the two groups of countries would be even wider if total R and D budgets, including expenditures for nuclear, aerospace, and military R and D were taken into consideration. However, it is also necessary to point out that between 1955 and 1965 the growth rate of the GNP (in adjusted dollars) was palpably lower in the United States and the United Kingdom than in the other three countries.[8] Comparisons made on the basis of the industrial production index give essentially similar results. This means that there is no necessary or direct connection between the size of funds allotted to R and D and the growth rate of the economy or of industrial production.

Since the positive benefits of R and D are unquestionable, this leads one to believe that R and D plays only a small part in the imperialist countries' efforts to enlarge their productive forces. Without making a full study of the matter, which would take us too far from our real subject, I should at least mention, for example, that, for the period 1960–1964, gross formation of fixed capital was on the order of 17% of the GNP (figured on un-adjusted price levels) in the United States, 16–17% in the United Kingdom, 24–26% in West Germany, 19–21% in France, and 21–22% in Italy.[9] These percentages are on an entirely different scale from those cited above for economically oriented R and D related to the same GNP (figured on unadjusted price levels), or even from the percentages for total R and D (3.4% in the United States and 2.3% in Great Britain, which spend more than the other countries by a wide margin). Without going more deeply into the matter than this, it is possible to see, by juxta-posing these two sets of figures, that R and D is only one element among many that go into making up a country's pro-ductive forces, and one of the least important at that. And to change this state of affairs significantly it would be necessary for the expenditures made on R and D in 1964 to be heavily in-creased. In the United States, for example, funds earmarked for R and D did not exceed 21 to 25 million (unadjusted) dollars be-tween 1964 and 1968.

Even so, technological progress does have certain effects on the functioning and the structure of the economy. I will now run rapidly over some of them.

1. The development of industrial technology brings with it changes in the structure of employment. J. K. Galbraith ob-serves, and he can be believed in this case since only figures are at issue, that between 1951 and 1964 the number of those employed in the United States increased by about ten million, but that there was no increase in blue collar workers. After examining statistics that relate unemployment and educational

achievement, he concludes: "The unemployed include the predicted concentration of the uneducated."

According to Galbraith the graph of labor's educational levels during the early stages of industrialization could be drawn "in the shape of a very squat pyramid," but with the introduction of increasingly sophisticated technology, the industrial system today requires a labor force structured like "a tall urn," whose lines "curve in sharply toward the base to reflect the more limited demand for those who are qualified only for muscular and repetitive tasks and who are readily replaced by machines."

He notes, moreover, that technological progress leads to the more rapid expansion of certain sectors that become key areas, and to a slowdown in other sectors. And he observes that the labor force is not adapted to the transfers of employment obliged by this change.[10]

2. Once again in the eyes of J. K. Galbraith, advanced technology implies the emergence of systematic organization and modern planning in large companies, which means that the entrepreneur is replaced at the helm by a collective entity, by "executives"—by management, which includes "all who bring specialized knowledge, talent or experience to group decision-making." It is this group of people, and no longer the traditional executives, who are now the reigning intelligence, the brains of the company. Galbraith calls them "the Technostructure." He sees "the divorce of the owner of the capital from control of the enterprise," in other words, "a shift of power from the owners of capital."[11]

Galbraith is developing a theory here which is the rage among many of the champions of neo-capitalism: business is no longer run by the capital investors and for this reason no longer has profit maximization as its goal. (In the same way, the technocracy which dominates public administration is supposed to have wrested real control of government from the politicians.

It goes without saying that I reject such interpretations, for the real question is not who makes the decisions, but for whom they are made.

Of course it is J. K. Galbraith who gets himself into a tight spot by asking this question, because he categorically refuses to answer it. He realizes that for highly-placed technocrats "pecuniary compensation becomes generous," he speaks of "spectacular" emoluments, but adds immediately that the executives "associate motivation with this high compensation," as if he who pays does not insist, always and everywhere, on being served. According to Galbraith, the goal and motivation of the technostructure is "to achieve the greatest possible rate of corporate growth," and he comes a cropper trying to show that the objective of growth can be pursued by executives apart from the consideration of profit. He concedes, though, that to achieve "esteem" a company has to have "a secure earnings record," and that "any firm that fails this requirement is a dog." But if he only talks about a minimum, it is because he places the highest importance on rapid growth. He states this more directly in another passage: "A rate of earnings that allows, over and above investment needs, for a progressive rise in the dividend rate will also regularly be a goal of the technostructure. This return must not be achieved by prices which would prejudice growth." [12] In other words, the technocrats are cleverer than the owners at defending the owners' interests. They do not want to compromise their chances for a steady stream of profits continuing on into the future by an inept and dangerous quest for too much profit too soon. This is a strategy for maximizing profits, which Galbraith wears himself out trying to conceal behind the concept of growth rate.[13]

The two other effects of technological development which I shall discuss seem to me to be of much greater importance to the subject of this study.

3. All the authorities I have consulted are in agreement about the fundamental and growing role played by the state in the organization and expansion of R and D.

"When investment in technological development is very high," writes J. K. Galbraith, "a wrong technical judgment or a failure in persuading consumers to buy the product can be extremely expensive." The costs and the risks "can be greatly reduced if the state pays for more exalted technical development or guarantees a market for the technically advanced product . . . Modern technology thus defines a growing function of the modern state." [14]

Geoffrey Owen not only notes that in the United States "over 60% of" the huge expenses of R and D "has been borne, not by industry itself, but by the federal government," but he also makes a point of illustrating how the state intervenes in R and D, as when, for example, the federal government plays "a catalytic role in the development of the 'scientific complex,' which is potentially one of the most effective instruments for bridging the gap between academic and industrial research." Finally, he adds, "As the Federal Government takes a more active part in promoting economic growth, it is likely to become more closely involved in the advancement of science, in industry and in the universities . . ." [15]

The OECD manual, to which I have already referred,[16] gives information and comparative data about the amount of public funds devoted to R and D in most of its member countries (1963–1964). State funds make up more than 60% of the total in the United States and France, 60% in Canada, more than 50% in Great Britain, 40% in Germany, 37% in Italy. The U.S. percentage remained essentially the same in 1968, while that of France seems to have risen slightly.

The same manual also offers helpful information about the use of public funds. In the United States around 54% of public funds spent on R and D were used by private enterprise (this rose to 69% in 1968), as were 48.5% in Great Britain, but barely 28% went to private research in France and roughly 23.5% in Germany. France spends most of its public funds on state-run research, and West Germany allocates half of its budget to research carried on within institutions of higher education.

But the general tendency is to pass on more and more public funds to industrial companies. As a matter of fact, in the course of its account of the preliminary work done on the French Sixth Plan, the newspaper *Le Monde* wrote that the decision made in favor of intensifying applied research was going to "push the government into having more and more research work done in industry, whether or not the company doing the research belonged to the private or public sector. This is a necessity, because research, especially if it is applied or developmental, can only bear fruit within the company where it has been done." [17]

The point of this section has been that the importance of the state's role in the field of R and D, and its support, have become an essential part of monopoly state capitalism (cf. Chap. VIII).

4. According to E. Varga, "The concentration of production facilitated the introduction of new techniques. The introduction of new techniques required, in turn, the further concentration of production in giant factories." Varga goes on to say: "The new equipment is very expensive. It requires the investment of large sums and the organization of production on a large scale." Therefore it is reserved for the powerful firms produced by concentration. Furthermore: "Today a small factory working with old machinery cannot long exist in competition with a big enterprise working in the same field and employing modern techniques." Therefore this small business is condemned to be swallowed up by a new merger, or to disappearance pure and simple, which also helps the giant, amalgamated companies. In conclusion, Varga writes: "The new production techniques are strengthening the domination of the monopolies in present-day capitalist economy." [18] That is a dialectical, Marxist analysis.

I have already pointed out, incidentally, that in the principal industrialized countries, funds earmarked for applied and developmental research, in other words those directly designed to aid industrial production, are greater by far than those that go to basic research. In the United States and Great Britain these direct subsidies to industry represent about 88% of all money from all sources spent on R and D. In France and Italy they come to about 80%. The *Le Monde* article just quoted reveals, moreover, that in France from now on heavier emphasis will be placed on the profitability and efficiency of R and D.

But the benefits of this expenditure do not reach all sectors and all businesses in equal amounts. G. Owen notes that in the United States, "There is a wide gulf between the research-intensive industries such as electronics, chemicals and aerospace on the one hand, and low-research industries like textiles, machine tools, metal fabrication and building on the other." [19] But the allocation of R and D funds on the basis of a company's size is characteristic. Thus, in the United States in 1964, research programs budgeted at more than 100 million dollars were reserved to 28 firms and absorbed 63% of all funds, and programs costing more than 10 million dollars were distributed among 130 companies and took up 83.5% of all funds. In France, in 1963, programs costing between 1 and 100 million dollars (there weren't any more expensive than that) affected 113 firms and swallowed up 83% of all funds. In the United Kingdom, the 20 firms engaged in the largest programs used 47% of the funds, and in Italy 70% of total expenditures were controlled by the 20 companies with the biggest programs.[20] This data confirms the fact that R and D everywhere, with variations in detail, is the almost exclusive perquisite of the "giant companies," even (and especially so, except in Italy) in countries where the major funding comes from the state.

And so, to round out E. Varga's conclusion: the new technology, with the aid of the monopoly capitalist state, is strengthening the domination of the monopolies in industry. And, moreover, I completely accept the conclusion of Harry Magdoff which follows: "Our argument here is not that the new technology determined the size of the corporation and the monopolistic trends that accompanied Big Business. Rather, the new technology provided the framework, and often the opportunity, for the quite normal tendencies of capitalist industry toward concentration of power." [21]

Notes to Chapter 5

1. *Op. cit.*, p. 29.
2. *Planification et croissance acceleree*, p. 75, "Petite Collection Maspero," 1967.

3. *Op. cit.,* p. 175.
4. *The New Industrial State,* Houghton Mifflin, 1967.
5. *"Réflexions sur le rôle actuel de la science," Économie et Politique,* no. 161, Dec. 1967.
6. *The Overall Level and Structure of R and D Efforts in OECD Member Countries,* OECD, 1967. This is the source for all other figures concerning R and D.
7. *Op. cit.,* p. 157.
8. *Economic Growth 1960–1970,* OECD, 1966, table I.
9. U.N. Statistical Yearbook, 1965, table 181.
10. *Op. cit.,* Chap. xxi.
11. *Op. cit.,* p. 50 and p. 71.
12. *Op. cit.,* pp. 158, 167–8, 175–6, 177, 181.
13. Recommended reading on this subject: Paul A. Baran and Paul M. Sweezy, *"Monopoly Capitalism,"* Monthly Review, 1966, Chap. II.
14. *Op. cit.,* page 5.
15. *Op. cit.,* Chap. IX.
16. *The Overall Level and Structure of R and D Efforts . . .* etc.
17. Issue dated April 28/29, 1968.
18. *Twentieth Century Capitalism,* Progress (Moscow: 1962?).
19. *Op. cit.,* p. 157.
20. Same OECD publication previously cited, tables 3 and 4.
21. *"The Age of Imperialism,"* Monthly Review, June, 1968.

6

Concentration
of Production

THE TRANSFORMATION of competition into monopoly, the growth
of monopolies engendered by the concentration of production, is,
according to Lenin, "a general and fundamental law of the present stage of development of capitalism." (cf. Chap. I)

It is the fashion for many bourgeois economists to refute Leninist theory on this subject by claiming that the facts do not support
it. For instance, Henri Peyret, after taking the precaution of
protecting himself with a quotation from Lenin, declares that
"the development of the largest U.S. corporations, in a country where the law should certainly have shown its effects soonest
and most thoroughly, proves on the contrary that, far from
evolving in some indefinable way toward a more and more perfect
state of monopoly, large companies grow, increasingly eliminate
their competition, assume a prominent place in the market, and
then see other companies spring up all around them, which
gradually begin to resist them, nibble away at their share of
the market and force them back within more reasonable limitations." Henri Peyret cites the cases of Standard Oil, U.S. Steel
and ALCOA, which have seen their share of the American
market reduced in recent decades, and which are, he says, far
from being the only examples. He concludes that their experience runs "counter to the Marxist law." [1]

One of the best ways to disprove a precise law is to make it
mean something it doesn't mean. You scrutinize every word

written by the author of the law until you find the quotation that suits your purposes, you pick it apart out of context, and win the argument with no trouble. As long as we're on the subject of quotations, it should be pointed out that if H. Peyret had kept on reading further in Lenin, he would have discovered this passage, along with many others like it: ". . . monopoly, which has grown out of free competition, does not abolish the latter, but exists over it and alongside of it, and thereby gives rise to a number of very acute, intense antagonisms, friction and conflicts." [2] Lenin repeatedly comes back to this contradiction between monopolies and free competition, to the conflicts that result from it, and to the redivisions of markets on the basis of the new relationship of forces which it brings about.

It is clear from the start that Lenin, like many others, myself included, does not employ the term "monopoly" in its strict sense, but gives it an expanded meaning that encompasses monopolies and oligopolies. And lumping them together is not so vulnerable to criticism as it might seem at first. J. K. Galbraith, who himself distinguishes between the two, concludes a comparison of monopolies and oligopolies by saying: "An oligopoly is not as iniquitous as a monopoly. But that is not because of aspiration but ability. Oligopoly is an imperfect monopoly." [3] One might add that an oligopoly is a monopoly which has not, or at least has not yet, succeeded. Therefore, there is no essential difference between the two. What separates them, Lenin would say, is a question of the relationship of forces. The relationship of forces has permitted the elimination of competitors in one case, and has not permitted it in the other.

But Peyret has truly delightful moments too. He ascribes a theory to Lenin which is very much like one of Kautsky's ideas, which Lenin, in fact, tore apart in a long and implacable attack. The idea that large companies evolve "in some indefinable way toward a more and more perfect state of monopoly" fits in exactly with the Kautskyan theory which Lenin criticized fundamentally for "obscuring and glossing over the most profound contradictions." [4] Anyone who needs more proof should go back to the full text of Lenin.

In any case, this discussion has enabled us to touch on the

importance of the problem of competition *versus* concentration, which was already an issue in Lenin's time and continues to be now, since it is inherent in the capitalist system. Competition leads to concentration by a process of selection, which does not, however, eliminate competition but sharpens the contradictions. Competition and concentration are dialectically opposed and consequently the conflict between them cannot be resolved once and for all by the victory of one or the other. But the *tendency* persists, today more than ever, for competition to be transformed into a monopoly (or oligopolies). This tendency toward concentration is, of course, neither uniform nor continuous.

Accordingly, Geoffrey Owen divides the development of concentration in the United States into three major periods: 1. The apogee of the first great era of concentration, from 1898 to 1902, which occurred in spite of the Sherman Antitrust Act of 1890. This first push toward concentration "imposed on American industry the basic structure that has persisted to this day." 2. A second antitrust law, the Clayton Act of 1914 made no headway either in preventing "the nation's second merger movement, which reached its peak in 1926–30 and would have continued but for the Depression." 3. Even with the passage of the Celler-Kefauver amendment, which reinforced the Clayton Act in 1950, a third wave of mergers began to pick up speed around 1948 and is still going on today.

In concrete terms, between 1947 and 1962, "the share of the hundred largest manufacturing firms in the 'value added' by manufacturing industry as a whole rose from 23 per cent to 32 per cent . . . As for mergers, more than 11,000 of them were recorded by the Federal Trade Commission between 1950 and 1964.[5] Since 1950, the 200 largest industrial corporations acquired more than 200 other firms, and 257 of the largest manufacturing corporations disappeared through merger during this period." [6] These overall figures totally undercut the conclusions which some people have thought it was possible to draw from isolated examples of an opposite trend, however impressive they may be. Owen states specifically, moreover, that many of these mergers were "conglomerate" and caused big corporations to enter new fields. I shall come back to this.

In Japan, the period between the two wars was marked by a powerful trend toward concentration, mentioned by Peyret himself, which led to the supremacy of two giant firms: the Mitsui and Mitsubishi trusts. After 1945, antitrust legislation that was inspired, if not imposed, by the Americans was unable to prevent the rebirth of trusts, and especially not the two giants just mentioned. "The Japanese trusts tended to recreate the old monopolies," writes Peyret. "By now 0.4% of the 400,000 Japanese corporations, according to *Fortune* magazine, earn more than 56% of the total profits." [7]

More recently, Alain Bouc has written about the creation of a gigantic iron and steel producer in Japan which was formed through a merger of the fourth and fifth largest producers in the world. This vast company is now the world's second largest steel producer, just behind U.S. Steel, and ranks with Japan's biggest industrial complexes. Along with this information Alain Bouc also mentions "the duality of Japanese industry," which is typified by giant firms on one side and a host of small and average-sized enterprises on the other. But within this mass of more modest companies, there has been a disquieting growth of bankruptcies: less than 2000 in 1962, 6000 in 1965, 8000 in 1966 and around 10,000 in 1967. "The problems of small business are in part the result of the prosperity of big business," the specter of the great pre-war monopolies looms once again on the horizon and government authorities "give evidence of going along with the trend." Alain Bouc also points out that in January 1969 the Mitsubishi and Dai Ichi Banks were to merge and thereby become the fifth largest bank in the world. [8]

In Great Britain, Christopher Layton counted 3384 mergers between 1958 and 1962, as against 1000 in the EEC, [9] while Jean Declemy, in July 1968, entitled an important article "The Trend Toward Industrial Concentration in Great Britain Progresses at a Pace Unequalled Anywhere Else in the World." Business mergers for the first half of 1968 involved more than 1.8 billion pounds sterling as against 1 billion for the entire year of 1967. And in 1967 there were mergers involving almost three times as much capital as the annual average for the period 1959–1963, and eight times more than the average for 1954–1958. "British

industry, which is already the most centralized in Europe in several areas, is thus in the process of becoming a band of
giants . . ." and "no branch of it is immune to the trend." [10]

The same process has been going on recently in the Netherlands. A news dispatch from there in September, 1968, began:
"The tendency toward concentration which has been going on for
several years in the Netherlands, has accelerated abruptly in the
course of the last few weeks." [11] An article in the same paper states
that in West Germany "mergers take place, most often, in those
sectors of the economy undergoing full expansion." In the course
of the last decade there were 46 mergers in the electronics industry, 44 in the chemical industry, and 29 among firms that make
machinery. While a total of only 19 mergers were recorded in
1958, there were 65 in 1967. The most intense merger activity
is going on among basic industries.[12]

In France, finally, according to a report submitted to the Economic Council by François Lagandré in February, 1967,[13] although 5% of French businesses are responsible for 67% of the
total national payroll, concentration has not yet made important
progress in the country (1965):

	GROSS INCOME BY COMPANY (in millions of francs)	% OF TOTAL GROSS INCOME
86 companies	more than 500	17.6
513 companies	more than 100	31.7
8,074 companies	more than 10	53.4

But France too is undergoing a process of concentration, which
is illustrated by these figures: 1017 mergers between 1950 and
1960 (annual average: roughly 100); 816 mergers between 1960
and 1965 (annual average: about 160).

But Henri Claude notes, and rightly so, that big mergers and
very big corporations have a special significance. He thinks that
"the tendency toward the merger of big businesses is a characteristic of the period following the establishment of the Common
Market." "Since the end of 1965," he adds, "we have been witness-

ing the acceleration of a process which is profoundly changing French capitalism." After examining the process as it affects the main industrial sectors, he concludes that "in each branch and for each product, production tends to be monopolized by one or two big firms along the lines laid down by the Fifth Plan." [14]

The accelerated trend noted in France by Henri Claude has continued. According to the magazine *Entreprise,* "1967 will be known as the year of the mergers . . . There has been a clearcut increase in the number of mergers, both those that occur spontaneously and those that are promoted by the state. . . . About 250 instances of concentration (mergers, reorganizations of activities, joint multinational companies) were recorded in 1967. This spate of agreements, whose pace continues to increase, is changing the face of the French economy month by month, is systematically upsetting the most dynamic as well as the most conservative sectors, slicing up business and shaking up personnel. An important step was thus taken during 1967 toward the adaptation of the French economy to international competition." [15]

This overview of the trend toward concentration in the principal industrialized capitalist countries leads to the conclusion that since the Fifties there has been a general movement in the direction of concentration, which first picked up speed significantly in the United States and Great Britain, and got started a little later in Japan and in most West European countries other than the United Kingdom. But however widespread it may be, this trend has not progressed uniformly in all places or gone on everywhere at the same time, which is not at all surprising.

Because it is a result of the contradiction between competition and concentration, this trend has been variously encouraged or impeded by governments and supranational organizations, whose laws, regulations and decisions are capable only of reflecting that contradiction. The importance of the trend quickly caused national and international codes governing concentrations to be drafted. We have observed already how this occurred in the United States (Sherman Act of 1890, Clayton Act of 1914, Celler-Kefauver amendment of 1950) and in Japan. In Great Britain since 1965 the Board of Trade has been able to submit merger projects to a special supervisory Monopolies Commission when it considers the projects to be incompatible with free competition in the domestic market. There are other regulations or national laws (antitrust laws in West Germany), as well as international codes. Article 85 of the Treaty of Rome, for example, condemns "any decisions by associations of enterprises and any concerted practices which are likely to [cause] . . . the restriction or distortion of competition within the Common Market . . ." Article 86 condemns "action by one or more enterprises to take improper advantage of a dominant position within the Common Market . . ."

Since free competition is a sacred principle, all these laws and regulations essentially aim at preserving the free play of competition (and, additionally, at defending the rights of shareholders: United Kingdom, France). But since concentration tending toward monopoly is the result of competition and favors the interests of the capitalist bourgeoisie, which employs the state as its tool, governments, both through their actions and, generally speaking, in every way (which does not mean that there are no exceptions, some of them even quite spectacular) not only do not oppose concentrations, but most often favor them, as long as they are aligned with the state's interests of the moment. We have seen that in the United States, as even the bourgeois authorities I have referred to testify, the antitrust laws have prevented nothing. According to G. Owen, "the antitrust laws are often violated," and they "have not prevented some firms from growing to enormous size . . . and from acquiring considerable power." [16] And Christopher Layton himself perceives something of the dialectical nature of the competition/concentration process when he states: "any policy designed to foster concentration must also seek to retain an element of competition." [17] In Great Britain, despite an apparent commitment to the Monopolies Commission and its trust-busting activities, the state has supplied itself with the means to encourage concentrations, especially by creating, in 1966, an Industrial Reorganization Corporation which has funds of its own and has, in effect, caused, aided or chaperoned several important industrial marriages.[18] We have seen that in France, according to the magazine *Entreprise* which is in a good position to know, the acceleration of the trend toward concentration has been "stimulated by the government." In Italy, various quasi-governmental agencies (IRI, EFIM) play an important role in the promotion of concentrations.

The ambivalent action of governments which sometimes find themselves "trapped" by the competition/concentration contradiction can produce curious results. For instance, the largest English tobacco manufacturer, Imperial Tobacco, was forced by the Monopolies Commission to divest itself of a 36.75% interest it had in Gallaher, the second-largest British tobacco company. But the Commission was powerless to prevent American Tobacco, which owned 13% of the Gallaher shares, from buying 50% in a public offering. And so British law prevented one British firm from controlling another, but it could not do anything against an American takeover bid.[19]

In the case of the EEC, André Marchal notes that "there is a basic contradiction in the European treaties: while they favor the broadening of markets, they limit as much as possible the broadening of companies." But he adds, "For some time these positions have appeared to be reversing themselves." Article 85 "today tends to be the object of a looser interpretation which removes concentration from its clutches." "A real transformation is at work," even within the famous Commission of the European Communities which does not hesitate to speak of "trends toward concentration which are necessary." For his part, André Marchal thinks that the concentrations and mergers seem "more necessary than ever in a European framework," notably to improve their ability to resist the invasion of American capital by creating multinational companies.[20] Thus competition within each of the Six creates pressures favorable to concentration at the national level, and a superconcentration at the multinational level of the Common Market becomes a part of competition on a global scale. The dialectical nature of the competition/concentration process makes itself felt, therefore, not only within a clearly marked off economic area, but also, and especially, when one moves from a given geographic division to a higher level.

If regional integration adds a new dimension to this process, it must be recognized that, viewed from another angle, it hinders the process through regulations and structures. In the case of the EEC, however, these seem to have become obsolete after only ten years. Certainly, Articles 85 and 86 of the Treaty of Rome are out of date already, and they are going to become more and more vestigial. A statement made by the Commission in July of 1968, among others, gives testimony of this,[21] and one can already point out that the number of new intracommunity subsidiaries, which were being established at the rate of 50 a year before 1962, rose to 280 in 1966.[22] But as many authorities have observed, intracommunity mergers are, strictly speaking, impossible, because no law governing joint international companies exists. "If a French and a German firm seek to merge," writes Christopher Layton, "the new group has to become a French company or a German one," [23] which causes all sorts of inconveniences. The law is always out of date. It only changes under pressure from events. This pressure is sufficiently strong today to force the law to change soon, despite the objections which will inevitably be raised. Already, at the request of the Commission, Professor Sanders of Rotterdam, with the assistance of five experts, one from each of the other countries of the Six, have written a draft of a law for European corporations. This draft, declares the Commission, "ought to be a very effective aid in speeding the creation of new legal powers, which European businesses, saddled with the difficulties of restructuring, need more and more every day." Doubtless we are on the brink of a strong swing toward "restructuring," in other words, toward concentrations and fusions, at the level and within the framework of the EEC. Already, for that matter, veritable matrimonial agencies for industrial marriages are springing up here and there, and large merchant banks are setting up specialized services or divisions. From this perspective, the Gaullist regime's refusal to permit the quasi-merger of Fiat and Citroën seems to have been only a "peripety." It is of greater importance that the magazine *Entreprise* saw fit to say that agreements between French and foreign firms "represent an important tendency which is bound to become more so in the future. The logic of the Common Market and of the economics of competition leads, in effect, to the creation of multinational groups." [24]

We have already touched on the fact that the term "concentration" stands for a whole range of agreements whose legal details and economic objectives are highly diverse.

The principal legal or contractual forms in use, in addition to mergers in the strict sense, are: absorption, which in reality amounts to a merger; mutual participation (exchange of shares and executives), which is often the prelude to a merger; seizure of control, which establishes a united management and uniform policies for both the controlling and the controlled companies; a subsidiary owned in common by two or more principal companies; combines and cartels that are designed to corner a particular market, to specialize in a particular area of production or to fix prices; all sorts of associations, finally, designed to facilitate joint research programs, joint sales efforts, standardization, etc.

Henri Claude concludes that in France and in the EEC, mutual participations (which he calls "quasi-mergers") and the various sorts of associations are the forms that concentration has taken most frequently in recent years. Mutual participations have been used mainly to combine the efforts of firms from different Common Market countries and help them circumvent the legal obstacles that still stand in the way of mergers, as well as to get around various difficulties which an immediate merger between powerful and complex financial groups would have faced. The other types of association have, among other things, made it possible to simplify the problem of creating mergers or quasi-mergers between public and government-controlled corporations (e.g., Renault-Peugeot, Charbonnages de France and Produits Chimiques d'Auby). This confirms the fact that when the pressure for concentration becomes irresistible, ways will be found for circumventing the obstacles before ways are found to get rid of them altogether. Claude notes, moreover, after his analysis of the two examples I have just borrowed from him, that in the case of a government favorably inclined toward monopolies, "an association between a government-controlled firm and a large private capitalist enterprise, the privately owned company necessarily has an advantage, because "parity" enables it to profit from the technological, industrial and, in certain cases, the financial strength of the state-owned company." [25]

Depending on their economic objectives, concentrations can be either vertical or horizontal, as is well known. But this classic distinction seems somewhat pedantic today, at any rate it seems so to Geoffrey Owen, who thinks that the reasons behind the establishment of both kinds of concentrations, in the United States at least, are becoming more and more similar. If we exclude cases of vertical concentration in which integration takes place from the top down (this essentially occurs in processing industries seeking to possess their own sources of raw materials, which seems to have been the original form of concentration and was done to achieve security), the other types of concentration, according to Owen, are a consequence of the importance assumed by "marketing" and indicate a "reorientation, on the part of a large section of American industry, towards the customer."

Owen cites the case of Du Pont, whose president has said: We must be prepared to carry our development closer and closer to the ultimate customer." And so the company decided, instead of selling its new product Delrin to processors, that it would make its own pipes out of Delrin and sell them directly. Likewise, Union Carbide "decided that the best way to promote the use of polyurethane foam in mattresses was to acquire a mattress maker and participate in the business directly." These examples of integration from the bottom up (vertical concentration) reflect, in Owen's view, a policy common in many industries, where the pressures of competition oblige the maximum use of resources. "A producer of oil and natural gas, for example, is no longer content to sell products to a textile company for conversion into nylon; . . . it acquires the textile company." Conversely, aluminum users are turning to basic aluminum production.

Concentration also takes place horizontally, of course. Metal producers, for example, now face competition from manufacturers of plastic, wood, paper, glass and textiles over numerous finished products that were once only made out of metal. This makes the metal producers eager to annex their new competition. "Start with the customer and work for him" is the principle that many companies follow. For instance, the two big can companies,

Continental Can and American Can "aim to cover the whole packaging field, with interests in steel, aluminum, glass, plastics, and paper." Similarly, copper producers (Anaconda) go into aluminum, Coca Cola has invested in coffee and orange juice, etc. One industry invades another; "distinctions between markets and between industries have become blurred." [26]

Outside the United States, the same processes are at work. In France, between 1957 and 1966, according to Henri Claude, Pechiney, the aluminum producer, absorbed or gained control of all aluminum processors; Saint-Frères, which dominated jute manufacture, extended its empire to take in carpet production; and Dollfus-Mieg, which monopolized the production of cotton thread, "took over companies that make cloth, hosiery, household linens and zippers." [27] Here too old barriers are breaking down.

This overly quick survey of a general tendency toward concentration that especially affects large firms, which are growing steadily more powerful and diversified as a result, conflicts sharply with the theory given out by certain people who claim that concentration runs into technological, economic and financial limitations, and that "there is an optimum amount of concentration, and once it is exceeded, overall costs rise prohibitively. If a business grows too large, its effective profitability has a tendency to decrease." [28] According to André Marchal as well, "Size is not a panacea," and if U.S. Steel was convicted of violating U.S. antitrust laws, it was not, said *Entreprise* "because it had acquired a position of domination, but because it had not known how to take advantage of that position and had become an *inert giant*." [29]

It is certainly possible that some day or other big companies will face a crisis of overdevelopment. But it would be a mistake to lose sight of the conclusions drawn in the preceding chapter, namely that the new technology accentuates the fundamental tendency of capitalist industry to become concentrated, and that it is particularly favorable to big business. Moreover, the two opinions quoted above are contradicted by Christopher Layton, who believes that when large, internationally oriented companies are completely integrated they provide "greater mobility of men, research facilities and other resources than any customs union." [30]

J. Magniadas feels this way even more. In his analysis of the
problem of size in business, he notes that the cumulative effect
of several factors encourages an increase in size. Some of these
factors are: the use of technological innovations, which require
heavy investment; and the internationalization of markets, which
raises the threshold below which a business ceases to be competitive under the conditions of multinational competition, given
the fact that businesses achieve greater "economies of scale" in
production and sales when their size increases, etc. He concludes
that the concentration of businesses and their increasing size have
nothing to do with notions of an "economic optimum" or a
"technological optimum," but are, in the final analysis, conditions
imposed by monopolistic competition and determined by it. A
business occupying a dominant position, "or finding itself in a
particular set of economic circumstances, etc., could be led to
cut down its rate of growth. On the other hand, the exigencies of
monopolistic competition can also lead it to achieve too much
productive capacity." [31]

I should also point out that having numerous foreign subsidiaries allows giant companies to play on these subsidiaries like a
keyboard. It is no secret that, depending on the economic climate
in the various European countries, Remington increases or de-
creases the emphasis it puts on this or that subsidiary in France,
the Netherlands, or elsewhere in such a way as to concentrate its
efforts on those that happen to be operating under the most
favorable conditions at the moment. The big U.S. copper companies were able to withstand an almost total strike during 1967–
1968, because the heavy losses they suffered were compensated for
by the growth of their subsidiaries' earnings in the Third World
where prices almost doubled in the absence of North American
production. An equally striking but altogether different sort of
example is offered by Imperial Chemical Industries, which has
welded its British factories and around forty European subsidiaries into an extremely profitable unit. The Dutch subsidiary,
for instance, receives its raw materials from a British factory, but
in return it markets finished products manufactured in Britain
as well as its own.[32]

For his part, Henri Claude observes that quite recently France has begun to experience "an unprecedented acceleration of concentration at the highest level," leading to an increase in the size of companies that are already very big. For this reason, he says, "capitalist leaders are occupied with the problem of determining the 'critical mass' beyond which the survival of a company would be assured. This concept of critical mass can be applied to research and development, marketing, production and financing." In addition, H. Claude emphasizes the fact that horizontal concentration tends to assume a more and more heterogeneous character among corporate groups. The groups attempt "to unite under their control the largest possible number of companies specializing in very disparate areas. [. . .] Specialization within diversification is the slogan of the day.

"This policy of diversified specialization," Claude continues, "is an attempt to overcome the contradictions of modern competition. To be competitive one must specialize. But specialization makes a company dependent on only one market and because of this the company becomes more vulnerable. By specializing in a certain number of very different sectors, capitalist groups try to eliminate the negative aspects of specialization. Consequently, the current tendency is toward multimonopoly."

But this is getting us into a subject that involves the action of the financial oligarchy, which we shall be investigating in the next chapter. Since the present chapter and the next chapter are very closely related, I shall wait and make concluding remarks about both of them at the same time.

NOTES TO CHAPTER 6

1. *La Strategie des Trusts*, pp. 119–120, *"Que sais-je"* collection, P.U.F. (Paris: 1966).
2. *Op. cit.,* p. 88.
3. *Op. cit.,* p. 182.
4. *Op. cit.,* p. 122.
5. The number of mergers rose from 4460 in 1967 to 5400 in 1968.
6. Owen, *op. cit.,* Chap. III. Cf. also Celso Furtado, "La Concentration du pouvoir," *Esprit*, April, 1969.
7. *Op. cit.,* Chap. III.

8. *Le Monde,* 4-19-68 and 1-12/13-69.

9. *Op. cit.,* p. 59.

10. *Le Monde,* 7-30-68.

11. *Le Monde,* 9-11-68.

12. E. W. Maenken, *Le Monde,* 6-26-68.

13. *Perspectives,* 5-20-67.

14. *Économie et Politique,* no. 149–150, Dec. 1966/Jan. 1967.

15. *Entreprise,* no. 642, 12-30-67.

16. *Op. cit.,* p. 20 and p. 53.

17. *Op. cit.,* p. 54.

18. Jacqueline Grapin, *Le Monde,* 3-5-68.

19. *Le Monde,* 7-18-68.

20. *Problèmes économiques,* no. 1,070, 7-4-68, La Documentation française.

21. *Le Monde,* 7-24-68.

22. *Le Monde,* 10-29/30-67.

23. *Op. cit.,* p. 58.

24. *Entreprise,* no. 642, 12-30-67.

25. *Ibid.,* pp. 95–97.

26. Owen, *op. cit.,* pp. 24–28.

27. *Op. cit.,* pp. 99–100.

28. Peyret, *op. cit.,* p. 120.

29. *Entreprise,* no. 642, p. 13.

30. *Op. cit.,* p. 119.

31. *Économie et Politique,* no. 149–150, Dec. 1966/Jan. 1967, pp. 70–71.

32. *Le Monde,* 10-8-68.

33. *Op. cit.,* p. 100.

7

The Financial
and Industrial Oligarchy

A HALF-CENTURY ago, Lenin and Bukharin pointed out a new feature of imperialism: the close ties that had sprung up between bank capital and industrial capital, and which almost always worked to the advantage of the banks. Lenin observed that "the industrial capitalist becomes more completely dependent on the bank." (41) Following Hilferding, he defined "finance capital" as bank capital which, through various means, transforms itself into industrial capital, giving rise to a "financial oligarchy" which is based on "the supremacy of finance capital over all other forms of capital" (59) and which uses this supremacy to insure its own hegemony.

Does this picture still correspond to reality today? It would be of very great interest to find out, and the best way to do that seems to me first to study the recent development of business finance, in other words, the current sources of industrial capital. Then I will direct my investigation, in more detail, toward the relationship of finance capital and industrial capital, before moving on to a third area, the evolution of the banks, and especially the evolution of merchant banks (Tr.: *Banques d'Affaires*), which is now in progress. Finally, I will attempt to effect a synthesis of the arguments of this chapter and the preceding one.

In a message to the Académie des Sciences Morales et Politiques of November, 1967, André Piettre recalled that "during the entire length of the 19th Century, credit, savings and property advanced together in the same direction." [1] While savings were directed more readily into the capital of business enterprises, credit was extended with increasing frequency to the same enterprises for working capital.

But since the Second World War, this arrangement has undergone radical changes. From then on, savings have forsaken long term investment for the money market. Business has filled the gap with its own savings, that is, it has financed itself with its own profits. After reminding us that the rate of reinvestment is the ratio between a business's gross savings (depreciation plus undistributed earnings) and its investments plus any variation in its inventory, A. Piettre calculates that, for the period 1962–64, the average rate of reinvestment in the private sector was 99.3% in the United States, 109% in Great Britain, 79% in West Germany, and 61.8% in France.

This analysis is confirmed by B. Lelièvre, who states that stock and bond issues by European and Japanese firms are running into serious difficulties, generally, and that the problem is even greater for American companies.[2] J. K. Galbraith adds further support to this. According to him, in 1965, personal savings in the United States totalled 25 billion dollars, while business savings, which include mainly the savings of big companies, rose to 83 billion dollars, or more than three times as much as personal savings. "Compared with the early fifties," adds Galbraith, "personal savings had increased by about fifty per cent; business savings had nearly tripled." [3]

Even Geoffrey Owen writes that "stock or equity issues appear to be declining in importance as a source of finance for corporations." In the United States "in the decade from 1954 to 1963 net new security issues (both equity and debt) declined from 26.3 per cent of total corporate sources of funds to only 11.6 per cent. There has been a steady surge in retained earnings and depreciation." [4]

Though he documents the "tragically reduced" role of individual savings in corporate investment as compared to reinvestment, Piettre does not hesitate to find fault with the theories of Marx and Lenin on the concentration of capital, because of

the extremely widespread nature of what he calls "property ownership" (Tr.: *propriété-avoir*), that is, because there are 17 to 20
million shareholders in the United States out of slightly more
than 45 million families. Piettre should have taken the precaution of rereading Lenin, particularly pages 48 and 49. Lenin
refers there specifically to "small, scattered shareholders" and
to the so-called " 'democratization' " of the ownership of shares
which some people claimed even then led to the " 'democratization of capital'," although it "is, in fact, one of the ways of increasing the power of the financial oligarchy." G. Owen also
notes that in the United States the role of institutional investors
(insurance companies, savings banks and retirement funds . . .)
is growing faster than that of individual private investors.
J. K. Galbraith goes even further. He argues that in the United
States the major portion of personal savings belongs to wealthy
or comfortable people; that in 1950 "households in the lower
two-thirds of the income range . . . did no saving at all"; that
"more than half of all personal savings were supplied by those
in the upper five per cent income bracket"; and that there is
"no reason to suppose that saving has become more democratic
since that time." And he says in conclusion: "The individual
serves the industrial system not by supplying it with savings and
the resulting capital; he serves it by consuming its products." [5]

Despite the so-called democratization of capital, mutual funds
were created, first in the United States and then in Europe, in
order to mitigate to a certain extent the inability of private
savings to take part effectively in corporate investment. Piettre's
comments are quite perceptive in this instance. He says: "It is
here that the gap between *power* and *ownership* is most fully
visible. The private investor delegates not only the supervision
but even the choice of his investments to the mutual fund, and
abdicates, along with this authority, all control over the corporations of which he is technically a part owner."

Mutual funds first appeared in France in 1964, and by September, 1968, there were 19 of them in existence. They represented about 300,000 shareholders and managed total net assets
valued at more than three billion francs. During the same period,

similar American institutions, which were generally older and numbered about 350, had a total investment of 40 billion dollars, the equivalent of 200 billion francs. In the final analysis, this figure is quite small compared to the total assets of institutional investors in the United States in 1962: 356 billion dollars.

Ninety-nine per cent of the shareholders of the French mutual funds (Tr.: called *sociétés d'investissements à capital variable* or SICAV) are private investors. The principal shareholders are heads of businesses, retired people and executives. They own one-fourth of the bearer securities and one-fourth of the registered shares. Workers and ordinary employees own 9% of the shares and 5% of the bearer securities. (Tr.: Contrary to the practice of U.S. mutual funds, the SICAV offer both registered shares and bearer securities to the public.)

With the principal exception of the three SICAV's created by the Crédit Lyonnais, a nationalized commercial bank, which operates them independently, almost all other French SICAV's were founded by the largest merchant banks, which are often associated with loan societies and insurance companies. Their investments are concentrated in chemicals and oil, and, to a somewhat lesser degree, in banks and electric companies. Their results are good. Using April, 1964, as a base of 100, the average price of SICAV shares reached 106.1 by the end of 1967, while the price index of French equitable securities with a variable rate of return had fallen 18.5% during the same time, and the price index of debt securities with a fixed rate of return had fallen 1.6%. We can say, therefore, that the SICAV's knew how to invest in the most prosperous companies, which is certainly not incompatible with being controlled by merchant banks.[6]

To sum up, the SICAV's and similar institutions abroad have not disrupted the stock market. They have only slowed the decline in the amount of personal savings invested in business. Generally controlled by merchant banks (at least in France), they have merely reinforced the power of the financial oligarchy.

If corporate reinvestment began to take the place of private individuals and the stock market as the major source of financing more or less everywhere after World War II, obviously industrial profits were large enough to make this possible. But this would seem to contradict the Marxist law that projects a growing tendency for the overall rate of profit to decline. E. Mandel seems to have interpreted this law in a special sense when he wrote: "It is the 'control' of the free flow of capital, or the elimination of competition, that enables the monopoly sectors to escape from participating in the general equalisation of the rate of profit." [7] Similarly, E. Varga states that "the profits of the monopolies fail to participate in the levelling of the general rate of profit." [8] The law is challenged much more directly by P. A. Baran and P. M. Sweezy, who argue that it presupposes a competitive system and would no longer apply to a system of monopoly capitalism.[9] This last interpretation has provoked critical reactions from Charles Bettelheim (in his preface to Baran and Sweezy's book) and Étienne Balibar.[10] Bettelheim emphasizes that the law of the profit rate's tendency to decline does not depend on competition but derives, according to Marx, "from the essence of the capitalist mode of production." Without getting into this controversy, I would like to point out that there is no reason, however one looks at the question, why the principle of the general equalization of the rate of profit cannot be reconciled with a rate of profit for monopolies that is higher than the average rate of profit (monopoly superprofit), or with the fact that during certain periods these superprofits can increase faster than total profits. In France, for example, between 1963 and 1967, gross profits grew by an annual average of 7.6% for business in general and 9.4% for corporations, while reinvestment rose to a record rate of 72.7%.[11] This data shows what is true in France and in general, that reinvestment is a method adopted almost exclusively by monopolies or firms verging on monopoly.

After noting the remarkable recent growth of reinvestment, André Piettre then presents some figures relating to the financing of business by banks. In France in 1966, business financed itself from the following sources (in round figures):

bank loans—short term: 67 billion francs
   —medium term: 20   "   "
    —long term: 30   "   "
reinvestment: 27   "   "
offerings of negotiable
  securities: 5   "   "

In the same way, in the United States in 1966, medium term and long term loans reached 36 billion dollars and reinvestment rose to 59 billion.

Relatively speaking, therefore, medium and long term credits extended to businesses by banks are larger in France than in the United States, but they remain quite sizable in both places. Although these bank loans are earmarked for financing the expansion of production, and do not constitute capital, they are just as effective a means of keeping the debtor companies under the thumb of the banks. André Piettre puts it quite well—he echoes Lenin here almost exactly, perhaps without knowing it—: ". . . Business leaders must adjust to the control of their creditors and must share their power with that of private finance. Aren't concentrations created today under the aegis of the big banks? But, here again, economic power draws further away from individual people." The only thing that needs to be added to that is: . . . for the benefit of the financial oligarchy.

Turning now to the problem of the relationship of finance capital and industrial capital, it seems to me essential to begin with this long quotation from E. Varga:

"Hilferding, in his *Finance Capital,* said that 'a constantly growing part of industrial capital does not belong to the industrialists that use it. They obtain use of the capital only through the banks . . .' In this way the industrial enterprises were kept dependent on the banks. In the subsequent period, especially after the Second World War, the situation changed. . . . There were two factors that played the decisive role in this respect. During and after the war the monopolies were able to set aside for themselves tremendous reserves out of their high profits. The inflation strengthened the position of the industrial monopolies since the greater part of their property consisted of buildings, machinery and equipment, raw materials and manufactured goods whose prices increased together with inflation; they were able to pay their old debts to the banks in devalued currency. . . .

"Industrial monopolies have become more or less independent of the banks and as a rule expand their constant capital by using their own reserve funds. . . .

"The big monopolies now create such huge reserves from their superprofits that they, as a rule, not only have no need for the banks but are able to establish or purchase banks themselves. The Rockefellers bought up the Chase Bank, one of the biggest in the U.S.A. The German concern, I. G. Farbenindustrie, had its own big banking house even before the Second World War." [12] In Varga's view, ever since the war the banks have played a secondary role compared to the industrial monopolies, and he sees proof of this in the disparity between their net earnings in the United States: the net income of financial institutions amounted to one-eighth the net income of industrial monopolies in 1957 and one-sixth of it in 1958.

He goes on to say: "The question of the relations between banks and industrial monopolies, however, is becoming of less and less significance because a very small group of financial magnates is gaining control over both banks and industries."

The reduced dependence of the industrial monopolies on banks since the time when Varga wrote those lines (probably 1960, since books published in the Soviet Union have not been dated for some time), is due to the recent proliferation of groups of industries or of common carriers, which are set up as (openly or not), or are associated with, holding companies. A complete list of them, for France alone, would be an impressive affair. Take for example the powerful Schneider group, whose president declared at the general shareholders' meeting of June 17, 1968: "Given the diversity of our investments, I think I am in a position to say emphatically how much the distribution of our assets, and the consequent distribution of risks, used to justify and still justifies categorizing Schneider S.A. as an investment company." (Tr.: *sociétés de portefeuille*)

Closely related to holding companies are the so-called conglomerates (companies that own or control a number of highly diverse businesses). In the United States, big companies that were prevented from expanding in their original area by the antitrust laws have oriented themselves toward growth through diversification, which is unrestricted. At the moment, more than 70% of American mergers are of the conglomerate type.

A number of these holding companies are taking a path diametrically opposed to the one Lenin once described. Instead of being taken over by banks, they are becoming like banks themselves. The president of Schneider informed his stockholders that 43% of the group's assets were non-industrial and invested in banks, real estate and finance. The Michelin holding company controls 100% of the Compagnie Financière Michelin. The Dassault group controls the Banque Commerciale de Paris, a merchant bank. The Chargeurs Réunis group controls several specialized financial institutions, including the Financière de l'Armement; it also has an interest in COCEPI, the investment company, and in the Société Financière pour les Industries de Tourisme. In Italy, the Fiat holding company manages a portfolio of which 21% is given over to banking and finance. It seems that Rockefeller and I. G. Farbenindustrie, the companies Varga mentioned in this connection, started a trend.

The result of all this is that big businesses now have their own internal, self-generated momentum, that they grow mainly through reinvestment, that their undistributed profits often permit them to turn themselves into conglomerates or holding companies and even to become sources of finance capital. In a word, industrial capital tends to free itself from finance capital. But just how far does this tendency go, and can one speak of a true decline of finance capital? That's what I shall try to determine by looking at recent developments in investment banking.

In the opinion of Owen, "the decline of equity issues and the growing importance of 'private placements' with institutional investors have had the incidental effect of lessening the significance of the investment banking firms which in the early years of the century played a dominant role in American industry."[13]

But this view, which in any case is weakly argued, is denied categorically by a 1968 report of the House Subcommittee on Domestic Finance, which states that the nation's biggest banks "are emerging as the single most important force in the economy." The report points out that large American banks are unaffected by antitrust legislation and that banks control 607 billion dollars in assets, or 60% of the total amount of institutional investment. Insurance companies, which are the second largest source of investment funds after the banks, only possess 162 billion dollars in assets. The report adds that 49 banks control 5% or more of the capital of the 147 largest industrial companies as well as 5% or more of the capital of the 17 most important merchandising companies and the 17 biggest transportation companies. "Because of the widespread distribution of capital, these 5% interests are sufficient to control many boards of directors." [14]

As for French merchant banks (Tr.: *banques d'affaires*), Henri Claude maintains that quite recently there has been "an unprecedented acceleration of concentration at the highest level, at the level of the leading financial groups." He shows that three clusters of concentration were formed in France in the course of 1966, around the Compagnie Financière de Suez, the Banque de l'Indochine and the Banque de Paris et des Pays-Bas. I should add that the Banque de Paris et des Pays-Bas, with total assets of 7 billion francs, is the largest merchant bank, not only in France but also in Europe. H. Claude also points out that the principal shareholder of the Compagnie Financière de Suez is Great Britain itself, which has a 29% interest in the bank.[15]

This is not the only example that reveals a tendency toward the internationalization of the capital of merchant banks. The Banque Worms, which is connected with the Banque de Paris et des Pays-Bas, joined forces in 1968 with the Philadelphia National Bank, thus bringing the portion of its capital controlled by English, Scottish, German, and American associates to around 30%. The Banque de l'Union Européenne Industrielle et Financière is partly controlled by the Banque de l'Indochine, partly by the Marine Midland Bank, which has a 20% interest in it, and partly by seven European partners with a 10% interest. The Compagnie du Nord, which is controlled by the Rothschild Bank, absorbed the American firm, the Amsterdam Overseas Corporation, in 1968. And the Agnelli family (FIAT) is supposed to be in the process of acquiring one-sixth of the stock of the Rothschild Bank.[16]

The internationalization of the business of the merchant banks is equally remarkable. According to H. Claude, at the end of 1953 the geographic distribution of the Banque de l'Indochine's portfolio of securities was as follows: France and Europe, 23%; Africa, 27%; America, 26%; Southeast Asia, 15%; others, 5%. But in 1965, it broke down this way: France and Europe, nearly 60%; America, nearly 20%; Africa, 9%; Southeast Asia, less than 5%. This change seems to me very significant: the bank has been interesting itself directly in international monopolies based in the imperialist countries.

As for the Banque de Paris et des Pays-Bas, it has interests in the United States, Great Britain, Luxembourg, Canada, Norway, Morocco, and South America, in addition to branches in Holland, Belgium, Switzerland, Algeria . . .

During 1967 and 1968, the large French merchant banks reorganized their structures thoroughly. The changes they made were almost the same in every case, and, according to Gilbert Mathieu's analysis, the salient points of the transformation were: a) One division was created for *foreign investments* of all kinds; these investments are governed by the laws of the foreign country where they are made and require contributions of local capital. b) A second division was formed to handle domestic *banking activities;* what had been merchant banks became commercial banks (Tr.: *banques de dépôts*). c) A financial holding company was set up to coordinate and direct the entire complex.[17]

Gilbert Mathieu sees three reasons for this metamorphosis: 1. The one that is most generally advanced is that the adoption of the status of a commercial bank makes it easier to open teller's windows and amass large sums of money. This argument seems highly overrated to Mathieu. 2. "By multiplying the number of its subsidiaries and permitting partial public ownership of each of them, the bank acquires a great deal of capital without losing control of its subsidiaries." 3. By differentiating their industrial activities from their other activities the banking groups can obtain the collaboration of a greater number of partners, notably employers' associations (Tr.: *syndicats patronaux*) and industrial groups. Mathieu gives examples of this.

But, in Mathieu's view, none of this was really that much of an innovation, and as far as he is concerned the main reason behind the change was political: the nationalization of merchant banks was a plank in the platform of the French left. By changing their title from merchant banks to commercial banks, and by expatriating their subsidiaries on foreign soil, the banks protected themselves from this threat.

All these reasons seem sound to me, but in my opinion Mathieu is wrong to minimize the importance of the first one. Making money and multiplying its power with other people's money has always been the policy of merchant banks. And the scarcer money becomes, the greater the efforts that must be made to pry it loose. I have shown that personal savings are increasing at a slower rate than they once did, and, in addition, that they are held as liquid assets more and more instead of being put into long term investments. This trend is what prompted the creation of the SICAV's. It is also what made merchant banks interested in crisscrossing entire countries with branch offices open to the general public. And the so-called "war of the banks" that occurred in France during the fall of 1968 showed how eager the large merchant banks, and especially the Banque de Paris/Pays-Bas, were to fight for control of the Crédit Industriel et Commercial (CIC) and the Crédit du Nord because they were both old commercial banks that, directly or through their subsidiaries, had networks of branches already in operation and a faithful clientele, which the old merchant banks lacked. To take over these banks was a much less difficult and risky way of draining off more money into industrial investments than setting up new branch offices. The fact that the war finally ended with a polite meeting, or so the story goes, at which the various belligerents agreed to split up the booty, should come as no surprise. The important thing is the energy which the big merchant banks exerted up until that moment.

Can one, then, speak seriously about a decline of the merchant banks? In terms of absolute power, no. In terms of relative influence, probably yes. But it would still be an error to exaggerate the extent of the decline. The comparison of the respective earnings of financial institutions and industrial monopolies that Varga uses is not entrely convincing, because the earnings of merchant banks are an insignificant measure of their power. Lenin estimated in his day that one could control a business with only 40% of its capital. But we have seen that, according to the House Subcommittee on Domestic Finance, 5% is enough in many cases today to control a board of directors. Even if this figure is too low, it is still abundantly clear that interlocking directorates have become quite common today, and that they make it possible to control the subsidiary of a subsidiary with a very small amount of capital. Profits are lower, in accordance with the smaller size of the actual investment, but control is nonetheless total.

Though it is undeniable that many industrial companies generate their own momentum these days, through reinvestment, by transforming themselves into conglomerates or holding companies, and by going into the investment business in their own right, it should not be forgotten that a great number of them still remain under the control of merchant banks. The Banque de Paris et des Pays-Bas still has interests in businesses as large and diverse as the CSF, the Compagnie Française des Compteurs, Esso-Standard, the Compagnie Française de Raffinage, Penarroya, Bull, Pierrefitte, the Compagnie Française des Pétroles, Usinor, Le Nickel, Hachette . . . If, moreover, as we have seen, the large French merchant banks thoroughly modified their structures in order to adapt themselves to a new situation, if they showed that their appetites were as voracious as ever during the "war of the banks," that really proves that they have no intention at all of throwing in the sponge. Of course, most of our examples have to do only with French banks. But it is difficult to accept the idea that France is an isolated case. In any case, the great American authority on the subject, to whom I have already referred, reminds us that the big American banks have always been "not just the most important, but the only economic power" in the United States. Perhaps this judgment is exaggerated, but it is impossible to believe that it is entirely inconsistent with reality. And during the period 1967–1968, 34 of the 100 biggest banks in the United States organized holding companies.[18]

The lesson that ought to be retained from all this is that the interrelationships of finance capital and industrial capital have become much more complex and more important than they were in Lenin's time, and that they no longer exist for the exclusive benefit of finance capital. Varga is undoubtedly right when he says "a very small group of financial magnates is gaining control over both banks and industries." And in the final analysis, just as the opposition between capital exports and commodity exports seems to have lost its meaning today because the two overlap so closely, in the same way the opposition and even the distinction between finance capital and industrial capital seems to me to have become somewhat idle. The time has probably come to abandon the notion of a financial oligarchy and to substitute for it that of a financial and industrial oligarchy.

In summing up this chapter and the previous one together, it is essential, first of all, to note that the universal tendency toward concentration, which was proceeding at breakneck speed at the beginning of the century, when Lenin called attention to it, then slowed up considerably between the two wars, but began an extraordinary advance once again in the Fifties. It picked up momentum first in the United States and Great Britain, then in Japan and Western Europe, where it is meeting with unprecedented success at the present moment.

This trend is the result of the basic contradiction between competition and concentration. It does not occur uniformly in all places or at all times; it is alternately, and sometimes simultaneously, restrained and encouraged by national governments and multinational institutions. These governments and institutions have reacted to concentration with regulations and practices whose ambivalence reflects the fundamental contradiction mentioned above.

But the growth of productive forces, their internationalization, and the heavy increase in exports of commodities and capital, together with worldwide and regional integration and technological advances, are all interrelated factors that accentuate the tendency for competition to be transformed into monopoly. Monopolies cannot be contained within national boundaries, and increasingly their goal is to set themselves up as giant firms with an international orientation.

The action of governmental monopoly capitalism primarily encourages concentrations at the national level. Domestic competition tends to be suppressed or curtailed to help the nation's monopolies compete internationally. Sometimes the state puts up obstacles in the way of concentration which is developing in the direction of multinational monopolies.

But the great vigor of the trend and the pressure of North American capitalism combine to force the creation of such monopolies, especially within already internationalized spheres like the EEC. Undoubtedly, we are at the beginning of a new phase during which multinational concentrations will multiply in various forms.

The high rate of profit of companies that are monopolies or that verge on monopoly, as well as the concentration and augmentation of their gross revenues, cause corporate savings to increase more rapidly than personal savings. Reinvestment has become the rule and recourse to the stock market the exception, despite efforts undertaken (SICAV) to drain off as much personal savings as possible into investment. The new importance of reinvestment, combined with the exigencies of the marketplace, militates toward more and more heterogeneous concentrations (conglomerates). Big businesses, in addition to their growing internationalism, are also more and more frequently carrying on their activities in several economic sectors simultaneously. The pursuit of profit through professional specialization is being replaced more openly by direct specialization for profit, wherever it comes from. A ceaselessly growing number of large industrial firms are turning themselves into holding companies, and the most powerful among them are participating in banking or financial activities.

The result of this is that industrial capital is now a self-starting enterprise; the hegemony of finance capital is no longer as absolute as it once was. The role of the banks remains important, however; their medium and long term loans are far more important to business than capital acquired through the stock market. The merchant banks are also concentrating themselves in more powerful groups. They are reorganizing themselves in order to adapt to a new situation. The distinction between merchant banks and commercial banks is fading.

Finance capital is defending its position. Industrial capital, meanwhile, is breaking through old barriers, pushing its way into the investment business and engaging in banking and financial activities. Ultimately, the two are merging and becoming largely interdependent. The oligarchy remains and, through this pincer movement, grows stronger as it unifies its functions. It begins to be, and soon will be, a financial and industrial oligarchy.

Notes to Chapter 7

1. *Revue politique et parlementaire,* Dec. 1967; *Problèmes économiques,* no. 1,060, 4-25-68.
2. *Banque,* Jan. 1968.
3. *Op. cit.,* p. 37.
4. *Op. cit.,* Chap. V.
5. *Op. cit.,* pp. 37–38.
6. The data for the SICAV's is taken for the most part from studies and documentation published in *Le Monde,* 9-24-68.
7. *Marxist Economic Theory,* Monthly Review, 1968, vol. II, p. 419.
8. *Politico-Economic Problems of Capitalism* (Moscow: 1968), pp. 161–2.
9. *Monopoly Capitalism,* Monthly Review, 1966, Chap. 3, sec. VI.
10. L. Althusser and E. Balibar, *Lire le Capital,* "Petite collection Maspero," 1968, vol. II, p. 199 *et seq.*
11. Data compiled by INSEE (Institut national de la statistique et des études économiques).
12. *Twentieth Century Capitalism,* pp. 118–121.
13. *Op. cit.,* p. 90.
14. *Le Monde,* 7-13-68.
15. *Economie et Politique,* no. 149–150, Dec. 1966/Jan. 1967, pp. 101–106.
16. Source: various financial reports.
17. *Le Monde,* 5-7-68.
18. J. Grappin, *Le Monde,* 2-13-69.

8

Monopoly State Capitalism

IN *Imperialism, the Highest Stage of Capitalism,* Lenin declares that "private monopolies and state monopolies are bound up together in the age of finance capital; both are but separate links in the imperialist struggle between the big monopolists for the division of the world." (73) He is much more explicit about the role of the state in *State and Revolution*: "Imperialism—the era of bank capital, the era of gigantic capitalist monopolies, the era of the development of monopoly capitalism into state-monopoly capitalism—has demonstrated with particular force an extraordinary strengthening of the 'state machine' and an unprecedented growth of its bureaucratic and military apparatus." (p. 38)

But one must admit that, on this subject, Bukharin goes further. Pages 149 to 160 of his book *Imperialism and World Economy* are devoted to "the interference of the state in economic life" by the creation of state monopolies or of businesses in which the state is part owner, by "state control over the production process of private enterprises," by "regulation of distribution" and by the organization of credit and national consumption. He shows, with the aid of examples, that "the interests of the state and the interests of finance capital coincide more and more" and that *"a maximum of centralisation and a maximum of state power are required* by the fierce competitive struggle on the world market." (155) His analysis leads him to conclude that "(as far as capitalism will retain its foothold) the future belongs to economic forms that are close to state capitalism." (158) ". . . the state becomes a direct entrepreneur and an organiser of production." (160)

The tendencies that Lenin and Bukharin perceived already in their day have progressed considerably in the ways that they foresaw, which gave E. Varga the opportunity, in a book that was published in France in 1967,[1] to analyze monopoly state capitalism in the light of recent developments.

First of all, Varga brings up the fact that, in Marxist theory, monopoly capital is considered a *single force*. Then he quotes Lenin to the effect that monopoly capital " 'introduced the beginnings of state-controlled capitalist production, combining the colossal power of capitalism with the colonial power of the state into a single mechanism and bringing tens of millions of people within the single organization of state capitalism.' " [2] Then Varga adds that "the coalescence of *two forces*—the monopolies and the state—forms the basis of state-monopoly capitalism." But in his view *"Monopoly capital and the state are independent forces"* [emphasis Varga's] that join together without involving the state in simple, unilateral subordination to monopoly capital. This conjunction of two independent forces has two objectives: 1. To safeguard the capitalist system; 2. to proceed through the intermediary of the state toward a new distribution of the national economy in such a way as to favor monopoly capitalism.

Although monopoly capitalism is considered a single force, a more complete analysis leads Varga to "discover that the monopoly bourgeoisie fully agrees on some questions, but sharply disagrees on others." This is because competition survives, "and that excludes a complete community of interests among the bourgeoisie." Varga gives some concrete examples of "contradictions between the monopolies of a single branch, or between separate monopoly enterprises and the interests of monopoly capital as a whole . . ." These contradictions account for possible conflicts with the state. Varga also thinks that the formulation of monopoly state capitalism based on the ideas of Stalin is inexact: " 'state-monopoly capitalism implies the subordination of the state apparatus to the capitalist monopolies.' "

I find it definitely unpleasant to have to express some reservations about Varga's argument as it bears on Stalin. But it really seems to me that Varga does not distinguish sufficiently between essentials and side issues. If Varga was right to say that, in Marxist analysis "*all* capitalist laws are no more than tendencies which are *always* opposed by counter-tendencies," doesn't this conflict with what he says against the Stalinist formulation? For, if it is true that competition survives under monopoly capitalism, "and that excludes a complete community of interests among the bourgeoisie," Lenin said over and over again, and the facts have always confirmed that, given the dialectical opposition of the tendency toward competition and the tendency toward monopolistic concentration, it was the latter that appeared to be stronger and was more characteristic of the highest stage of capitalism. To neglect competition and its consequences would be an error, but to give it too much importance is also a mistake, which leads to the belief, held by Varga, that monopoly capitalism and the state are independent forces. This belief is difficult to square with the Leninist theory of the nature of the state. According to P. A. Baran and P. M. Sweezy, a theory that views the state as an independent social force is "seriously misleading," because "in reality, what appear to be conflicts between business and government are reflections of conflict within the ruling class." [3] And when Varga sees in monopoly state capitalism the simple *coalescence* of two forces, the monopolies and the state, he seems to me once again to contradict Lenin, who, in the statement quoted by Varga himself, speaks of *combining* these two forces into a single mechanism.

This is not just a semantic quibble. The notion of *combination* (an expression used in the Leninist theory of the nature of the state) emphasizes the fundamental identity of the objectives of monopoly capital and the state. The notion of *coalescence* gives too much importance to the disagreements that can arise between government policy and the interests, not of monopoly capital as a whole (Varga recognizes this elsewhere), but of a branch of monopoly capital. If, moreover, two independent forces are simply conjoined, nothing guarantees that this conjunction will last, since it is not structural. However, certain evidence I will be presenting later on proves that this so-called coalescence is not only lasting but growing more pronounced, and Varga himself recognizes that it is permanent. In short, the Stalinist formula seems to me a correct statement of the situation—"state-monopoly capitalism implies the subordination of the state apparatus to the capitalist monopolies"—because it affirms what is the very *essence* of monopoly state capitalism, and because it does not seem to me to run counter to a more profound analysis that puts secondary contradictions in their proper place.

The United States is undoubtedly the industrialized country in which monopoly state capitalism had to face the greatest difficulties. The absolute primacy of free enterprise, whose praises are sung there in every key, once appeared to present insuperable obstacles to the direct intervention of the state in the organization of the economy. The obstacles have, however, been surmounted. Geoffrey Owen offers some very interesting information on this score.

Referring to the New Deal of the Thirties, which "shifted the major sources of economic power from private to public institutions," Owen observes that "it was an unnerving experience for American businessmen," and that "since then, the instinctive reaction of many businessmen to any proposed enlargement of Government authority has been vehement opposition." Not only did the legislation of the New Deal remain essentially intact, however, but the Employment Act of 1946 formally recognized the federal government's responsibility to " 'promote maximum employment, production and purchasing power.' " And since the beginning of the Kennedy administration in 1961, "the Federal Government showed a greater willingness to innovate in the field of economic policy and to intervene in the decisions of businessmen." For their part, businessmen still kept up a show of resistance, but in the last few years, there has grown up among them "a more rational, less dogmatic attitude . . . toward the Government's involvement with the economy." The result of this is what Owen calls a " 'dual' or 'mixed' economy, in which government and business bear a joint responsibility for economic progress," none of which prevents the continuation of a constant debate "over such questions as how to reconcile the advantages of competition with the need for Government supervision in steel, electricity supply and other key industries." [4]

Moreover, when the United States met with serious difficulties over its balance of payments, President Johnson addressed the business community in these terms: "I am asking you to join hands with me in a voluntary partnership. I am asking you to show the world that an aroused and responsible business community can close ranks and make a voluntary program work." There was, of course, some resistance, notably from the Chase Manhattan Bank, which claimed that what Johnson was asking for amounted to "a giant step in the direction towards Federal domination of the economy." But the giant step was taken, since 500 large companies agreed (and few others refused) to send a report every quarter to the Department of Commerce describing their "individual" balances of payments. [5] This was an important and characteristic event: the voluntary, non-institutionalized cooperation of big business with the state.

In commenting on the preponderant role of the American government in regulating the economy, J. K. Galbraith points out, among other things, that federal expenditures for goods and services, which are an important aspect of governmental intervention in the economy, rose from 1.7% of the GNP in 1929 to 8.4% in 1965. And he goes on to say that this increase "has been with the strong approval of the industrial system." No one objected because the increase went mainly for defense and the space program (which accounted for 50 to 60% of the federal budget between 1960 and 1965, as against 10 to 15% between 1930 and 1940), and these expenditures directly profited big business. Galbraith insists on this point: "These expenditures are strongly supported by businessmen," and he adds that probably the majority of the large industrial corporations "would . . . approve other areas of government activity, including in particular those that support advanced technology." This is because, "no more than any other social institution does the industrial system disapprove of what is important for its success." [6]

Galbraith does not neglect to mention, moreover, that those who resist governmental intervention are, for the most part, "entrepreneurs," a category which he opposes to big business and the technostructure, and which he places on the margins of the industrial system. He has, in fact, painted the picture of an internal contradiction in the capitalist system that is of secondary importance, since if the American government is sometimes forced to pay attention to this declining category, its actions fundamentally conform to the interests of the monopolies. For, in the United States, where government leaders and the leaders of monopolies are interchangeable, the state is a direct expression of the monopolies, and, one could even say, an integral part of them.

Elsewhere, J. K. Galbraith states that "the market for the most advanced technology and that which best allows planning is also in the public sector," that "much scientific and technical innovation comes from, or is sponsored by, the state or by publicly supported universities and research institutions" (cf. the end of my Chap. V), that "the state regulates the aggregate demand for the products of the industrial system [which is] indispensable for its planning," and that "the state provides the wage and price regulation." Galbraith concludes his argument as follows:

"Clearly the modern organized economy was designed with a perverse hand. For how, otherwise, could so many needs seeming so inescapable conspire to make a system which still rejoices in the name of free enterprise in truth be so dependent on government.

"The industrial system, in fact, is inextricably associated with the state. In notable respects the mature corporation is an arm of the state. And the state, in important matters, is an instrument of the industrial system." [7]

France is the industrialized country where monopoly state capitalism in the form of direct governmental intervention in production is the most prevalent and has the longest history. The magazine *Entreprise,* which expresses the point of view of French business circles, reveals, in an article by Jacques Rigaud, that for thirty years now, the French government has been intervening in the structures of the economy and has played the role of a "producer of riches." Rigaud divides those thirty years into two periods: from 1936 until the end of the war, the government's actions were characterized by their *direct impact*. For the last several years, additional state intervention has made itself felt through *indirect radiation*.[8]

In the first phase, state intervention in the economy took a "compact form," thanks to three processes: a) nationalization, which sometimes affected entire industries (coal, electricity, gas), sometimes only an important part of an industry (loans, insurance) and sometimes, under special circumstances, an individual business (Rénault); b) expropriation, to a virtually total extent, of a private business, which resulted, in theory at least, in joint ownership, by the state and by private individuals. This occurred principally in the transportation industries (Railroads, Air France, Compagnie Générale Transatlantique, Messageries Maritimes); c) creation from the ground up of a nationally owned organization designed for a special new purpose: Caisse Nationale des Marchés de l'État, Atomic Energy Commission, etc.

In the second phase, state intervention "took a more subtle and often less visible form": 1. On the one hand, the traditional public sector proliferated, through subsidiary operations and investments; it created for itself "a secondary sector of joint ownership" either through partnerships between state-owned businesses (Air Inter), or in partnership with private capital (Auby-Charbonnages, SEREB, Aérotrain). 2. On the other hand, the state practiced what Rigaud calls "remote-controlled intervention," the best example of which is the Plan Calcul: an official organization of moderate size, supported by a research institute, and charged with putting into operation the government's plan [Tr.: to develop a competitive French computer industry] through private enterprise. "More and more," concludes Rigaud, "there is a place for the state to function not only as a customer and a producer, but also as an instigator," and he adds that "the future undoubtedly belongs to these flexible forms of intervention."

In West Germany in 1962, according to Varga, the government owned 74 industrial corporations, each capitalized at more than 100 million marks, and with a total capitalization of 20 billion marks. But Italy is probably an even better example of a govern-

ment equipped with powerful, clearly defined and efficient official organizations that allow it to intervene, either directly or
indirectly, in order to propel the country's economy forward and
steer it in the desired direction. The state-owned holding company ENI. (Ente Nazionale Idrocarburi) has played a well
known role in this and has extended its activities outside the
oil business, through 175 companies that are involved in chemicals, machinery, textiles, cement, rubber and, now, nuclear combustibles. The IRI (Institute for Industrial Reconstruction) is a
state-owned investment company which is often held up as an
example of state intervention. Created in 1953, it ranks fourth
today among European businesses and controls, directly or
through five specialized holding companies, 130 corporations,
three of which are large banks. It applies the directives of the
state while reserving to itself the choice of the appropriate means
to accomplish them. Decentralization, flexibility and the rights
of private capital are its rules. The EFIM group is an organization
that administers government investments in the manufacturing
sector. It controls three holding companies through which it is
associated with important private Italian groups (Fiat, Monte-
catini-Edison, Pirelli . . .) and with foreign companies (Fire-
stone, Westinghouse . . .). There is probably no other country
besides Italy where monopoly state capitalism has expanded its
influence so broadly and vigorously over production itself in the
energy-producing and industrial sectors.

The IRC (Industrial Reorganization Corporation), which the
Labor government created in Great Britain at the end of 1966,
seems less ambitious. But, thanks to an article by Alain Jacob,[9]
it is clear that the IRC, whose name is reminiscent of the Italian
IRI, is every bit as much a typical instrument of monopoly state
capitalism. A government agency with 150 million pounds in public funds at its disposal, the IRC's purpose was to "aid British
industry in adapting itself, through structural and organiza-
tional reforms, to modern conditions of international competition,
to promote plans for the rationalization of industry from which
the national economy can derive substantial benefits . . ." More
concretely, its resources were supposed to allow it to grant loans
to various private businesses "in order to encourage certain

mergers or the creation of entirely new enterprises." In effect, the IRC has made its influence felt in several mergers brought about since its creation: e.g. through a loan of 3 million pounds to Rootes for its merger with Chrysler, of 25 million pounds for the Leyland-B.M.C. merger, of 15 million pounds for the English Electric-Elliot Automation merger, etc. In other cases, it has acted through more subtle and indirect means. And it received, Jacob tells us, a qualified welcome from the City, which led it to "take up a position a little closer to the City than to Whitehall." This led the Labor government, in turn, to promulgate a law affecting industrial expansion, which "authorized the government to make direct and permanent investments in certain corporations." Finally the situation evolved "toward a kind of acceptance of government intervention, as well as the services which it offers through the IRC on the one hand and the Industrial Expansion Bill on the other." The result has been "a liaison between the government and the City," and according to the Communist paper, *The Morning Star*, as quoted by Jacob, the IRC is a supplementary device "for making private industry more profitable and encouraging the growth of monopoly." That is a conclusion I find it difficult to argue against.

This British point of view is echoed by J. Magniadas in an article in the French Communist periodical *Économie et Politique*: "Today, intervention by the state in order to accelerate concentration and create companies of great size has become an essential objective of Gaullist policy. One of the main goals of the Fifth Plan is the restructuring of the French economy around 20 or 30 dominant groups." He goes on to say: "State intervention therefore really seems like an essential element of the process of capitalist concentration in our time." But Magniadas also makes it clear that the ambitious objectives of the financial oligarchy can not be attained "without increased pressure and intervention by the state, not only to have them accepted by certain monopolistic groups, to the extent that concentrations imply changes in the existing balance of power between groups, but also to make their economic and social consequences acceptable to the working class, to the middle class and also to non-monopolistic businesses." [10]

Here again, then, we find an expression of the fact that, if monopoly state capitalism fundamentally and universally serves the interests of the financial and industrial oligarchy, it can find itself in contradiction (albeit a secondary contradiction) with certain monopolistic groups and especially with non-monopolistic businesses.

P. A. Baran and P. M. Sweezy give a theoretical Marxist explanation of the development of monopoly state capitalism in their extremely interesting book, to which the reader, himself, should refer since I will limit myself here to a brief, and inevitably distorted, synopsis of it. According to Baran and Sweezy, "monopoly capitalism is a self-contradictory system," because it tends to create an increasing surplus that, under normal conditions, cannot be absorbed and therefore will not be produced. As a result, there is a tendency toward chronic underemployment of available resources and toward stagnation. But there are remedies for this, which the system must use in order to survive. Among these remedies the authors include, on the one hand, what they call "sales efforts" (advertising, diversity in the presentation of products, planned obsolescence, model changes, credit arrangements, etc.) which become an integral part of the total surplus and consequently increase it; on the other hand, and of particular importance, are government expenditures (especially military spending) which absorb a more and more significant portion of the potential surplus and thereby create an actual surplus, which private consumption would be incapable of doing. From this point of view, therefore, monopoly state capitalism (which consists to an important degree of public expenditures) is not a matter of choice, it is a course of action which the monopolies and the monopoly state must adopt in order to insure the survival of the system.[11]

To sum up, we have seen that monopoly state capitalism is a system in which the apparatus of the state is subordinated to the financial and industrial oligarchy, a system which, though beset by contradictions, resistance and hesitation, has nevertheless developed vigorously in recent years, not only in Italy, which seems to be the leading example of this process, but in most of the other industrialized capitalist countries, and especially in the United

States, France, and Great Britain. In the United States, the largest companies have not only universally accepted the growing intervention of the state, but they have also agreed to collaborate voluntarily with the state in order to protect the system. In France, the president of the *Patronat,* himself, first referred to the expansion of international competition and the changes in the overall situation which force business to face the same scientific and technological problems as the rest of the world, and then called on the state to play a greater role in helping business confront these challenges. "The main feature of this new phase in our economic development," he declared, "is the determining role that governments are going to be called on to play in it. Competition today is an international struggle that involves the entire nation. Business can not fight the battle alone." [12] It doesn't seem as if there is any risk in predicting that monopoly state capitalism will continue to increase its influence over the economy.

After remarking on what I have called the resistance and hesitation that impede the growth of monopoly state capitalism, as well as what he refers to as its "uneven development," Varga advances the theory that this uneven process of development is characterized by great leaps forward when the capitalist system is in crisis or feels itself threatened, and by partial retreats when the danger is removed.[13] This analysis seems to correspond to the historical facts for the whole period, roughly speaking, that lead up to the Second World War. But during the last decade, monopoly state capitalism has taken hold in a more general way and with greater force than in any other period; however, it can not be said that those ten years included any crisis or danger to the capitalist system. The reverse is true. Localized and limited recessions did not impede favorable development in general, the average rate of growth of the GNP for the industrialized countries of OECD was significantly higher between 1960 and 1966 than between 1950 and 1960, and, politically speaking, it was an era of détente in international relations.

It seems to me instead that the state's function in the class struggle is to be a tool of the power of the ruling class. During a period when liberalism alone was enough to achieve bourgeois economic goals, the dominant capitalist bourgeois class first used the state essentially as a means of political coercion and repression, except insofar as the state enjoyed certain traditional economic responsibilities such as currency and customs regulations, etc.

Then, in a second phase, the phase of imperialism and monopolies, the internationalization of economic life has forced the state to intervene increasingly as an instrument of the economic supremacy of the ruling class, the oligarchy. This has not happened all at once or without difficulty, which is the reason for the uneven development of monopoly state capitalism, which is not uniform geographically or chronologically, and which can proceed by leaps and bounds during a period of crisis or external threat. But partial or relative retreats do not impede the overall advance, and we have probably now arrived at a new stage where the merger of the state and the oligarchy is permanent, organized institutionally and irreversibly in all respects. The state has become the instrument of the oligarchy's economic as well as its political power. And this is true at all times, whatever the circumstances. Unfavorable circumstances only make it more obvious and perceptible.

Varga goes much more deeply into another aspect of this, and he is right to speak of "supra-national monopoly-state capitalism," which seems to him *an important new phenomenon.* From before the First World War and up until the Second, various kinds of monopoly state organizations involving several countries were set up, but in Varga's opinion—and mine too—they were an exception then, while now they are a normal part of life. Varga mentions the International Monetary Fund, the World Bank and its subsidiaries, the ECSC, the EEC, NATO, CENTO, and the international agreements on basic products, to which I would add GATT, OECD, the "Club of the Ten," the International Court at The Hague, SEATO, and the Kennedy Round. The reason for this whole jumble of organizations, as Varga has seen, is that all the supranational economic organizations are also political.

But Varga's analysis of this new and important phenomenon seems to me quite inadequate. According to him, and he insists on this point, the causes and the objectives of the supranational organizations "are identical to those of state-monopoly capitalism on a national scale—the defence of the capitalist social system and the securing of high monopoly profits." Although he barely mentions the neo-colonial policies of the imperialist countries, he does put heavy emphasis on the serious contradictions that divide the members of the Common Market, and which set them off as a group from the United States. And he concludes his discussion of monopoly state capitalism *on a supranational scale,* with this quotation from the program of the Communist Party of the Soviet Union: " 'The dialectics of state-monopoly capitalism is such that instead of shoring up the capitalist system, as the bourgeoisie expects, it aggravates the contradictions of capitalism and undermines its foundations.' " [14] As far as I am concerned this is an erroneous conclusion because it leaves the essential point obscure.

If, in fact, the appearance of a multitude of diverse but mutually coherent multinational organizations after the Second World War is "a *new and important* phenomenon," [15] obviously this phenomenon is a response to a new situation and its causes and objectives can not simply be "identical" to those which brought about the rise of monopoly state capitalism at the beginning of the century. The contradictions of capitalism that exist both within the imperialist countries and among them (Varga concerns himself primarily and almost exclusively with these supranational contradictions) are the sort of evidence that no one can attack. But their importance at the present time can only be understood by referring to new contradictions that have appeared during the recent past: the rise of China as the recognized leader of the authentically socialist countries and the widespread revolutionary opposition to imperialism which is beginning throughout the Third World. One notable result of this is that what Varga calls "supra-national monopoly-state capitalism" is something quite different from a simple extrapolation of monopoly state capitalism as we used to know it to the supranational scale. Only the blind will not see it as an attempt at worldwide imperialist integration under the direction of American superimperialism, which is a response to new causes and aims at almost completely new objectives. I shall discuss this crucial subject in detail in Chapter X.

NOTES TO CHAPTER 8

1. *Politico-Economic Problems of Capitalism,* the chapter called "Problems of State-monopoly Capitalism."
2. "War and Revolution."
3. *Monopoly Capitalism,* p. 67.
4. *Op. cit.,* pp. 18–19.
5. *Op. cit.,* p. 174.
6. *Op. cit.,* pp. 228–30.
7. *Op. cit.,* p. 296.
8. *Entreprise,* no. 642, 12-30-67.
9. *Le Monde,* 7-9-68.
10. *Économie et Politique,* no. 149–150, Dec. 1966/Jan. 1967.
11. *Op. cit.,* Chaps. 4–7.
12. Statement made by M. Huvelin, President of the French employers' organization before a meeting of the Centre de recherche des chefs d'entreprises, as reported by *Le Monde,* 11-12-68.
13. *Op. cit.,* pp. 59–64.
14. Varga, *Politico-Economic Problems . . . ,* pp. 68, 69, 71, 74.
15. P.J.'s emphasis.

9

Imperialism, the Third World and the Socialist World

WE HAVE seen in the course of the preceding chapters, and especially in Chapters II, III, and IV, that the economic relationships between the imperialist countries and the countries of the Third World boil down essentially to relationships of domination and exploitation: the huge reserves of raw materials in the Third World are controlled by imperialism and exploited for its profit; three-quarters of the Third World's trade is transacted with the imperialist countries, and it is characterized by a special kind of exploitation known as "unequal exchange"; investments of private capital enable imperialism to siphon off a large economic surplus produced in the Third World, and foreign aid, which makes it possible to perpetuate this exploitation, also strengthens imperialism's political domination of its local staffs and of local social groups which are dependent on it.

As a result, the economies of the Third World countries become satellites of the imperialist economy as a whole (but, in numerous cases, one Third World country is especially dependent on a "special relationship" with a particular imperialist country), and consequently the Third World becomes integrated into the worldwide imperialist system. But such conclusions seem to me to require various refinements, to which most of this chapter will be devoted. It will also include a discussion of the relationship between imperialism and the Socialist world.

A. Imperialism and the Third World

The best way of exploring this subject seems to me, first, to examine the effects that the domination and exploitation of the Third World has on imperialism, and, second, to examine what effects the same process has on the Third World.

1. CONSEQUENCES FOR IMPERIALISM

Marxist writers for a long time considered the underdeveloped countries as an outlet for the surpluses of capital accumulated in the imperialist countries. Then, they came to realize the considerable importance of capital repatriated in the form of profits; so that today they often discuss the problem from a perspective that is exactly the reverse of their former position. They hunt for statistics, make calculations, and set up balance sheets.

I want to say right away that their calculations and balance sheets are very useful from certain points of view, but that they are an insufficient basis for arriving at a solution to the problem at issue. This is also an opportunity for me to criticize myself, for I gave too much importance in my two previous books to the strictly financial and book-keeping aspects of the problem. Although I wrote in *The Pillage of the Third World* that "it seems to be a vain undertaking to make even a rough estimate of the tribute which imperialism exacts from the Third World, or of the contribution such tribute makes to total capital accumulation" (I meant tribute through the repatriation of capital), I did so less because the method seemed dubious to me than because the necessary data were unavailable (*p. 79*). In *The Third World in World Economy*, I wrote out a balance sheet for imperialist investment in the Third World that no longer seems to have quite the significance it did at the time, when I felt able to conclude from it that "it is not the imperialist countries which aid the Third World, but the Third World which aids imperialism." That is an inexact statement. It reduces the problem of the relations of the Third World and imperialism to a question of finance, which is a limited and distorted perspective. Fortunately,

I added that in any case "this pedestrian arithmetical calculation has the sole purpose of exposing the myth of aid, and it is clear that it is quite powerless to give a real idea of the enrichment imperialism derives from the pillage of the Third World." (p. 117)

To approach the problem in terms of capital flow, one must keep in mind that the countries of the Third World are almost all always very poor in foreign exchange reserves, and that it would be impossible for these reserves to be used on a permanent basis for transfers of capital to the imperialist countries. And so, this time I think I have finally succeeded in demonstrating, in Chapter IV-A, that in view of the enormous annual deficit in the external accounts of the Third World, caused by the repatriation of profits realized from investments of private capital, imperialist foreign aid was *the only solution* to the imbalance of external payments, that is, it was the only way to perpetuate exploitation, because it made up for the deficit.

Of course, this general description, which applies to the situation of the Third World as a whole over a certain number of years, does not apply with mathematical exactitude to every place at all times, and it would be a simplistic view of things to think that foreign aid exactly covers each year's balance of payments deficit in each country. Aid for a given year, moreover, is generally decided upon, and its exact amount is settled, before the external account balance is known. There is also a certain amount of juggling that goes on between foreign aid and the other major elements affecting the balance of payments. For example, a Third World country might permit itself to enlarge or reduce its trade deficit according to the amount of foreign aid it expected or hoped for.[1]

Nevertheless, generally speaking, foreign aid is the fundamental reason for the continuing relative equilibrium of the Third World's external payments today. Only if foreign aid did not exist could one speak of a contribution by the Third World, through transfers of capital, to the accumulation of capital in the imperialist countries. But this hypothesis is completely unrealistic, because the system would collapse very quickly from lack of reserves. In order to prevent such a collapse and also to perpetuate the imperialist exploitation of the Third World, the imperialist countries provide foreign aid as an indispensable counterweight to the various financial depredations of their monopolies.

Unequal exchange is another important form of imperialist pillage, which is a permanent feature of relations between the two groups of countries. For most Marxist writers, unequal exchange between industrialized capitalist countries and Third World countries is a particular case of the law of value. "By sending their goods to the backward countries," writes Ernest Mandel, "and using them, in turn, as sources of raw materials, food, etc., the industrially advanced countries are able to sell their goods for more than their value and buy what they need at less than it is worth." Elsewhere Mandel says that unequal exchange represents "the exchange of less work for more work, or, what amounts to the same thing, a transfer of value from the backward to the advanced country." [2] As Charles Bettelheim sees it, products sold to the exploited countries by the industrialized countries are "quite generally sold for more than their value," while the exploitation of underdeveloped countries by unequal exchange results "frequently in the purchase of the products of these countries at a price lower than their value." [3]

There is a thesis written by A. Emmanuel, but unfortunately still unpublished at this writing, which, I have heard, is a contribution of the greatest importance to the Marxist analysis of unequal exchange. I have been able, however, to familiarize myself with the thesis's broad outlines, at least, in an article also written by Emmanuel.[4] As he describes it, he has conducted an analysis that leans heavily on the works of Marx and that is consistent with his law of value. Unequal exchange, according to Emmanuel, "is the result of contact between underdeveloped countries and developed countries, regardless of the products they exchange with one another." Unequal exchange does not exist within a national framework or as a general rule but only at the international level. It is a result of the difference between rates of surplus value. "The difference in salaries is essentially due to a difference in the cost of labor," since the requirements of workers in underdeveloped societies have generally remained at the minimum level necessary for mere survival, while the cost of labor in the advanced countries today includes the cost of satisfying needs which capitalism has been forced to fulfill. In a very lively paragraph, Emmanuel goes into this in greater detail:

"What an incredible windfall it was. At a certain moment in its history, capitalism came across underdeveloped man, who, as far as his material needs were concerned, had just emerged from the tribal stage, although he had the same ten fingers and two arms as developed man and a brain that functioned in the same way too. *In the final analysis, the surplus profit from unequal exchange is the result of the fact that underdeveloped man can manage modern tools, while he is still far from having modern material needs.*"

Finally Emmanuel proposes the following definition:

> If allowance is made for all fluctuations in price that are produced by the imperfections of the marketplace, "unequal exchange" is the relationship between prices established by virtue of the law of the equalization of profit rates in areas with basically different rates of surplus value, that is, where surplus value is, for whatever reason, unaffected by the equalizing force of competition.

According to Carlos Romeo, in his analysis of the same phenomenon, inequalities of exchange between one market and another reflect:

> . . . an exploitative relationship between technoeconomically unequal producers who exchange their products according to a formula of equivalence that implies the mutual recognition of their inequality. In short, unequal exchange means trading a small amount of highly paid work for a large amount of poorly paid work.[5]

Despite these varying definitions or the reservations felt in certain quarters,[6] no one questions the existence and the importance of unequal exchange nor the fact that unequal exchange results in a concrete "transfer of value from the backward country to the advanced country." However, even though unequal exchange is a matter of record, it is not figured into the trade balance, which is a component of the balance of payments of a given country in a given year. It can only be evaluated as a changing quantity, by plotting the deterioration of the terms of exchange against the figures for a single base year, and, in my opinion, this year ought to be fairly remote from the present in order to minimize circumstantial variations. In Chapter III-A, on the basis of official documentation, I was able to calculate that the deterioration of the terms of exchange between the countries of the Third World and the developed capitalist countries between 1954 and 1965 had amounted to a decline of 19%. This means that the losses incurred by the Third World in this way in 1965 had risen, by comparison with 1954, to the equivalent of 19% of their exports to the developed capitalist countries in 1965, or to about 5 billion dollars. But according to François Luchaire, the loss for 1965 came to around 14 billion dollars if, instead of using 1954 as a base, one chooses the economic situation of fifty years ago.[7]

Summing up, it is not possible to arrive at an *absolute* measurement of the extent of the transfer of value brought about by the operation of unequal exchange in a given year. One can simply deduce, from the *relative* figures above, that the amount is of considerable size, and one can also determine how the process operates, and that it operates differently for imports than for exports. In the case of imports to the Third World, there is, in effect, a monetary transfer involved, since the invoice includes the surplus value of the product purchased in an industrialized country. This surplus value is thus actually transferred in currency when the import bill is settled. On the contrary, when a Third World country sells a primary product to an industrialized country, the transaction is characterized by an absence of transfer, which is the equivalent, for the exporting country, of a loss of profit equal to the difference between the value of the product and its undervalorization in terms of the price obtained. In this case, the surplus profit due to unequal exchange is only realized by the importing country at the moment when the imported product is integrated into that country's internal economy. Unequal exchange is therefore definitely a component of the trade balance of the Third World countries. It increases the amount spent on imports and reduces the amount received for exports, but in my opinion there is no way whatever to calculate its effect exactly in either area. Price curves by category of product only permit the supposition that the loss from exports is much larger than the gain from imports.

It must, however, be pointed out that despite the fact that unequal exchange brings about an effective transfer in one direction and an absence of transfer in the other, when all is said and done it has repercussions in every case in the balances of payments of the countries involved, since it tends to improve the total trade balance of the industrialized capitalist countries and to worsen the trade balance of the Third World countries. Therefore it has a positive effect in maintaining the stability of the capitalist countries' balances of payments and a negative effect on Third World balances, which often forces the Third World countries to curb their imports in order to achieve equilibrium.

Though it is impossible to calculate the transfer of value effected by unequal exchange, one can still theorize about it, somewhat absurdly perhaps, in the following manner: in 1966, the OECD countries as a group recorded a total gross formation of fixed capital of 288 billion dollars.[8] In the same year, exports from the Third World to the industrialized capitalist countries were equal to around 28.4 billion dollars. If one assumes, purely for the sake of argument, that half the value of these exports represented unequal exchange, which, in turn, went in its entirety into the gross formation of fixed capital in the countries receiving it, it would still only account for roughly 5% of the total. It goes without saying that this hypothesis has no scientific value. It has no other purpose than to provide a comparative basis for evaluating the importance of unequal exchange vis-à-vis the group of countries—the imperialist ones—which it benefits. And it allows me to conclude that its importance is relatively minimal,[9] which does not, of course, prevent it from being of very great importance to the Third World because of the immense difference in economic strength between the two groups of countries (from 1 to 5½ or 6).

According to E. Varga, there is a "long-term tendency of capitalism towards a decline in the growth of production," and for Baran and Sweezy (cf. Chap. 8), monopoly capitalism, undermined by its internal contradictions, tends to create a growing surplus which can not be absorbed under normal conditions and therefore will not be produced. This creates a tendency toward the underemployment of resources and stagnation. These authors are thus in agreement about the essential tendency at issue. Baran and Sweezy, moreover, add that counterforces exist: "sales efforts," and government expenditures, which allow a portion of the potential surplus to be absorbed, and consequently counteract the essential tendency toward stagnation. It seems to me that one should also follow Varga in adding to these counterforces "the expansion of the world capitalist market resulting from the development of capitalist relations in the less advanced countries," which is going on now in Asia, in Africa, and in Latin America.[10]

It is certain, in fact, that the Third World offers the imperialist countries a market for their industrial products and, therefore, that it absorbs some of their surplus. Earlier I estimated that this surplus absorption amounted to about 5.5% of the total value of imperialist industrial production. But Varga's theory has to be qualified, for, as we have seen, this market shows a tendency to contract, since, because of the deterioration of their terms of exchange, the Third World countries' capacity to absorb imports is constantly shrinking in terms of relative value (Cf. Chap. III-A). If, then, sales to the Third World constitute one of the elements that counteract the essential tendency toward a slowdown in the growth of production in the imperialist countries, their countervailing effect is currently diminishing. The monopolies (cf. Chap. IV-C) often react to this by substituting industrial production within the Third World, through capital exports and industrial investments, in place of the exportation of commodities, which has become a more difficult proposition. But this substitution produces yet another. While commodity exports absorb a portion of the potential surplus of the imperialist factories, imperialist industrial production within the Third World, and this includes assembly plants, creates a new

source of productive capacity, which tends to enlarge the potential surplus. Imperialism thus reverts to its fundamental
tendency. It can not shake itself loose in this way from its contradictions.

The point of the foregoing is that all the various ways in which
the imperialist monopolies have siphoned off the resources of
the Third World have, in all cases involving transfers of money,
roughly speaking, had to be compensated for ultimately by foreign aid, which represents the forced contribution made by the
salaried classes of the imperialist countries to their monopolies
so that they can continue to plunder the Third World. But since
there is monetary compensation, these forms of plunder do not
play a direct part in the accumulation of capital in the imperialist countries. They bring about an internal transfer between social classes. As for unequal exchange, it undoubtedly
comes down to a transfer of value from the despoiled country to
the monopolies of the despoiling country. Only a modest portion
of this transfer (overvalorization of imports in the Third World)
occurs in the form of a transfer of money. And the largest part
of this (undervalorization of exports from the Third World)
contributes to the accumulation of capital within the imperialist
countries. The size of this transfer cannot be reliably calculated.
It is far too insignificant a feature of the overall formation of
savings or capital in the countries in question.

From another point of view, sales made by the industrialized
countries in the Third World counteract the essential tendency
toward a slowdown in the growth of production by imperialist
factories. But the significance of these sales is diminishing, and
their partial replacement by the production of monopolies
within the Third World itself tends to re-establish the essential
tendency all over again.

One might almost be tempted to conclude from all this that,
in the final analysis, plundering the Third World has only a
moderate effect on the overall economy of imperialism. But I
have not yet referred back to the data in Chapter II. They boil
down, remember, to this: the overall economy of the imperialist
countries as a group depends, with respect to their overall needs,
on the contributions of the Third World:

————to a very great degree in the case of edible oils (notably peanut and palm kernel oils), and to a great degree for rubber;

————for all its cocoa needs;

————in 1964, the imperialist countries depended on the Third World for 48% of their oil requirements. By 1980, they will depend on the Third World for at least 65% of their needs. Oil from the Third World accounted for about 19% of the total energy from all sources used by the imperialist countries in 1964, and will account for 30% by 1980. The energy balance of the imperialist countries depends on a rapidly growing supply of Third World oil;

————Third World iron ore now fills one-third of imperialism's requirements. This dependence grows greater every year (it tripled during the last decade and a half).

————imperialist dependence on imported chrome and manganese ore from all sources is almost complete (Third World + socialist countries), and on the order of at least four-fifths from the Third World alone;

————in the case of cobalt, the imperialist countries depend on the Third World for at least three-quarters of their current needs, and this dependence is growing;

————dependence is almost complete for tin;

————the imperialist countries fill 40% of their copper requirements from the Third World, and they will depend on the Third World more heavily in the future;

————dependence for bauxite supplies has reached the level of 67%, is growing rapidly and will continue to do so more and more.

In order to assure themselves the best possible conditions, from every point of view, for covering their indispensable requirements in oil and basic raw materials, the imperialist monopolies control almost all the irreplaceable sources situated in the Third World.

Given the situation of dependence, of growing dependence, which is brutally obvious from the above data, it would be pointless to calculate the amount of the Third World's contributions to the economy of the imperialist countries and the enormous additional value which they create for it. All figures for surplus profits, in terms of capital formation for dollars or whatever, even if they could be arrived at, would serve no purpose, for without the contributions of the Third World, the economy of the imperialist countries would simply collapse. The Third World provides imperialism with a unique elixir of life.

2. CONSEQUENCES FOR THE THIRD WORLD

If the exploitation of the riches and, in particular, of the energy resources and raw materials of the Third World is a vital necessity for imperialism, and if the result of this is imperialism's fundamental and constantly growing dependence on the Third World, the Third World, for its part, depends and depends increasingly on the imperialist system, for, as we have seen, its economy is a satellite economy integrated into that system.

I would like to discuss briefly——a detailed investigation would lead us away from our subject——the consequences that result from all of this for the Third World.

The notion of underdevelopment comes to mind immediately. But this notion is ambiguous and misleading. Here is what Charles Bettelheim has to say on the subject:

> In fact, the phrase "underdeveloped countries" suggests ideas without scientific validity. It suggests that the countries it is applied to are simply "backward," or "behind" the others, which are known as "advanced countries."
>
> This vision of different countries running a race for economic and social progress, with greater or lesser success, is purely imaginary. But when this vision of international relations is intellectualized, it tends to be expressed statistically, as a rank list of standards of living, which substitutes for historical explanation and scientific analysis. Neither history nor analysis could treat as abstractions the domination and the exploitative relationships that exist among the various countries of the world today.
>
> If one wishes to act scientifically, in my opinion, it is necessary to eliminate the expression "underdeveloped countries" in favor of the far more exact term, "exploited and dominated countries with crippled economies." [11]

In a chapter that ought to be read in its entirety, Bettelheim shows that the present situation in the so-called "underdeveloped" countries is in no way comparable to what the "advanced" countries experienced before their industrialization, for the economies of these countries were not at all dependent. They "were not crippled and tottering, but on the contrary, they were homogeneous and self-sufficient." He shows that "in fact the so-called underdeveloped countries 'developed' over the same length of time as the developed countries, but they did not grow in the same direction or in the same manner." This evolution occurred as a function of the imperialist domination which Bettelheim analyzes: the *dependence* of the Third World countries and the *exploitation,* of which they are the object, lead jointly to a halt in development caused by the dislocation of the various sectors of the economy.

This analysis is essentially similar to the analyses of numerous other Marxist economists, in particular that of André Gunder Frank, which is the result of a thorough study of the Latin American countries and especially of the Chilean and Brazilian situations, to which he devotes what amount to separate monographs. According to Frank, the combination of the processes of domination and exploitation in the Latin American countries has led to the creation of structures whose effect is to reproduce these processes. This is the basis of the theory of the "development of underdevelopment," since what is called underdevelopment can only grow worse while these processes are in operation and these structures remain in force.[12] In other words, there is no exit from the imperialist system for the peoples of the Third World. This same analysis and these same conclusions appear in the work of Ruy Mauro Marini, who, like A. G. Frank, lingers over the problem of the so-called "national" bourgeoisies.[13] According to Marini, the influx of imperialist capital into local businesses is what lies behind the growth of the industrial Latin American bourgeoisie, which started out with an idea of autonomous development that turned, in effect, into integration, giving rise to "a new type of dependence that was much more absolute than what had existed previously." This integration not only "denationalized" the local bourgeoisie, it even "increases the split between the bourgeoisie and the working classes by intensifying their hyperexploitation." The combination of tend-

encies which produce integration and the abandonment of as-
pirations for autonomous development "leads to the fall of the
democratic liberal regimes . . . and to the establishment of
technico-military dictatorships." In a word, as soon as economic
integration is combined with joint capitalization, it leads straight-
way to political integration of the crudest sort.

Frank also insists that the common interests of the indigenous
bourgeoisie and imperialism have not only a long term but also
a short term effect: "Even in the short run, the Latin American
bourgeoisie cannot be national . . . in alliance with Latin American workers and peasants—as the Popular Front rule book
would have them do—because the same neo-imperialist encroach-
ment is forcing the Latin American bourgeoisie to exploit its
supposed worker and peasant allies ever more and is thus forcing
the bourgeoisie to forego this remaining source of political support." [14]

This analysis based on Latin America is essentially applicable
to all the countries of the Third World. In places where an indigenous bourgeoisie has not yet arisen, experience shows that
one will spring up rapidly with the help of the ruling bureaucracy, since a bureaucracy and a nascent bourgeoisie are intimately
interrelated. A merchant class appears first and enriches itself
in trade and especially in foreign trade, thanks to the "facilities"
which the bureaucracy arranges for them, and from that moment
on, they generally operate in association with the imperialist
companies active in international trade. The wealth obtained in
this way is invested at first in real estate ventures; then comes an
association with foreign capital in businesses that produce goods,
light industries for the most part. From that time on, the em-
bryonic bourgeoisie can no longer grow except as an integral
part of the imperialist system. The Latin American experience
is repeated in all its aspects and with all its consequences.

In countries like those of Latin America, where the "national"
bourgeoisie has developed the closest symbiosis with the imperialist system, because of the hyperexploitation of the common
people, the inequality of the distribution of the national income
goes well beyond similar inequalities in the developed capitalist
countries. The result of this, among other things, as Frank points

out, is a loss of potential economic surplus through the non-use or under-use of the labor force and other resources and through the unfortunate orientation of investment. This loss of potential surplus, added to the portion of the actual surplus transferred or realized in the imperialist countries, causes a structural clogging of the economy that stands in the way of any real growth in those countries with at least the beginnings of industrialization.

The incompatibility between the exploitation of a country's principal resources by foreign monopoly capital and the development of that country were illustrated recently once again by the case of Iran. Remember, first of all, that in 1951 the government of Dr. Mossadegh, which was only receiving 16% of the profits earned from Iran's oil by Anglo-Iranian, proclaimed the nationalization of oil when that company refused to consider proposals for a fairer division of profits. Anglo-Iranian organized a boycott of Iranian oil, and then, in 1953, the Mossadegh government was overthrown under conditions which observers termed "ambiguous." The new Iranian government negotiated with Anglo-Iranian and the other exploitative companies, which rewarded Iran with a fifty-fifty split of the profits, an arrangement that soon began to spread elsewhere.

Fifteen years afterwards, in 1967–68, the oil companies, grouped together as the Iranian oil consortium, ran up against the Shah himself, who was working out a five-year plan covering the period 1968–1973. Sixty per cent of the cost of the plan was to be covered by oil income, and he expected it to produce rapid economic development. The contribution requested from the oil industry required that that industry double in size in five years. The consortium was in strict opposition to the plan because, as master of the extraction and the sale of oil throughout the entire imperialist zone, it intended to direct production in the various oil-producing countries according to a strategy governed by its interests alone. In other words, Iran was no more the master of its resources in 1968 than it had been in 1951. The Shah fulminated against companies "which arrogate to themselves the right to dispose with the natural resources of Iran according to their whim," and more cautiously he made the most of the fact that because his country was not embroiled in the Arab-Israeli conflict, it offered a more secure source of supply than certain others . . . , a rumor circulated that the Soviets had made an offer to develop the oil fields of South Iran. Compromises were spoken of, denials made, and at the time of this writing, it is not clear if a solution has been found. The latest news, however, leads one to believe that an arrangement much closer to the interests of the consortium than to those of Iran is likely.[15]

This conflict seems to me all the more relevant because it involves a country whose strategic position would lead one to expect the greatest amount of flexibility from an essentially Anglo-Saxon imperialist consortium. For it is clear that, although imperialism dominates and exploits all the countries of the Third World, it establishes hierarchies and makes distinctions among them to such a degree that Marini and Frank, for example, believe they have discovered an attempt by North American imperialism to set up certain Latin American countries as "sub-imperialist centers linked to the mother country's exploitation of their neighbors."[16] Frank thinks that the United States has chosen Brazil, and to a lesser extent Mexico, "as economic and political fifth columns or beachheads in Latin America from which American monopoly capital and its government capture the markets and governments of the lesser countries, after American technology, foreign finance and political influence have created the necessary expansionist conditions there. This integrationist or sub-imperialist development of course augments the economic and political disequilibrium both within these Latin American countries and among them . . ."[17]

It is obvious that in one very precise and extremely concrete area, foreign aid, imperialism in general and the imperialism of the United States in particular is highly discriminatory. A beneficiary country's geographic situation is the criterion for deciding how crucial it is that the country's political submission be guaranteed and total. Without even mentioning South Vietnam, which is almost too perfect a case, one can, for example, observe that South Korea receives three times more net economic aid from the United States than Indonesia, which has a population four times larger. This aid enables South Korea to cover a considerable budgetary deficit and to maintain a fanastic trade deficit. At the other end of Asia, Turkey receives more net American economic aid than the entire Middle East (including Israel). And the Dominican Republic, with less than four million inhabitants, received from its North American protector in 1965 more than half the amount received by 85 million Brazilians, who themselves are not neglected. The objective of this policy is openly admitted by the Congress of the United States, which votes special appropriations each year (in addition to military aid) called "supporting assistance" for countries located on the periphery of the Communist world.

I have mentioned *en passant* the unequal development—or rather underdevelopment—of the Third World countries, the differences that can be observed among them in terms of productive strength. I have remarked, for example, that several Latin American countries enjoy some industrial development, which is equally the case for certain countries in North Africa and Southeast Asia (India). Taking this observation as their starting point, certain writers conclude that the industrialization of the Third World is inevitable. According to the bourgeois journalist and economist Jean Lecerf, whom I have already quoted at the end of my last book, the inroads made by the Third World into the steelmaking sector [which are still quite limited. P.J.] are a sign that similar incursions will be made in other areas, which will push the most developed capitalist countries "toward more complex and more remunerative activities," but they will also oblige them to "abandon, at the price of terrible difficulties, a large part of their labor-intensive industries, which are more suited to the new countries." [18] Marxist economists follow suit. "The industrialization of the colonial and semi-colonial countries," writes Ernest Mandel, "is an irreversible process. It undermines one of the pillars of the old colonial system—the role of outlet for goods of current consumption, which is played by the backward countries." Exports of these products are falling and are replaced more and more by exports of goods used by industry. The result is that "at the heart of the imperialist bourgeoisie, the interests of those who regard the industrialization of the underdeveloped countries as the reinforcement of a *potential competitor* conflict with the interests of those who regard it principally as the source of *potential customers.*" [19]

But Marini who also sees the outlines in Latin America of "a new arrangement of the international division of labor," according to which certain inferior stages of the production process would be shifted toward certain countries while the central imperialist countries would reserve the higher stages for themselves, does not neglect to add immediately afterwards, however, that "every advance made by Latin American industry confirms . . . more strongly its economic and technological dependence on the imperialist centers." [20] Within the framework of the imperialist system, in fact, the Third World countries can not auto-industrialize themselves in any way, since this concept of auto-industrialization has to do with the origin of the capital invested as well as with the notion of autonomous development. To create *some* industries in a Third World country is not the same thing as industrializing it. In the majority of cases, the new creations are not part of any overall plan or even a program for the development of the country where they are located, but on the contrary they are part and parcel of the strategy of the imperialist monopolies that control them in collaboration, most often, with local private or public capital. The motivation behind them is almost always an imperative of the marketplace. And so in general, the picture is one of a variegated sampler of new industries decided upon because they would benefit foreign interests or local class interests. Between 1959 and 1966, the production, properly speaking, of automobiles in Latin America (more than 60% locally owned) grew from 130,000 to 410,000 units (+215% in seven years) and car assembly by itself tripled, but underproductive Latin American agriculture used 15 to 20 times fewer tractors than Great Britain or France and 8 to 10 times fewer than Italy, per equal surface area.[21]

Under such conditions, to claim that the industrialization of the Third World is an irreversible process is a bit hasty, and to see in this process the reinforcement of certain potential competitors for certain imperialist firms (producing consumer goods) and the emergence of potential customers for others (producing equipment for industry) is a dubious vision, since in the great majority of cases (frequent exception: the textile industry) businesses producing consumer goods in the Third World are only the antennae of central imperialist monopolies and have been created for the express reason of holding on to, enlarging, or sometimes taking over, a market.

Of course, these disparate new factories have led to a growth in the production of manufactured goods, which achieved an average annual rate for the period 1960–1966 of 5.9% for Africa, 7% for South Asia, 5.9% for East Asia, 5.6% for Latin America, and 9.3% for the Middle East (arithmetic mean: 6.7%), as against 6.3% for the industrialized capitalist countries. (Again these figures can only be appreciated when the starting point is known: an advance of one, going from 10 to 11 is a 10% rise, but going from 1 to 2 it is a gain of 100%.) But the possibility of true industrialization is excluded under present conditions, if only by the small amount of savings available: 12.9% of the GDP was the arithmetic mean of total savings in the groups of Third World countries listed above, as against 21.4% for the industrialized countries.[22] The growth of industrial production in the Third World can not continue even anarchically under today's conditions without large amounts of foreign capital investment. However, private imperialist capital flows in the direction of the already developed countries have been five to six times greater in recent years than private imperialist capital flows directed toward the Third World. No upheaval, then, seems to threaten the existing economic structures: imperialism will not deliberately "abandon" any industrial sector to the Third World. It will continue to invest only what it must in order to control the sources of raw materials and in order to hold on to its markets.

It is quite clear, all the same, that, however anarchic they may be and will remain, these new Third World industries as well as those that will be created at the initiative of the Third World countries themselves—they exist in spite of everything—will not be engaged in electronics but in technologically crude sectors requiring large amounts of unskilled labor. When they have gradually multiplied over the years, the international division of labor will be somewhat modified. It will continue to exist at a slightly higher *absolute* level. Already exports of virgin metals from the Third World are replacing exports of ore. But as the industry of the very advanced countries develops toward ever higher technological levels, the new international division of labor that will result from this will continue, at a *relative* level, much like that of yesterday and today and it will preserve a quantitative gap between exploiter and exploited that is comparable in size if not wider. It will remain typically imperialist in character. It can not be otherwise.

Imperialism can not transform itself into its opposite. The domination and exploitation of the Third World are its essence and necessary to its survival. The essence cannot change, by definition, but the necessity, especially for raw materials and energy sources, has become so severe that it is already a matter of life and death and will be so increasingly. The economic development of the countries of the Third World is "blocked" by imperialist exploitation. It can not be un-blocked unless the stranglehold of that exploitation is broken. The peoples of the Third World have no other choice than to struggle to break free, but imperialism also has no choice. It must struggle to keep the Third World from breaking free. Otherwise, it has every chance of hearing its own death knell. What for one side is the only path to survival leads directly to the destruction of the other. No reconciliation is possible.

B. IMPERIALISM AND THE SOCIALIST WORLD

The socialist countries or those called socialist, as I defined them in my earlier books (USSR, the people's democracies of Europe, including Yugoslavia, the socialist countries of Asia, Cuba), represent one-third of the world's population and enjoy a total gross domestic product on the order of 30% of the world's GDP. Although imperialism can no longer dominate the socialist world as it increasingly dominates the Third World, it still cannot disregard the socialist world.

Although capital investments in these countries seem out of the question for the moment (subject to what will be mentioned further on), trade with them remains possible. Moreover, it has never stopped since the end of foreign intervention against the young Soviet Union. In 1924–1925, the USSR bought 28% of its total imports from Germany, 15% from Great Britain, 14% from the United States, and trade with the West developed further during the first two five-year plans, since the USSR could not carry on construction programs and industrialization except with equipment imported from the great capitalist countries. It succeeded quite well at these objectives, and the portion of national consumption taken up by imported machinery fell from 30% in 1927 to 13% in 1932.[23]

Since the Second World War, the socialist countries' foreign trade has developed as follows:

	1948	1958	1967
Total export (in millions of dollars)	3,690	12,080	21,630
Total exports as a % of world exports	6.5%	11%	11.5%
Trade with developed capitalist countries (% rounded off)	41%	17%	24%
Trade with socialist countries (% rounded off	47%	72%	62%
Trade with the Third World (% rounded off)	12%	11%	14%

Obviously it is the figures for trade with the industrialized capitalist countries that are the most interesting for us. The high percentage for this kind of trade in 1948 is clearly due to the same reasons that caused the USSR to import large quantities of goods from the same countries at the end of the period of foreign intervention after the First World War: the economies of the USSR and of the new people's democracies had been generally ravaged during the war against Hitler, and it was therefore a matter of necessity for those countries to import otherwise unavailable goods from the western countries, which had suffered only slightly or not at all from the war. But trade with the capitalist countries fell from a peak of 41% in 1948 to only 17% in 1958. Then, in 1959, came the effusions of Soviet-American good-will at Camp David, which marked a new turning in the relations of the USSR, and the pro-Soviet countries, with imperialism. The revival of East-West trade between 1958 and 1967 was thus the result of essentially political causes. This trade, which was carried on for the most part between the USSR and the West, rose from 17 to 24% of the total trade of the socialist countries, while exports from the same bloc only rose from 11 to 11.5% of world exports. During the same period, trade between the socialist countries (in which the Soviet Union again played the preponderant role) fell from 72 to 62% of total trade in the socialist world, which simply reflects the abrupt decline of trade with China. Speaking very crudely, the countries of the Soviet bloc shifted their foreign trade quantitatively from China to the imperialist countries.

East-West trade still remained relatively small compared to the total trade of the imperialist countries: 4% in 1967. In that year, the OECD countries imported goods worth 660 million dollars from China (of which 150 million went for food products, 325 million for raw materials and chemical products, 146 million for manufactured articles) and sold China goods worth 980 million (of which 83 million went for food products, 280 million for chemical products and raw materials, 614 million for transport equipment and manufactured articles).

Total trade between the OECD countries and the Soviet bloc in 1967 broke down as follows, in millions of dollars:[24]

PRINCIPAL CATEGORIES	OECD IMPORTS CIF		OECD EXPORTS FOB	
	Value	%	*Value*	%
Food products	903	20	466	11
Raw materials	1,049	23	351	8
Combustible minerals	857	19	15	
Chemical products	226	5	544	13
Transport equipment	236 ⎫		1,549 ⎫	
Manufactured articles	1,108 ⎭	30	1,158 ⎭	64
TOTAL TRADE	4,525		4,189	

OECD trade with the countries of the Soviet bloc is therefore four times greater than with China, in the case of exports, and seven times greater in the case of imports. But the question especially worth asking is how important an addition is this trade to the imperialist countries on the one hand and to the Soviet bloc on the other, and also to what degree is East-West trade capable of interfering with trade between the imperialist countries and the Third World?

The balance of trade between the two groups of countries, for the categories of transport equipment and manufactured articles, was favorable to the imperialist countries (taking into account the discussion below) only to the ultimately insignificant extent of a 1.8 billion dollar surplus. Thus the Soviet bloc makes an almost negligible contribution toward the absorption of the surplus industrial potential of the imperialist countries, and, on the other side of the ledger, the imports are without any doubt basically profitable to the economies of the East European countries. Leaving aside the sales of combustible minerals from these countries, which have involved mainly coal and are thus of slight interest, let's stop for a moment and look at the case of raw materials, where the balance expressed in terms of its dollar value (+700 million dollars, in favor of the countries of the Soviet bloc) may be an inadequate measure of the real importance of these transactions. Half of these sales involved wood, more than a quarter involved leather, skins and pelts, textile fibers, fertilizers and crude minerals (probably phosphates), and only a little more than a tenth involved metal-bearing ores. Sales of these ores by the pro-Soviet countries to the imperialist countries, which I mentioned in Chapter II, are therefore of practically no importance at all in the overall economic picture. In 1967, they represented exactly 5% of corresponding imperialist transactions with the Third World.

It is true that the category "manufactured articles" includes sales of non-ferrous metals to the OECD countries. These sales totalled 260 million dollars in 1967, but three-fifths of that amount was spent on silver, metals of the platinum family, and nickel. Interference with Third World exports was therefore negligible. Finally, one can safely say that, under present conditions, the large and growing dependence of the imperialist countries on Third World exports of energy resources and basic ores is not threatened in any significant way by similar exports either from the Soviet bloc or, speaking more generally, from the socialist countries.

It is a curious fact, however, that the imperialist countries grudgingly purchase certain basic raw materials from the countries of the Soviet bloc. The case of nickel is typical. The Third World is deficient in nickel (with the single but noteworthy exception of New Caledonia), while the socialist countries are well provided with the metal, and in addition, the leading producer of nickel among the imperialist countries (Canada) does not produce enough of it to satisfy imperialist requirements. In recent years, it has been necessary to supplement imperialist production with annual imports of about 30,000 tons from the Soviet bloc. However, it seems significant to me that quite recently the imperialist countries have gone to considerable effort to speed the development of New Caledonian production (which enjoys vast reserves) in order to free themselves from even partial dependence on the Soviet bloc. This program of expansion was deemed so important that the Gaullist government was even persuaded to pool the public capital at its disposal with private capital from the United States in order to promote it.

But the reality of the recent past, as recorded in statistics, may be an insufficient basis on which to try to predict what will happen in the future. There are those who would like to enlarge East-West trade. A. N. Kosygin himself declared before the 23rd Congress of the Communist Party of the Soviet Union: "If our partners in trade take into consideration the changes that have taken place and those that are now being made in the economy of the Soviet Union, it will allow us to increase substantially the volume of our purchases in the capitalist countries."

Their capitalist partners are taking those changes into such serious consideration that, very recently, economic cooperation between East and West has moved in several new directions: 1. The tendency toward long term commercial transactions has been confirmed, within the framework of trade agreements whose duration very often extends over several years. 2. It makes possible certain new kinds of activity such as the sale, construction, and launching of complete industrial installations (FIAT, Renault, ENI, etc.) which require the co-operation of both governments. 3. In numerous imperialist countries, private or joint organizations with governmental participation are being set up to engage in trade with Eastern Europe. In France, for example, such a company has been created under the aegis of the Centre National du Commerce Extérieur, with the participation of Schneider, Renault, etc., and of the Banque de Paris et des Pays-Bas. 4. Scientific and technological exchanges, as well as technological and economic cooperation are underway on both sides of what used to be called the iron curtain (France, Sweden, Italy).

And since A. N. Kosygin invites us to take note of the changes being made in the economy of the Soviet Union, it must be confessed that such changes indeed exist, not only in the USSR, but in the people's democracies (notably Czechoslovakia, Hungary, and Poland, not to mention Yugoslavia, which amounts to a model for the rest): material incentives have received official consecration, the market is used to regulate the economy, profit has been rehabilitated as a business concept and businesses are competing on a profit basis, etc., and the net effect of these changes is to sanctify the abandonment of the basic principles of socialism. At the same time, and once again following in the footsteps of Yugoslavia, Poland and Rumania are asking to be included in GATT, a commercial instrument of imperialist integration. And Ota Sik, who simply pushed forward too quickly in Czechoslovakia with the economic reform undertaken in the USSR at the instigation of Liberman, has said that he envisaged the creation of a freely convertible currency,[25] which is a logical step, once the others have been taken, and which leads just as logically to membership in the IMF, the monetary instrument of imperialist integration. Many western observers, like Jacques Dumontier, have gone right to the heart of the matter. According to Dumontier, an influential member of the Conseil Economique et Social, "As soon as the concept of profit and a concern for truth in prices become the golden rules of the countries formerly referred to as countries with centrally planned economies, then a kind of communication will inevitably spring up between the countries of the West and those of the East."

And he went on to say:

"The efforts underway to develop Europe all the way to the Urals, together with the needs felt by the countries of Eastern Europe, will gradually contribute to the creation of a free world stretching from San Francisco to Vladivostok [. . .] with the Atlantic in between." [26]

Of course, someone will say, at least state ownership of the means of production will continue to stand in the way of foreign capital investments in the countries of the Soviet bloc. But that is only conjecture at this point, and besides, recent Soviet-Japanese agreements that provide for the common exploitation of the diverse riches of Siberia open the door to investment by Japanese monopoly capital.

The process of economic and political evolution now going on in Eastern Europe is a treacherous path that could lead far and also makes one want to ask the countries of the Soviet bloc whose side they are on. Without going into the multifarious aspects of this problem, which would take us too far afield, we can at least try to see which cause the socialist countries embrace in the mounting conflict between the peoples of the Third World and imperialism, since that confrontation is the fundamental and dominant issue of our time.

There is no simple answer. If on the one hand the USSR is giving aid to the Vietnamese while they are at war, as well as to Cuba, on the other hand it also gives aid to various pro-American and anti-Cuban regimes in Latin America, as well as to a pro-imperialist and anti-Chinese India, and to the ultra-reactionary regime of the King of Morocco, which was mixed up in the assassination of Ben Barka while he was preparing the first Tricontinental Conference. But if giving aid to Vietnam and Cuba is an unavoidable political necessity for the USSR, with which it must comply in order to preserve its anti-imperialist image, the aid it gives to twenty or twenty-five Third World governments, run by political prostitutes in the service of imperialism, is deliberate. Without attempting to delve into the qualitative or quantitative nature of the aid given to Vietnam, Jean Baby shows, in

the course of a succinct analysis, just what political motivations
this aid implements: the USSR does not seek to inflict defeat on
the American aggressors, but only to exert pressure on them to negotiate for peace, which is indispensable to the continuation of
peaceful coexistence as defined by the Soviets. They want to
force the Americans to find a way to an armistice that will not
force them to lose face and will result in a compromise, however
shaky. Hasn't N. Podgorny, President of the Presidium of the
Supreme Soviet, said: "Only the situation in Vietnam prevents
us from establishing truly good relations with the United
States?" [27]

Light years away from the great confrontations in the arena
of world politics, a book modestly entitled *Les Problèmes de la
Croissance du Tiers Monde Vus Par les Économistes des Pays
Socialistes* offers us some revealing points of view. Its Polish
author, M. Falkowski, warns us at the outset that this is not an
expression of his personal ideas, but a systematized version of the
opinions of the economists of the socialist countries, especially
those in the USSR, Poland and Yugoslavia.[28]

I should say immediately that this book strikes me as mon-
strous. Certainly not because it is ignorant: the East European
economists are not unaware either of the imperialist international
division of labor or of unequal exchange,[29] etc. But the theory
which they propose is that thanks to the combined efforts of East
and West, the countries of the Third World can undertake their
own development without having first broken loose from the
chains of imperialist exploitation. Indeed, "the former colonizers
are more disposed to make political and economic concessions
to the backward countries." (139) The East European economists
also have confidence in GATT, the U.N., UNCTAD, and think
that the importance of the struggle in these forums "is immense."
(155) There is absolutely no discussion of the problem of the
state in Third World countries run by lackeys of imperialism, and
it is argued that the local bourgeoisies are capable of playing a
progressive role. Everything can be handled in a nice way: "The
changes now underway in the world economy ought to improve
the structure of relations between countries with different systems; they ought to eliminate any sort of domination and bring

about a new integration of the world economy that will respect the interests of existing groups and, in particular, those of the developing countries." (140) In short, this solemn work dedicated to "those who seek to deepen the dialogue between 'East' and 'West,' in order to apply the appropriate solutions to the urgent problems of growth in the countries of the 'Third World,'" simply bears witness to the ideological putrefaction into which revisionism has led certain economists in the socialist countries to sink. I say "certain," because I am not yet ready to admit that they all—especially among those who cannot make themselves heard—are of the same stripe.

Notes to Chapter 9

1. Poul Høst-Madsen writes in the June, 1967, issue of *Finance and Development*, a joint publication of the IMF and the World Bank, that "the low level of reserves and credit facilities available to these countries [the developing countries—P.J.] explains why deficits cannot persist." Deficits are "covered over the long run by an almost equivalent inflow of long-term financial resources (including government transfer payments), leaving, again over the long run, an approximate balance in the over-all balance of payments."

2. *Op. cit.*, vol. I, p. 200.

3. *Op. cit.*, pp. 36–37.

4. "Échange inégal et politique de développement," in Cahier no. 2 of the Centre d'étude de planification socialiste, Paris.

5. *Sur les classes sociales en Amérique Latine*, Maspero, 1968, p. 30.

6. The caution with which Emmanuel begins his definition annoys me a little bit, because "imperfect competition" is practically the rule in most of the exchanges concerned.

7. *L'Aide aux pays sous-développés*, P.U.F., "Que sais-je" collection, p. 20.

8. Based on data from *Basic Statistics of the Community*, 1967, Table 18.

9. According to Varga, *Politico-Economic Problems* . . . , p. 160, "the additional profit from foreign trade with the less developed countries constitutes an important part of monopoly superprofits but not a decisive one."

10. *Ibid.*, p. 194.

11. *Op. cit.*, Chap. 3.

12. *Capitalism and Underdevelopment in Latin America*, 1969 (revised).

13. "Sous-développement et revolution en Amérique latine," *Tricontinental*, French edition, no. 4, 1968.

14. *Op. cit.*, p. 313.

15. *Le Monde*, 10/11 and 15 March, 23 and 30 April, 1968.

16. R. M. Marini, in the article cited.
17. *Op. cit.*, p. 302. This notion of "sub-imperialist" countries does not concern only Latin America. India seems to play a similar role in Asia.
18. *Le Figaro*, 11-1-66.
19. *Op. cit.*, vol. II, p. 480.
20. Article cited.
21. According to a report issued in July, 1967, by the Banque française et italienne pour l'Amérique du Sud (Rothschild group).
22. World Bank Annual Report, 1968, Table 2.
23. *Problèmes économiques*, no. 1054, 3-14-68.
24. Source: OECD statistics on external trade.
25. *Le Monde*, 12-19-68.
26. *Le Monde*, 11-12/13-67.
27. Jean Baby, *La Grande controverse sino-soviétique*, Grasset (Paris: 1966) Chap. V.
28. Published by Payot (Paris: 1968).
29. The socialist countries also profit from their trade with the Third World. This perhaps is why Falkowski's book slides over these problems somewhat.

10

Imperialist Contradictions and Integration. American Superimperialism

For Lenin, writing in 1916, one of the characteristic features of the imperialist phase of the capitalist system was that monopolies and capitalist associations were dividing up the world's economy, while nations were proceeding to divide up the land in their struggle for colonies, "for economic territory." He states that by the beginning of the Twentieth Century the division of the world was complete. But that does not at all mean that the division was definitive. The relations of forces bring about a redivision of the world by unpeaceful means. "For there can be *no* other conceivable basis under capitalism for the division of spheres of influence, of interests, of colonies, etc., than a calculation of the *strength* of the participants in the division, their general economic, financial, military strength, etc." And so the alliances among imperialist powers are "*inevitably* nothing more than a 'truce' in periods between wars." (106)

It is certain, in fact, that the First World War was caused by a conflict over the division of the world, and that it was settled, moreover, by a territorial redivision that benefited the conquerors. And though the Second World War had more complex causes because of the existence of a powerful socialist state, it is nevertheless beyond dispute that one of those causes was the lingering problem of the redivision that occurred at the end of the First World War.

In 1951, Stalin grandly reaffirmed the theory of "the inevitability of war between imperialist countries," but E. Varga attempts to show, in a chapter of the book already referred to,[1] that this theory, which was correct in Lenin's day, had become erroneous by 1951 and is even more so today. His most noteworthy argument to this effect is based on the existence of a socialist world whose rapid growth has caused the disappearance of mutually hostile coalitions of imperialist powers and forced all the western imperialist powers to replace these coalitions with a single military alliance (NATO). And so, although the contradictions of imperialism remain, a war between imperialist powers seems to him highly improbable because it would lead to the end of capitalism in the defeated countries and therefore would weaken the world capitalist system.

In refuting Stalin, who believed that the economic superiority of the United States was bound to continue and would therefore oblige the other imperialist countries to fight the United States in order to get out from under its thumb, Varga argues against the necessity of perpetual American economic supremacy by invoking the law of unequal development under imperialism. According to him, "the unequal development removed this domination by peaceful means." The other imperialist powers are developing faster than the United States. American exports are in a state of relative decline. American gold reserves are declining absolutely. The United States has to call on the aid of other countries in order to maintain the stability of the dollar. In a word, the United States *"can no longer dictate"* in economic affairs, while the Common Market will further reinforce the position of the United States' principal competitors.

This point of view seems to me very much open to attack. And though I share Varga's conclusion as to the great improbability of wars between imperialist countries, the analysis which leads him to that conclusion seems to me quite inadequate. The Third World, for example, plays virtually no part in it; and China, of course, none at all. But since the law of unequal development has come up, this is a good place to stop and spend some time on that subject.

A. Unequal Development

There is no doubt that as far as Lenin was concerned, unequal development brought about changes in the balance of forces and generated contradictions and rivalries within imperialism. He notes that the young capitalist states in his day (United States, Germany, Japan) were advancing much more rapidly than the older ones (France, England). He observes that finance capital and the trusts "are increasing instead of diminishing the differences in the rate of development of the various parts of world economy," (96) "for under capitalism the development of different undertakings, trusts, branches of industries, or countries, cannot be *even*." (119)

Let's try to see, then, first of all, how the principal imperialist countries have developed, comparatively, since 1950. The table below helps to make this clear:

	INDICES OF GDP (1963 = 100)		INDICES OF MANUFACTURED PRODUCTION (1963 = 100)	
	1950	*1966*	*1950*	*1966*
Developed capitalist countries	59	116	46	124
USA-Canada	64	119	64	127
EEC	49	115	40	118
EFTA	68	112	63	116
Developing countries	56	114	42	120
Latin America	54	117	46	123
South and Southeast Asia	59	111	39	115

SOURCE: United Nations Statistical Yearbook, 1967, Table 4.

From the above figures it is clear that from 1950 to 1963, the combined overall growth of the United States and Canada (from 64 to 100) was lower than that of the EEC (from 49 to 100), which supports Varga, while, in return, it was higher than that of EFTA (from 68 to 100). But it is also the case that, from 1963 to 1966, the United States and Canada[2] made a comeback (from 100 to 119) with respect to the EEC (from 100 to 115) and continued to stay ahead of EFTA (from 100 to 112). Development was therefore unequal simultaneously with respect to time and place, and, on the whole, Varga's contention that the other imperialist powers are developing faster than the United States appears insufficiently supported by the facts, at least for the period 1950–1966. There is even less support for Varga in the area of manufactured production, which is of special importance, since the comeback staged by the United States and Canada between 1963 and 1966 was more spectacular in that sector ($+27\%$, as against $+18\%$ for the EEC and $+16\%$ for EFTA).

The only variation in rate of growth that is really significant is that of Japan (absent my table because it is absent from its source) compared to all the other imperialist countries. Between 1950 and 1966, the average annual growth of the Japanese GDP was at least 9% higher than all others, and Japan has since gained second place among the imperialist powers in volume of GDP, far behind the United States (the ratio was 1:6.5 in 1968), but outstripping, in descending order, West Germany, the United Kingdom, France, Italy, and Canada.

With that one exception, it is a risky business to draw any hard and fast conclusions on the basis of the above figures about the unequal development of the United States vis-à-vis the other western imperialist countries. But, in the case of the "other" countries, it can be said that West Germany and especially Italy have tended to develop their economies more rapidly than France and the United Kingdom. Finally, however, one absolutely cannot lose sight of the enormous difference in economic weight between the United States and all the other imperialist countries, including Japan. In 1968, the GNP of the United States was higher than the total GNP of the 19 other members of OECD.

The table above also enables us to observe that, if the growth of the Third World (developing countries) is compared to that of the developed capitalist countries, between 1950 and 1966, both overall growth and the growth of manufactured production were essentially at the same level in both groups of countries, which indicates a significant slowdown in the Third World in terms of per capita growth, since the population has increased much more vigorously there than in the other group. The per capita growth of GDP between 1950 and 1966 was on the order of 65% in the developed capitalist countries and only 41% in the Third World countries. But the table also shows that in absolute terms the growth of GDP and of manufactured production were more rapid in the developed capitalist countries than in the Third World during the most recent period. The present tendency is therefore toward an aggravation of the inequality of development between the two groups of countries, not only on a per capita basis, but also on an overall basis.

But let us return to the imperialist countries and to Lenin, for whom unequal development within the capitalist system existed not only among countries, but also among industries and among trusts. This is the moment to recall that, among the 70 most important businesses in the world, some 55 are American and that the U.S. giants are extremely predominant in basic sectors such as oil, and in advanced sectors like electronics, not to mention nuclear industry, space and rockets. These U.S. giants, and many of the less gigantic firms, are present not only in the United States, but, increasingly, throughout the entire world and especially in the other imperialist countries.

I invite the reader to recall my earlier chapters and to consult when necessary my Chap. IV-B and C, which shows that the growing internationalization of business, of commodity exports and especially of capital exports indicates the increasing domination of the monopolies and of the economy of the United States over the monopolies and economies of the other imperialist countries. Let us remember only that almost one-fifth of American investments in industry are made abroad where these investments are multiplied by the increased use made of the local financial markets and banks (which quadrupled from 1967 to 1968); that American industry abroad constitutes the world's second largest capitalist power and that it is developing more vigorously than native industries in the countries where it is located; that its size and influence in those countries is beyond comparison with the size and influence of foreign investment in the United States. The result of all this is an increasingly rapid transition from economic independence to economic interdependence between imperialist countries, which makes certain data from these countries' statistical records seem more and more to the point, for interdependence does not work to the equal benefit of all, but for the profit of the most powerful and especially for the profit of the super-imperialist United States. The United States has assumed a leading role in world economy, both through the action of its international and integrationist monopolies, and through its monopolist government and the integrationist world institutions which it first promoted and which it still controls.

Of course, American supremacy and American leadership are often challenged, sometimes bitterly, and integration does not have the magic property of abolishing the inherent contradictions in the capitalist system. The rivalries which Lenin stressed remain. But world capitalist integration, which did not exist in his time, has appeared, and with it a new internal contradiction in imperialism that can be called "rivalries/integration." Before trying to get to the heart of what this entails, which will not be accomplished until the next and final chapter, it seems to me best to study its manifestations in the most important areas.

B. The "Rivalries/Integration" Contradiction

The essential object of this section will be to determine, in the light of the facts and from the perspective which Mao Tse-Tung[3] invites us to adopt: what is the principal element of the contradiction in question.

1. MONOPOLIES AND CAPITAL

The invasion of the economies of the other imperialist countries by American private capital has created anxieties and often even provoked acts of resistance which are too well known to go into them all once again. I shall, nevertheless refer to this reaction directly, as it concerns the Common Market, in the subsection that follows. For the moment I shall limit myself to a typical extra-European case—Canada.

Foreign investments in Canada, of which four-fifths are American, represent about 35% of the country's industrial property. At the beginning of 1968, a report on the effects of foreign investments on the structures of the Canadian economy, written by a group of experts at the request of a member of the government was presented to the House of Commons. This report, while recognizing that private investment from the United States could be beneficial in certain respects to the Canadian economy, observes that the country has still not derived all the advantages it expected from them, and that, in addition, it had been unable to overcome their disadvantages, which were: a tendency on the part of the United States government to subject Canadian subsidiaries to certain American laws (extraterritoriality); location of the centers of private decision-making outside Canada; utilization by the U.S. government of the connections between mother companies and their subsidiaries as instruments of foreign policy; American business and the U.S. government work their way into Canadian structures without the American subsidiaries ever ceasing to belong to the American industrial system, so that these subsidiaries indirectly become "the instruments of American foreign policy and the concern of American military planning." [4] But the journalist reporting this information added that the report in question did not seem as though it ought to win the entire and unanimous approval of the Canadian government, and that even its publication raised difficulties. Geoffrey Owen, who deals with the same problem in the same way, concludes that although anti-American attitudes are strong in Canada, "the country's need for outside capital to develop her resources is so great that very little defensive action has been taken." [5]

The general need for foreign capital is not all that is involved here. In certain sectors and within the framework of the capitalist system, recourse to giant foreign firms with superior resources, technology and procedures appears almost unavoidable. The creation of a totally integrated company, capable of developing the lands of the French region of Lower Languedoc, of undertaking the industrial processing of its products and selling them, was a project too vast for the scale of the economy of France, which was faced with many other pressing problems. Even the Gaullist government could not resist turning over the problem to the powerful American company, Libby's, which supplied everything that was necessary: capital, organization, technology, productive capacity and ready-made sales networks.

Although the relatively traditional sectors are capable of resisting American penetration, it is much more difficult to oppose it in the new sectors such as the computer industry. The American corporation, IBM, alone controls more than 70% of the world market. Bull in France and Olivetti in Italy have only been able to survive by calling on the capital and know-how of IBM's American rival, General Electric. And under the French "Plan Calcul," the 10070 computer is built under American license, while the first computer constructed completely under the aegis of the plan, the Iris-50, a model of limited capability that appeared at the beginning of 1969, itself included certain American parts.

In an area like aviation, integration seems to be a necessity for the middle powers, superseding individual rivalries when it comes to planes that require amassing considerable amounts of capital and setting in operation a whole galaxy of equipment, technology and expertise. The *"Concorde"* supersonic transport will be Anglo-French or nothing, the "Airbus" will be at least Franco-German, and in December, 1968, Great Britain, Italy, West Germany, and the Netherlands signed an agreement for the joint construction of a swing-wing fighter plane. The French company Dassault, the pride and mainstay of Gaullist power, joined forces with the Belgian firm SABCA, it established a relationship with Fokker, the Dutch concern, which itself was connected with two American companies, and it signed an agreement to cooperate with the American aerospace conglomerate, LTV.

A serious conflict took place within EFTA in 1968 between two member countries, Great Britain and Norway. It seems to me to provide still more evidence of the inevitable supremacy of the American monopolies. Great Britain, which produced practically no virgin aluminum and imported 30% of Norway's considerable annual production (about 330,000 tons), decided to create its own aluminum industry, which would cut purchases of

the metal from Norway. But this new "domestic" British industry, which was finally launched despite Norwegian protests, involved the creation of three factories, one by ALCAN, a Canadian
company in which the U.S. giant ALCOA has an interest, and
the two others by groups in which two other large American
firms, Reynolds and Kaiser, are involved. The Norwegian aluminum industry, however, is partly controlled by a domestic group
and partly by subsidiaries of American and Canadian companies,
doubtless the same ones just mentioned.[6] This affair, which was
on the surface an internal EFTA issue, was nothing less, essentially, after all, than an internal affair between the North American groups that dominate world aluminum production and
control the production centers which they own in accord with
a strategy that relates only to themselves. The incident bears a
curious relation to the Iranian oil affair I discussed in the preceding chapter and shows that the North American trusts that
dominate this or that sector on a worldwide scale don't play with
kid gloves any more readily in Europe than they do in the Third
World. Their goal, increasingly, is to take over everywhere, and
they are succeeding at it. The rivalries which they arouse vanish;
the integrationist zeal of the international monopolies prevails.
And Geoffrey Owen announces to us that "American industry
is still in the early stages of 'going international.' "[7]

This integrationist pressure from the monopolies, and especially from the U.S. monopolies seems so irreversible that a
French university professor, Jacques Houssiaux, seriously im-
agines institutionalizing it. ". . . The concentration of business
on a global scale," he writes, "leads us toward a new international
order. It is high time that theoreticians establish the outlines of
this new order and that a congress of heads of state and the leaders
of the two or three hundred industrial empires that will govern
the essential economic activities of tomorrow determine the constitution of a future society where the nations and the great companies will share the administration of men and things."[8]

Probably this delirious vision of world monopolist integration
does not represent anyone but its author. But the fact that it
could appear in as august a publication as *Le Monde Diplomatique* is symptomatic. And so, especially, is the fact that Pro-

fessor Houssiaux's views were essentially reiterated, only with more restraint, by Jacques de Fouchier, who, as vice president of the Banque de Paris et des Pays-Bas, does not only represent himself. De Fouchier recommends "a planetary strategy for the utilization of resources," a strategy which "obviously is scarcely within the capabilities of any companies except those established on a planetary scale." Judging that it is utopian to imagine the rapid dissolution of the nation-states, he too believes that "the essential problem is that of seeing that these structures do not enter into conflict with international business . . ." [9]

2. THE CASE OF THE EEC

I shall limit myself to recalling the fact that if West European business and government circles are all favorable to the EEC today, they are split between those who favor an Atlantic Europe, that is a Europe integrated with the American economy, and those who recommend a European Europe, that is a Europe which is independent, if not the rival, of the American economy. The arguments of both sides are unimportant. What counts is that they both are partisans of a Europe of monopolies, and it is also important to see, since such a Europe exists and is growing more so, in what direction, precisely, it is going.

I pointed out in Chapter VI that although Common Market-wide international concentrations run by various participants from the Six seemed destined to grow in the future, at least ten years after the Treaty of Rome, this process had hardly begun while a powerful tendency toward concentration had been felt in each of the Six. But I also showed in Chapter IV-B that during recent years, U.S. foreign investments had increased far more within the EEC than anywhere else: roughly two times more. I will say it again: American assets in the EEC increased from 1,680 to 7,000 million dollars between 1958 and 1966. As a result, while multinational concentrations among the Six remained potentialities, the American monopolies hurled themselves, in effect, on the EEC, despite the anxieties and even the active resistance sometimes raised by their invasion. As Geoffrey Owen points out, it was the formation of the Common Market itself that gave a new impetus to American investment. American exporters who had "often had to choose between withdrawing from the market and investing in local production," chose to establish themselves in the EEC and to adapt themselves "to the emergence of a tariff-free Continental market even bigger than the United States itself." [10]

For his part, Christopher Layton states that "the largest American firms are better placed today than European firms to seize the advantages of the Common Market." Provided with large subsidaries in several European countries, they are more flexible and "better able to rationalize their production . . . than European firms with one fixed home base." He cites the example of Ford and that of IBM, which integrated the manufacture of components in its different European factories. And he concludes that the American firms "have proved more 'European' than the Europeans." [11] I would add: because the U.S. monopolies disposed of infinitely greater means, notably in the areas of finance and technology.

But Layton, who is an advocate of transatlantic monopolies, sings the praises, moreover, of "the political value to Europeans of American direct investment." He does not understand why anyone should oppose it.

"American corporations," he writes, "with interests in different European countries have an immense interest in the stability and strength of Europe, and in good relations between the two continents. If they sometimes lobby European governments in their own interest, they will also be found lobbying the United States Government in favour of amicable policies which make for good relations. Direct investment enhances America's interest in the security of Europe, strengthening a commitment which most European Governments regard as vital. It is a cement of unity for the Atlantic world." [12]

I am certainly not going to argue against the idea that economic integration through the actions of monopolies leads to political integration. The result of this is that the United States is more and more induced to think of the Europe of the Common Market as *its* Europe, which makes good imperialist logic since its monopolies are becoming more and more influential there. In the final analysis, the fact that our modest European monopolists are divided into pro-American and pro-European camps is of secondary importance. What is essential is that an EEC which one intends to give over to monopolies in general can only continue to be ever more inevitably dominated by those monopolies which are by far the most powerful and which have free access to it, namely the American monopolies. Contradictions and rivalries will remain. Even new ones will arise when true Common Market concentrations appear. I mean those concentrations which the Commission of the EEC definitely favored in a communiqué of January, 1969. But the monopolistic integration, favored by those worldwide integrationist agreements, among which the Treaty of Rome is only a regional cog, can hardly fail, or fail to benefit the monopolies whose worldwide position is invulnerable.

That the Common Market is a part of the worldwide integration of trade was demonstrated splendidly at the time of the negotiations known as the Kennedy Round. Note, first of all, that the inclusion of the Common Market in those negotiations was no accident. It was foreshadowed by the Treaty of Rome, whose article 110 prescribes that the Six "contribute . . . to the harmonious development of world trade, the progressive abolition of restrictions on international exchange and the lowering of customs barriers." It was the United States, though, that proposed the negotiations, and this proved that although it had already penetrated the market of the EEC from within with its capital, it was not ready, nonetheless, to give up forever the idea of penetrating it from without, which it would do, in order to improve its chances of success, by bringing about a lowering of the tariff barriers. It is known that the confrontation was fierce, since unquestionable contradictions were involved among those interests present around the bargaining table, as well as among the Six themselves. But the important thing is that these contradictions were surmounted finally, amid advantages gained and concessions given on all sides, in order to arrive at an agreement which certainly did not close the door on new frictions, but did, none the less, constitute an important step in the direction of integration. Layton sees in this a partial application of certain grand principles that ought to be inscribed in an actual "Atlantic Code." [13]

3. TRADE AND MONETARY PROBLEMS

It is not irrelevant to point out that the Kennedy negotiations were carried on in the spirit of GATT, which I have already described in Chap. III-B as an international charter for international trade and an instrument of worldwide imperialist integration. It was, moreover, also in the aftermath and in the spirit of GATT that the two first meetings of UNCTAD were held, in Geneva in 1961 and in New Delhi in 1968. Although this takes us away from our subject a bit, it is impossible not to note that those two meetings both wound up as fiascos in terms of concrete decisions. And numerous bourgeois observers were not able to keep themselves from remarking that the representatives of the industrialized capitalist countries at these meetings refused the slightest tariff advantages to the underdeveloped countries, although they had been able to agree on similar compromises among themselves within the framework of the Kennedy Round. Worldwide imperialist integration in the spirit of GATT, therefore, tends, in fact, to reinforce the cohesion of the imperialist countries and, consequently, to reinforce their overall position of power, while it maintains the countries of the Third World in their state of commercial subservience.

But it is monetary problems that assume quite special importance and meaning in the framework of the intra-imperialist contradiction of "rivalry-integration." And at the heart of these problems is the role of the dollar as the principal international reserve currency.

Let us recall very briefly that, because of the dollar's role, the American balance of payments has constantly shown a deficit since 1950 (with the sole exception of the year of the Suez crisis). Dollars held abroad, whether by central banks or by private individuals, derive essentially from American capital exports or from exports of commodities to the United States, and they are, in fact, generally not turned in by those who hold them, because these dollars constitute a gold-credit for which there is, in principle, no reason to demand conversion. The result is that by agreeing to defer payment on their credit, foreign dollar-holders finance the American Treasury, which is in debt to them, and they themselves increase the deficit in the American balance of payments. Among other things, this allows the United States to make use of its own debts to spend money throughout the world on its economic and military aid, to continue its capital exports to creditor countries and to finance its aggression in Vietnam.

Another result of this is an inflationary process on a worldwide scale, for the dollars held by central banks can be used to back new issues of currency in the dollar-holding foreign countries while they still make up part of the currency of the United States. But this system has its limits, as a table taken from an article by Harry Magdoff [14] shows:

	GOLD RESERVES IN THE USA	DOLLARS HELD ABROAD
at the end of 1955	21.8	11.7
" " " " 1960	17.8	18.7
" " " " May, 1968	10.7	31.5

(billions of dollars)

These figures indicate that dollar credits held abroad have grown almost exactly in inverse proportion to the decrease in gold reserves at Fort Knox; and that if foreign dollar-holders had demanded gold for their credits at the end of May, 1968, the United States would have been short the equivalent of 20 billion dollars in gold. And so it is not surprising that a system founded on the dollar as an international reserve currency is beginning to show a few cracks.

Without going into details that would be out of place here, it should be said that the crisis which the dollar underwent in March, 1968, must therefore be attributed to this system's incapability of insuring durable monetary peace and prosperity throughout the capitalist world. It generated contradictions, since it made nearly all the currencies of the capitalist countries vulnerable to the dollar. And these contradictions have been expressed in various ways: France, for example, was not caught napping and had converted a large part of its dollar reserves into gold, while other countries did the same, though to a lesser degree and more surreptitiously.

But the most characteristic contradiction, in my opinion, was that when the dollar crisis struck, all the countries, beginning with France, flew to the aid of the ailing dollar, because that crisis endangered the world capitalist system itself. The *Times* of London wrote: "The international monetary system and *the free world economy which it sustains* face a major crisis of self-confidence." [15] And the *Wall Street Journal*: "It is by no means certain that anything like the comparatively free enterprise system in the U.S. and the West would survive. The impact of a drastic decline in trade on the commodity-selling developing nations would be staggering. The Communists would not only crow; they would have rich opportunities for economic and political exploitation." And so the governments of Western Europe bought the dollar to avoid its collapse. M. Albin Chalandon exclaimed before a gathering of Gaullist parliamentarians: "For the sake of the Western World, we must avoid both the war of currencies and the war of tariffs," while M. Jacques Rueff, the Gaullist government's great monetary adviser declared: "The depreciation of the dollar must be avoided at any price." Of course, both of them backed the theory of the revaluation of gold and a system that would not benefit the United States. But faced with this urgent common danger, they joined with everyone else to save the dollar first.

A few months later, in May and June, and then in November, 1968, when the French franc came down with a cold of its own, the roles were exactly reversed. When, in the spring of that year, Gaullist power struck some people as having been shaken, official circles in London discovered that the "order" created by a general whom they did not much like was preferable to disorder. President Johnson sent his wishes for success to General de Gaulle. And the American banks acted so as to avoid additional shocks to the franc.[16] In August, large credits were allocated to France by the IMF and the central western banks. The Undersecretary of the American Treasury "emphasized that the major contribution of the United States to this credit had been decided upon despite the attacks which the franc had made on the dollar for so many years," since the collapse of the franc could bring about a collapse of the whole western monetary system and of the pound in particular.[17] International solidarity came into play once again in November, when the franc alarmed everyone most severely. The emergency meeting of the finance ministers of the principal western countries in Bonn has remained fresh in every memory. Statements by President Johnson and the American Secretary of the Treasury made it known that the United States was ready to give France unconditional aid, through all necessary financial and monetary means. "Why," asked the magazine *Entreprise,* "has there been a total about face in the attitude of the United States?" Because, the magazine answered its own question, "it is imperative for the United States to defend the franc. The American government is afraid that a crisis in France will touch off an international monetary crisis which the United States would have to pay for." [18]

The moral of these events is clear. Antagonisms between the imperialist nations are unavoidable. But it is interesting to observe that these antagonisms are most evident when things are going relatively well, and that they fade from view when they are going badly for one of the antagonists: Great Britain, the United States, or France. That solidarity, indispensable for them all when one is faced with danger, is the keynote of all the statements I have quoted, and there are many more like them. This solidarity of intention is only the reflection of a real solidarity: the internationalization of productive forces, of the movements of goods and of capital, and of economic life in general, has grown to the point where every illness affecting one of the limbs of the imperialist body imperils the entire organism, which then reacts by reflex. The internal cohesion of the imperialist system itself is a necessity that supersedes all antagonisms. This necessity also has other causes, which we shall look at further on.

4. POLITICAL AND MILITARY PROBLEMS

It is well known, and admitted by everyone, that the close cohesion of the imperialist powers since the Second World War has resulted from their close political and military alignment with Washington. This solidarity has really only been challenged by one country—once again it was France—and France's disagreements with Washington have centered on two major problems: the war in Vietnam and NATO.

In several instances, the Gaullist government showed its disapproval of American aggression in Vietnam. Without attempting to establish the precise causes of this disapproval, without, in particular, attempting to determine to what degree the French position was essentially an obligatory gesture toward that immense section of the Third World for which France remains the "mother country," I shall confine myself to observing that the French position has never been translated into action. France never recognized Hanoi, made no official shipments of supplies, however small or symbolic, even of civilian supplies, and refused to initiate any diplomatic action whatever, even of an exploratory nature. The only French action that obstructed U.S. aggression even indirectly was, as I mentioned above, converting a significant portion of the dollars held by the Bank of France into gold. But it is extremely unlikely that this conversion was undertaken with that purpose in mind. Therefore, French hostility to the American presence in Vietnam ought to be seen for what it is—a simple matter of speechmaking.

France, however, went beyond oratory when it withdrew its forces from NATO in 1966. But France always said quite openly that it was remaining faithful to the Atlantic alliance, which "must continue as long as it will appear necessary," namely "unless events occur that modify relations between East and West in a fundamental manner." [19] France went further than that. Jacques Isnard informs us that despite her withdrawal:

"France continues to participate in the NATO air alert and exchanges information with its allies on the movements of Soviet ships in the Mediterranean. It uses the same broadcast codes, cooperates in keeping equipment uniform, and has the option of requesting support from NATO facilities in case of some future invasion. It is to test and apply this theory of potential conflict that joint maneuvers are held and that specialists at the level of general staff officer participate in working sessions."

Jacques Isnard also suggests the real significance of French withdrawal from NATO with this quotation from the French Minister of the Armies:

> In case of a serious crisis, we will certainly not turn away from NATO, because NATO will do what the Americans decide. It is better to speak directly to the chief than to his underlings. General Lemnitzer has never claimed that he would not telephone the President of the United States in the event of a serious crisis. It is better, then, that we should be in direct contact with the President ourselves.[20]

Observers have been unanimous in pointing to a shift—some have talked about a reversal—in France's political orientation toward a more definitely pro-Atlantic position at the end of 1968. And most of them also noted, with justification, that this return to the fold was not entirely unconnected with the promise made by President Johnson at the time of the franc crisis (and subsequently carried out) to provide France with unconditional assistance through all financial and monetary means. But that gives us a precise indication of the possible limits of Atlantic misbehavior for a country with 50 million inhabitants, even though it is in fifth place economically among the imperialist powers and is probably in third place from the military point of view. Imperialist political cohesion is ultimately dictated by the inescapable economic and financial cohesion of a world which calls itself free but can permit its members only minor departures from solidarity. And in the case of France, politically and militarily, as well as economically and monetarily, nothing more than minor acts of insubordination have ever been committed. Gaullism, wayward child of imperialism though it may be, is still a child of imperialism and certainly has not lost any of the basic family traits. And so the contradictions that Gaullism brought to the imperialist camp were only "non-antagonistic" contradictions, because they did not threaten the foundations of imperialism.

5. RELATIONS WITH THE THIRD WORLD

I have shown, in Chapters III-A and IV-A, that the exchange of goods and the flow of capital between the imperialist countries

and the Third World have shown a tendency for a certain number of years to escape from the bilateral channels inherited from
the colonial period and to follow new, intersecting multilateral
paths. This is another way in which the general tendency toward
increased internationalization of economic life throughout the
world is being confirmed. I did not neglect to mention, either,
that this tendency allows American rapacity to display itself
over a wider area throughout the world and gives freer play
to superimperialist America's ambition to have a finger in every
pie, especially in the Third World.

I have also shown, at the end of Chapter II, that although
imperialism is as careful as ever to make sure it controls the
principal sources of raw materials in the Third World, it has
been seizing control of them for a small number of years now
almost exclusively through multinational investments, as seen
most spectacularly in Africa.

Finally, although multinational official aid, in the strict sense
of the term—aid administered through the intermediary of organizations like the World Bank and its subsidiaries—has tended
to increase, though very slowly, in relative amount, I have also
noted (Chap. IV-A) that bilateral aid, by far the prevailing form
of aid, is being coordinated more and more by consortiums that
represent the countries giving aid to a particular Third World
country. It seems worthwhile, to me, to stop for a moment and
consider this new form of aid to the Third World.

The consortium that administers aid to India groups together
West Germany, Austria, Belgium, Canada, the United States,
France, Italy, Japan, the Netherlands, and the United Kingdom
under the aegis of the World Bank and with the assistance of
the IMF. The aid consortium for Pakistan is similar to it in
all respects. It includes, notably, the United States, the United
Kingdom, Canada, Japan, and West Germany. In addition to
these actual consortiums, "consultative groups" have also been
set up under the high authority of the World Bank. They exist
for South Korea, Ceylon, Malaysia, Thailand, Peru, Morocco,
Nigeria, the Sudan, Tunisia, and East Africa. This last consultative group is multinational twice over, both in terms of the
countries giving aid and of those receiving it, which include

Kenya, Uganda, and Tanzania, the three countries that constitute the East African community. There are also joint, coordinated financial mechanisms in operation for Colombia and Mexico. To be precise, the World Bank is associated with twelve countries in its aid program for Colombia and with eleven for Mexico. In 1968, the World Bank adopted a new plan. For the first time, it established a "resident mission" in a single country—Indonesia —charged with drawing up suggestions both for the preparation and implementation of development projects and for the coordination of aid in all its forms with the contribution of the consortium.[21]

It is unavoidable that these forms of aid should bear the mark of imperialism. M. Ali Bhutto, a former Pakistani minister who is now a member of the opposition party, has said of his country: "The powers that grant their financial support to the country within the framework of the consortium exert pressures on the entire economic structure. They are not content to intervene directly with the government. They also have their agents in the market place." [22] And so the creation of a resident mission in Indonesia seems to have accomplished nothing but make regular and official what was already generally in operation.

Collective organizations that administer private capital are also being created on a grand scale. For example, in 1969, an international investment company for Asia (Private Investment Company for Asia or PICA) was launched. It was inspired by the precedent of the Adela Investment Company and the prime mover behind it was probably Japan. Japanese and American private investors each contributed one-third of its capital. The final third was split between Canada, France, the United Kingdom, West Germany, Italy, Sweden, Norway, Switzerland, and Australia.[23]

Such an organization is essentially only an attempt to systematize what is increasingly practiced today, namely the association of private, multinational capital (often in combination with public capital) not only in mining but also in industry or for vast construction projects. For instance, the first big fertilizer factory built in Senegal, in 1968, brought together several French and German firms, SFI (a subsidiary of the World Bank), the

Banque Européenne d'Investissements (EEC) and the Banque National de Développement of Senegal. The capital behind the Algerian company CAMEL (a factory that liquefies natural gas from the Sahara) is only 26% Algerian; the rest is Franco-Anglo-American. In the case of the Brazilian steel industry, it is not correct to speak of an association of capital, but rather of a division, since American and Japanese capital is invested in two plants and the capital of a French group in a third. On the other hand, capital from various foreign countries together with Brazilian capital is jointly financing the construction of the Uniao petrochemical complex. In Pakistan, the construction of the Tarbela dam, which will be the biggest in the world, set a Franco-Italian and a German-Swiss group at each other's throats. In other words, there was a rivalry between two binational groups, but the World Bank, which was the administrator of the project, came to the aid of the highest bidder (the Franco-Italian group). Three consortiums competed to build the largest African dam in 1968. One consortium united German, Swedish, French, and South African firms (the South African company was linked to Anglo-American interests). The second was Anglo-Swiss. The third was a combination of American, French, Portuguese, South African, Italian, and Swiss capital. The first consortium won the contract. The extension of the Trans-Cameroon railroad was made possible by an association of American public capital, French capital and capital from the Common Market Fund for European Development.

In one and the same Third World country, even if it remains closely tied to a "mother country," it is common practice for capital to be solicited from various foreign countries, and different ones are involved in each sector. In the Ivory Coast, the construction of the port of San Pedro is being backed by Franco-Italo-German capital, France is going to finance the sugar cane plantations, the United States has put money into the rubber plantations, the Danes and the Norwegians have an interest in the fisheries, and the Kossou hydro-electric project is supposed to be financed by public funds from America, Italy, and the Ivory Coast.[24]

The result of all this is one glaring fact: the private hunting grounds of yesteryear in the Third World are indeed a thing of the past. This does not mean that the old ties do not still exist. Far from it. But these old ties are not, as a general rule, the exclusive relationships they were formerly, and they are crumbling everywhere. Each of the big imperialist countries— and even some of the smaller ones—now has direct interests, public and private, in twenty-five, thirty or forty countries of the Third World, and of course many more are involved in the case of the United States. The economies of the dependent countries have become joint ownerships. The direct consequence of this is that the open rivalries for the domination of the Third World countries, which were once flourishing conflicts, have faded and almost disappeared altogether. The United States has been left in peace to pursue aggression in Vietnam and in the Dominican Republic. It has overthrown progressive regimes in Indonesia and Ghana and it has intervened more or less secretly in twenty other situations, without any of the other imperialist countries so much as lifting a finger. France raised its voice only once. It was unable to do more, not only because of the reasons given above, but because it was doing the same thing as the United States. It sent its paratroops to Gabon and Chad. It overthrew the progressive regime in Mali with its own barely disguised agents. It intervened more or less secretly in ten other situations, and no one lifted a finger against France either, because *all* the imperialist countries had a direct or indirect interest in the imperialist interventions of the United States, of France, etc. Of course, there is still intra-imperialist friction that crops up here and there, but it is no longer anything but the exception that proves the rule. The rule is a fundamental agreement to keep the countries of the Third World within the integrated imperialist system, so that everybody's goods and, especially, everybody's capital can continue to circulate through the Third World with ever greater freedom. At the same time imperialist investors are tending to shift their capital away from competition and into associations with other imperialist capital so that exploitation can be mutually beneficial.

6. CONCLUSION

A conclusion is hardly necessary for this section. It should already be obvious from the discussion that has gone before. According to Harry Magdoff, what we have just been analyzing is the primary trait of imperialism today, or as he puts it: "the shift of the main emphasis from rivalry in carving up the world to the struggle against the contraction of the imperialist system." [25]

Since the Second World War, the imperialist camp has brought about an internationalization of economic life unlike anything previously on record. Because tariff barriers and import quotas have fallen and sometimes even been suppressed, because of the free circulation of capital and the convertibility of currencies, national economies have become more and more dependent on each other. They are tending to become nothing more than the components of a single entity or the pieces of a puzzle which is called the world imperialist economy and comes complete with its own constitution as expressed in the great global integrationist treaties. Every recession, every change in one of these parts affects the others, and it is significant that the problems of foreign trade and of international competition have taken on an unheard of importance in our time.

Just as the tendency toward the concentration of businesses and toward monopoly has not eliminated competition (cf. Chap. VI), but has simply outstripped it, and just as in the competition/concentration contradiction, the second element of the pair has become its principal element, so too in the rivalry/ integration contradiction, which arose at the time that integrationist tendencies first appeared, it is the second element of the pair that has become its principal element. It seems to me that the investigations I have just made of various sectors of the economic and political life of imperialism have factually demonstrated this. And if numerous authorities have given too much importance to France's action under the Gaullist regime, as a spoilsport in this respect, isn't this because France was practically alone in speaking out against what was happening and that its voice simply clashed with the rest of the chorus? The important thing in my eyes is not that there was sometimes a discordant voice, but that there was only one.

To parrot Lenin in 1970 is the surest way to do him ill. And to keep on stressing intra-imperialist rivalries, which certainly survive and will survive as long as imperialism does, is to refuse to see the facts as they are today and to evaluate them properly. But the facts demand an explanation and mine is still incomplete. In the next chapter, I shall try to explain why worldwide integration has become a predominant aspect of imperialism today. First I must still establish certain characteristics of American superimperialism.

C. AMERICAN SUPERIMPERIALISM

I have already talked a great deal about it, in particular, to point out the extreme predominance of American capital exports (Chap. IV-B), or to note the worldwide supremacy of the transatlantic monopolies. I will therefore only discuss aspects of U.S. imperialism here that I have not yet mentioned or that I have discussed insufficiently, and, in particular, I shall bring in additional information about the increasingly international role of the large American firms.

The income of American corporations abroad, which only amounted to 10% of the income of corporations inside the United States in 1950, had risen to 24% of domestic corporate income by 1964. Baran and Sweezy point out that from 1957 to 1963 sales by foreign subsidiaries went up 54% as against only 17% for domestic industrial sales. And so it is not surprising that U.S. News and World Report concluded in 1964 that "businessmen increasingly are deciding that markets abroad—not those in this country—offer the biggest potential for future growth." [26]

Four years later, Geoffrey Owen thinks that "the surge of interest in overseas business is not likely to be temporary," and he explains why at length. He notes that the recent wave of overseas investment has had the effect of " 'internationalizing' certain product markets and the companies which serve them," and that these corporations are orienting themselves "in the direction of a global strategy, whereby product planning, manufacturing and marketing are rationalized and integrated in a network of factories throughout the world." And he quotes an extremely revealing statement made by the head of a big company: " 'We think of ourselves, not as an American company with overseas interests, but as an international company whose headquarters happen to be in the United States.' " [27]

The American military presence throughout the world has increased in size just as aggressively as the invasion carried out by its capital and its monopolies. Harry Magdoff, who notes the obvious connection between the two developments, points out that American armed forces were stationed in only three foreign countries in 1929. During the Second World War, they were stationed in 39. And today they are distributed among 64, as follows:

Latin America	19
East Asia (including Australia)	10
Africa	11
Europe	13
Near East and South Asia	11

Magdoff insists on the fact that American military leadership has developed to the detriment of the other powers and, in this regard, he quotes Undersecretary of State, Eugene V. Rostow: " '. . . In many ways the whole postwar history has been a process of American movement to take over positions . . . of security which Britain, France, the Netherlands and Belgium had previously held.' " [28]

Magdoff does not neglect to mention that at the same time that American capital, monopolies and armed forces are invading the entire world, a similar, and by no means coincidental, invasion is being carried out by the American banks. In this table, he shows how the number of branches maintained by U.S. banks abroad has grown:

	1950	1960	1967
Latin America	49	55	134
Europe	15	19	59
Africa	0	1	4
Near East	0	4	7
Far East	19	23	63
U.S. Dependencies	12	22	31
	95	124	298

Of the 298 branches recorded at the end of 1967, 259 were the branches of only three banks: The First National City Bank, The Chase Manhattan Bank, and The Bank of America.

According to *Fortune* magazine, deposits in these foreign branches increased from 1.35 to 9.5 billion dollars between 1957 and 1967. Recently, they have been growing seven times faster than domestic deposits. Magdoff notes in particular that in the countries of the Common Market, the American banks are better represented than the banks of the other countries of the Six, and he quotes an article in *Fortune* which observes: "It has become a cliché in banking circles to say that 'the only really European banks nowadays are American.' "

Naturally, the field of operations open to the branches of the American banks is immense and various. They exist and develop in symbiosis with international investment and international trade. But they also form subsidiaries in association with foreign capital. They invest in a large area of business unrelated to banking. They acquire controlling interests in companies as minority stockholders. They cooperate with other local or international banks, and sometimes with the United States government.[29]

Their action is facilitated by the continuing attraction of the dollar and all that it represents. It is significant that the French magazine *Entreprise,* in its November 30, 1968 issue, which appeared shortly after the dollar crisis in the spring of the same year, should write that for the great majority of capital investors "the dollar remains the best currency in the world." There were three reasons given for this:

"1. It is covered by the unlimited industrial power of the United States; 2. the dollar's rate of monetary depreciation is traditionally very low . . . ; and finally, 3. the political stability of the United States and the liberal ideas of the government in Washington eliminate the possibility of any political disaster striking the American economy or the dollar . . ."

Returning to Harry Magdoff, he too goes into a long analysis, which is better than most, of the mechanics of the dollar's status as an international reserve currency and he outlines the advantages which the United States enjoys because of the deficit in its balance of payments. He insists on the fact that this deficit allows the United States to proceed with capital investment, military expenditures and foreign aid, and therefore serves to maintain and increase American control over all countries and all economic areas, while it helps build the "pax americana." But it is time to look at Magdoff's conclusions.

In his view, the United States "can be the world banker and supply the reserve currency, because of the cooperation its military and economic strength commands among the other industrialized nations. And, necessarily, within the United States this is accompanied by 'an inexorable entanglement of private business with foreign policy.' " (According to a report of the Council of Foreign Relations.)

As for the international monetary system:

What is at stake here is not mere adjustments in the credit mechanism of the International Monetary Fund . . . but the central issue of the dollar as the international currency. At the same time, the partners of the United States in this monetary system have their own necks to protect and their own competitive interests to pursue.

But:

Most of the nations in the imperialist network have no alternative: as creditors of the United States government and banks they must submit to being members of what is virtually the dollar bloc. The more independent metropolitan centers, however, do

have some options. Almost half of the dollar obligations to foreigners are concentrated in six nations: Britain, Japan, France,
West Germany, Italy, and Switzerland. They therefore have the
weapons with which to pressure the United States. Nevertheless,
under present circumstances, their options are limited. Their
interests are aligned with the United States to the extent that
United States military and economic power is used to secure the
imperialist system and push back, if possible, the borders of the
non-imperialist world. At the same time they are worried about
their own skin and the competitive threat of United States business and finance. Hence, the jockeying for power that does take
place operates within the limits of present international monetary arrangements.

I would like to say, parenthetically, here, that the United States
has been able to find certain partial remedies for the deficit
in its balance of payments. For example, it was, at least recently,
able to maintain the rhythm of its foreign investments, while
substantially reducing the outflow of capital, by considerably
increasing its use of foreign money markets. At the same time,
income repatriated from previously accumulated investments
continued to increase, especially the income earned in the Third
World, and in 1968 the American balance of payments was
deficit-free. It is true that capital placements for that year (net
purchases of securities) made in the United States by foreigners
reached the record amount of 3.5 billion dollars, giving evidence
of international confidence in the American economy and in
American currency.

Magdoff, taking another tack, observes that: "The tensions
within the centers of imperialist power show up in many ways.
Within the dominant business circles of the other industrial
powers are groups whose immediate business interests are tied
up with those of the United States, while others see their profit
opportunities shrinking in the face of United States expansion." [30]

Finally: "Circumstances and the striving of U.S. economic, political, and military activity have led to a situation in which
U.S. institutions can dominate the capitalist world. In the absence of a reshuffle of power between the imperialist and non-

imperialist worlds, the United States can call the tune as the main protector and organizer of the imperialist network." [31]

According to Magdoff, then, the United States dominates the capitalist world today; it protects and manages the imperialist system. For him that constitutes the second distinctive characteristic of imperialism today: "The new role of the United States as organizer and header of the world imperialist system."

Although a comparison of the growth rates of the American economy and the economies of the other imperialist countries over a long period of time did not at all seem to me valid proof of an unequal development that favored the other countries, Harry Magdoff's investigations of the increase in American power throughout the world, and my own investigations, particularly in the other imperialist countries, did lead to the discovery of an inequality of development on a worldwide scale which undoubtedly favors the United States.

Another result of this is that the United States is not only developing more rapidly than other countries, but at the same time that its own power develops, it is hypnotizing the other countries with its strength and locking arms with them in its role as dominator, protector and manager of the imperialist world system and the countries which belong to it. American imperialism has therefore become superimperialism, for it controls the other imperialist countries, in a way, like a mother company controling its subsidiaries. My comparison is not rigorously exact and that is why I added the phrase "in a way" to it, for U.S. control is obviously not absolute nor does it lack opposition. This is the time to note that although superimperialism is similar, it has nothing to do with the "superimperialism" (Tr.: *sur-imperialisme*) or the "ultra-imperialism" of Kautsky, which Lenin fulminated against more than a half century ago (cf. Chap. I). U.S. superimperialism was born out of competition, out of unequal development and out of interimperialist contradictions and rivalries, and it bears the indelible marks of its origins. Magdoff is right to observe that although most of the imperialist nations accept American leadership, they do so not with light hearts or out of "pure wisdom" but because they have no alternative; and that although the most powerful nations still have arms at their disposal and even sometimes use them, nevertheless they have "little choice." Can this lack of alternatives and this limitation of choice continue? And is the redistribution of power among the imperialist interests that Magdoff refers to a probability? I have already said: the answers to these questions will be found in the next chapter.

But I can't end this chapter before demonstrating that U.S. superimperialism also has its weaknesses. Although, in Chapter II, I pointed out the imperialist countries' great and growing dependence on the Third World for the fulfillment of their needs for basic metals, Harry Magdoff offers more information on this subject in connection with the United States. "What is new in today's imperialism," he writes, "is that the United States has become a 'have-not' nation for a wide range of both common and rare minerals." Here is Magdoff's table showing imports of all raw materials except gold:

PERIODS	NET IMPORTS IN % OF CONSUMPTION
1900–1909	−1.5%
1910–1919	−3.1%
1920–1929	0.7%
1930–1939	0.6%
1945–1949	5.5%
1950–1959	12.8%
1961	14.0%

It is clear from this table that, especially since the Second World War, the dependence of the United States on imports has increased rapidly. Moreover, it is characteristic that this overall situation should result much less from minerals which the United States always was short of, than from ordinary substances that were traditionally abundant there. The table below shows the growth of imports, for the most notable examples, figured in percentages of domestic production:

	1937–1939	1966
iron ore	3%	43%
copper	− 13%	18%
lead	0%	131%
zinc	7%	140%
bauxite	113%	638%
oil	− 4%	31%

Magdoff doesn't say where these imports originate. But it is only necessary to refer back to Chap. II to determine that the Third World is the exclusive or preponderant source of all these products, with the exception of lead and zinc, which it produces only in small amounts.

This dependence on imports is supposed to increase, in general, in the future. For example, specialists estimate that in the case of iron, without a technological breakthrough that would permit more practical utilization of domestic low grade ore, dependence will reach roughly 50% of consumption in 1980, and 75% by the year 2000.

But dependence also exists, and even more heavily, in the case of rare and strategic ores. For 38 out of 62 of these ores, dependence on imports is higher than 80% of total current requirements; for 14 other ores, dependence runs between 40 and 80%. According to a commission created by the President of the United States, three-quarters of the materials imported under the stockpile program come from the underdeveloped countries. For this reason, the chairman of the commission observed: ". . . it is to these countries that we must look for the bulk of any possible increase in these supplies. The loss of any of these materials, through aggression, would be the equivalent of a grave military set-back." H. Magdoff insists, moreover, on the importance of dependence in the case of various special metals used in the construction of jet aircraft.

Though it is super-powerful, then, American superimperialism is still vulnerable, because, among other things, of its dependence on the Third World for raw materials to supply its factories. What I said previously on this subject in reference to all the imperialist countries is equally valid, to the degree that it is justified by specific details, for the most powerful and most dominant country of them all.

Notes to Chapter 10

1. *Politico-Economic Problems* . . . pp. 79–80.
2. Canada accounts for about 7% of the total.
3. *Selected Works*, International, vol. II: "On Contradiction," section IV.
4. Jean Tainturier, *Le Monde*, 2-17-68.
5. *Op. cit.*, p. 140.
6. *Le Monde*, 5-10 and 7-26-68.
7. *Op. cit.*, p. 145.
8. *Le Monde Diplomatique*, Nov., 1968.
9. *Le Monde*, 10-1-68.
10. *Op. cit.*, p. 133.
11. *Op. cit.*, pp. 29, 56.
12. *Op. cit.*, p. 30.
13. *Op. cit.*, p. 140.
14. "The Age of Imperialism," Part 2, *Monthly Review*, Oct. 1968.
15. Emphasis by P.J.
16. *Le Monde*, 6-1 and 6-2/3-1968.
17. Jacques Mornand, *Le Nouvel Observateur*, 8-12-68.
18. *Entreprise*, 11-30-68.
19. Statement of Michel Debré recorded in the communiqué of the Atlantic Council, 11-16-68.
20. *Le Monde*, 12-25-68.
21. As reported in *Finance and Development*, the joint publication of the IMF and the World Bank.
22. *Le Monde*, 3-13-68.
23. *Le Monde*, "Avis financiers," 2-15-69.
24. As reported in *Le Monde*, in various articles.
25. *Op. cit.*, June, 1968.
26. *Op. cit.*, p. 198.
27. *Op. cit.*, Chap. 8.
28. *Op. cit.*, June, 1968.
29. *Ibid.* Oct., 1968. (Though "The Age of Imperialism" originally appeared in three issues of the *Monthly Review* [June, October and November,

1968]——the version read by Jálee——it is now available in an enlarged, book edition published by Monthly Review Press.—Tr.)

30. *Op. cit.*, Oct., 1968.

31. *Ibid.*, Nov., 1968.

II

The Main Contradiction.
Political Perspectives

WE HAVE already seen—and I think I have proved it—that in
the internal contradiction within imperialism that I have called
"rivalries/integration," the second term seems to be a predominant one at the moment. The result is that, if, as I believe, the
pre-eminence of integration is irreversible, there is definitely no
possibility that conflicts leading to war between imperialist
powers or groups of such powers will occur ever again. The
historical situation at the beginning of the century that Lenin
described has definitely been replaced by another.

But since an author's words are so often misinterpreted and
turned into something he never intended to say, I want to repeat once more, at the risk of being tedious, that this conclusion
absolutely does not imply that there will be no more rivalries
between imperialist powers. I simply think that these inevitable
rivalries, which will undoubtedly weaken the imperialist nations
as a group, will no longer be able to spill over into armed
conflicts or even into very serious antagonisms capable of shaking
the foundations of the system or the basic unity of the imperialist
camp. This is so because, as experience has already shown, when
these antagonisms threaten to explode into open conflict, the
integrationist imperative has stifled them and will continue to
stifle them in order to preserve the vitally necessary cohesion of
the imperialist mother countries.

In other words, to put it briefly, the "rivalries/integration" contradiction does not seem to me a major element in the convulsive movements that are beginning to give evidence of themselves in the world today. But it is still a factor, to the degree, for example, that its dominant element, integration, shores up the imperialist camp, which itself constitutes an element of an external contradiction that I will discuss later on.

But the integrationist imperative clearly is unable to suppress or resolve the inherent contradictions of the capitalist system, which arise out of the very essence of the system.

The most basic of these contradictions remains the opposition between the effective socialization of production and the private or capitalist form of the ownership of the means of production and of the appropriation of surplus value. This contradiction, it can be said objectively, is becoming more severe, since the socialization of production is indisputably broadening and intensifying, while private ownership, or, more exactly, the power that comes from it, continues unceasingly to be concentrated in fewer and fewer hands. But this growing contradiction, whose existence no one can objectively deny, only has revolutionary potential to the extent that it is felt inwardly by those who are its victims, namely, salaried workers and, especially, the proletariat. But this supreme contradiction, which is blindingly clear to anyone who reads Marx and analyzes the evolution of capitalist society in Marxist terms, remains relatively theoretical and abstract to the great mass of salaried people and to the working class. The history of the labor movement shows that it makes itself felt, subjectively, only through its concrete effects and does not generate vast struggles except when it causes a worsening of the conditions and the rate of exploitation of the working class, which happens mainly during recessions and depressions. The fundamental contradiction of capitalism is not perceived in its essence, but only through its most tangible and flagrant manifestations, and revolutionary ideology does not spring up spontaneously among the proletariat.

Marxists seem to me to be in general agreement that this fundamental contradiction comes out more clearly and crucially —whatever nuances may divide individual observers—in what Varga calls the "long-term tendency of capitalism towards a decline in the growth of production." Baran and Sweezy, for their part, express a similar point of view. Monopoly capitalism, they say, "tends to generate ever more surplus, yet it fails to provide the consumption and investment outlets required for the absorption of a rising surplus . . . Since surplus which cannot be absorbed will not be produced, it follows that the *normal* state of the monopoly capitalist economy is stagnation." [1] It is this tendency that is essentially (I'm compressing a very long argument here) behind cyclical and periodic crises of what are called overproduction and underconsumption.

The question I have been leading up to is: does this basic tendency toward a slowdown of growth, toward stagnation and the depressions it produces, does this most direct expression of the supreme contradiction of capitalism create any serious likelihood that the system will collapse in the foreseeable future? Or, to put it another way: is the contradiction in question, concretely and in a strategic sense, the main contradiction of our time?

It has to be said that a great number of writers on the subject, Russians, as well as pro-Soviet and anti-Soviet writers, seem to think it is. Their books, studies and articles are sprinkled with stereotype, incantatory references to the "deepening of the generalized crisis in capitalism" or to the "exacerbation of capitalism's inherent crisis." All this is supposed to mean or imply that the deepening of the crisis of capitalism or the exacerbation of its contradictions are facts that will lead directly to the dissolution of the system. No attempt at a proof of this is made; incantation takes the place of it. But it must also be said that, although these incantatory invocations have been made for dozens and dozens of years, capitalism does not seem to be headed toward a quick death by its own hand. It must be conceded, in particular, that the last great generalized crisis in capitalism took place forty years ago and that, since then, and especially since the Second World War, the motherlands of the capitalist system have experienced only recessions that have been limited in duration, in area, and in severity.

Although a Marxist cannot deny the importance of inherent contradictions, he also should not forget that all Marxist laws only express tendencies, which is why responsible and clear-headed Marxists have been led to consider the reverse tendencies, the restraints or palliatives which capitalism, in their view, has been able to use in order to counteract or slow down the action of the tendencies created by the operation of Marxist laws. That is what writers like Hamza Alavi have done.[2] And there is the more recent and fuller example of Baran and Sweezy, whose solid work I have already referred to in previous chapters. But although the analysis made by Baran and Sweezy is rich and persuasive, they did not occupy themselves with projecting the results of their investigation into the future. That is, they did not decide whether the countermeasures used by monopoly capitalism would be effective for long. Hamza Alavi, on the contrary, concludes, after looking into this question:

"I do not claim that capitalism will not experience any more crises, since the system is incompatible with the conditions which are theoretically postulated as necessary for the achievement of stable growth. I only say that a great catastrophic crisis that would produce the dissolution of capitalism *is not inevitable.*

"This change of perspective—from the theory of the final crisis to the theory of stagnation—is important, since it destroys illusions and complacencies. The theory of stagnation brings out the importance played by the conscious struggle of the people in the establishment of socialism. The contradictions of capitalism will not necessarily do it for us."

And Varga, whom I just finished quoting again, what does Varga think about this? I have discovered the existence of two Vargas. There is the Varga of 1960–1961, the probable publication date of his book *Twentieth Century Capitalism.* At the end of the last chapter, on the new or third phase of the generalized crisis of capitalism, he writes: "We may prophesy the following for the foreseeable future.

"The U.S.S.R. will overtake the U.S.A. economically and develop the world's most powerful economy . . .

"The world socialist system as a whole will surpass economically the capitalist system. This development will weaken and shake the capitalist system, will hasten its end. The world socialist system will become the deciding factor in the development of human society.

"The colonial system will disappear. The former colonies will be developing their economy rapidly with the aid of the Soviet Union and the other socialist countries."

And his final word is this: "The twentieth century will go down in history as the century of the death of capitalism and the triumph of communism." With this Varga, then, we are hip deep in stereotyped incantations.

But several years later, in a book whose aim is to attack dogmatism (cf. Preface), his *Politico-Economic Problems of Capitalism,* we encounter another Varga who is infinitely more circumspect. While discussing the changes that have occurred within the capitalist countries as far as business cycles are concerned, he takes note of the growing role of the state, of its controls and "anti-crisis" measures, which "lower the intensity and duration of the upward phase and the depth and duration of crisis in future cycles." And the last sentence of this fundamental chapter marks a basic retreat from his earlier position: "In any case, the long and powerful growth in output observed up to the present in the vanquished industrial countries is unlikely to continue in the future." [3] It would seem that Varga is definitely tending to align himself with Alavi and his change of perspective from the theory of the final crisis to the theory of stagnation.

If a conclusion of that sort is admissible—and I incline to agree with it—, it follows that the contradictions inherent in the capitalist system are not capable, in and of themselves, of causing the great catastrophic explosion which has been dinned in our ears for so long, and faith in such an explosion, as Alavi suggests, can even weaken the effort to build socialism. But if capitalism is not destined to collapse at the end of a somehow natural evolution, and if the idea of a struggle regains its former stature, we must concede that it can catch on, and catch on not only as an idea but in actual fact in certain milieux, such as the student movement, within the industrialized capitalist countries. The question to ask, then, is whether such struggles appear likely to develop into authentic revolutionary mass movements some day in those countries.

Now, first of all, it is necessary to attack a basic illusion. Although the role of revolutionary violence has been restored in a beneficial way to the essential position where it belongs, this has too often resulted in the identification of all violence with revolutionary action, which is a far too idealistic view. The recent history of France is rich in various explosions of violence— by peasants and small shopkeepers—which were not revolutionary in the least, not even prerevolutionary. The student revolt during May and June of 1968 probably kindled the largest strike that had shaken an imperialist mother country in twenty-five years. But one must look carefully at what happened and realize that, with the exception of an extremely marginal segment of the French working class, the movement was essentially reformist and not revolutionary, despite its size and determination. When the leaders of certain unions were circumvented or disavowed by the rank and file, this was not done because their membership opposed them over qualitatively different demands. Their demands were simply quantitatively more ambitious. It is also true in the case of actual violence that the size and toughness of a strike are absolutely no guarantee of revolutionary spirit. Otherwise the American longshoremen would be true revolutionaries in spite of their staunch support of the war of aggression in Vietnam.

It is always useful to reread Lenin and Mao Tse-tung; they should not, however, be consulted like Bibles. Their analyses should be referred to as a source of renewed strength. Lenin, especially in *The Lessons of the Revolution* (1910), in *Marxism and Insurrection* (1917) and in *"Left-Wing" Communism, an Infantile Disorder* (Chaps. IX and X), defines the objective conditions necessary for the triumph of the insurrection. Mao, in *Against Book Worship—IV* (1930), warns against idealistic temptations not based on a knowledge of the real conditions of society, which lead to opportunistic or putschist errors. In *Problems of War and Strategy—I* (1938), he follows Lenin in examining the conditions required for unleashing insurrection in the advanced capitalist countries. And in *On Contradiction—IV* (1937), he puts heavy stress on the dialectical interaction of the infrastructure and the superstructure and of objective and subjective conditions.

I refer to these texts in order to invite the reader to engage in private study and analysis rather than impose my own analyses on him, and to allow him to draw his own opinion of my conclusions, which I must now return to.

On the subject of objective conditions, it ought to be said, however unpleasant it may be to do so, that although most Marxist economists are increasingly in agreement that business slumps are tending to diminish in severity and that we are headed toward a sort of prolonged and latent recession, this is only a prospect and not a tendency indicated by the existing facts. The rate of economic and industrial growth in the imperialist camp has generally not shown any decline at all in recent years. Unemployment is at its lowest recorded level almost everywhere. It is also a fact that since the Second World War, imperialist capitalism has basically been able to maintain or even raise real salary levels, while also, of course, increasing the rate of exploitation of labor through gains in productivity. And it has succeeded in financing itself as never before. Capitalism's main problem today is the monetary crisis, a worldwide phenomenon that manifests itself at the national level. But is it pessimistic to think that, in the light of what actually occurred in this area in 1968 (cf. Chap. X), the imperative of cohesion and integration will come into play when the danger increases and that a new or altered system will be created at that time which will bring relief of undetermined duration to the imperialist camp?

And as far as subjective conditions are concerned, it takes no great powers of perception to notice that there is no imperialist mother country in which the workers are currently organized in an authentically revolutionary mass movement of any kind whatever. The only two large Communist parties, in Italy and France, have foundered in revisionism and "the peaceful way." (Tr.: *la voie pacifique*) Workers everywhere are hemmed in by union leadership that is reformist and usually part of the system. This is another obstacle (cf. Mao Tse-tung) to the ripening of objective conditions. And if a certain West European Communist Party was right in 1968 when it proclaimed that the revolution's powder was wet, it neglected to mention, of course, that one of the reasons it had got that way was that that same party had been keeping its own powder under water for twelve or fourteen years. Will the small revolutionary groups that flourish here and there be able to reverse this trend? Various conditions will have to be fulfilled beforehand. And then there is the problem of the so-called "labor aristocracy," which is more prevalent than ever in technologically advanced, consumption-oriented industrial societies. Because a serious discussion of this problem would take us too far afield, I will confine myself to referring the reader to Lenin (Chap. VIII and X) whose analysis has not dated in the least, as well as to Chapter I of this book.[4]

The result of all this is that although the contradictions inherent in the capitalist system must inescapably produce a revolutionary situation in the industrialized countries some day—and this will happen without an armed intra-imperialist conflict, which no one any longer believes will occur—still there is no basis yet for claiming that that day is already taking shape. For the foreseeable future, such an outcome is only a possibility. And so, viewed from the perspective of a concrete analysis of a concrete situation, the essential contradiction of the capitalist system does not seem to have matured sufficiently to be considered, *by itself*, as the main contradiction of our time.

The main contradiction of our time has, to be sure, already been present on every page of the preceding chapters, like a watermark. Now W. W. Rostow, an American economist and personal adviser to President Johnson will help me introduce it directly and define what it is:

> The location, natural resources, and populations of the underdeveloped areas are such that, should they become effectively attached to the Communist bloc, the United States would become the second power in the world. . . . Indirectly, the evolution of the underdeveloped areas is likely to determine the fate of Western Europe and Japan and, therefore the effectiveness of those industrialized regions in the free world alliance we are committed to lead. If the underdeveloped areas fall under Communist domination, or if they move to fixed hostility to the West, the economic and military strength of Western Europe and Japan will be diminished, the British Commonwealth as it is now organized will disintegrate, and the Atlantic world will become, at best, an awkward alliance, incapable of

exercising effective influence outside a limited orbit, with the balance of the world's power lost to it. In short, our military security and our way of life as well as the fate of Western Europe and Japan are at stake in the evolution of the underdeveloped areas. We evidently have a major national interest, then, in developing a free world coalition which embraces in reasonable harmony and unity the industrialized states of Western Europe and Japan on the one hand, the underdeveloped areas of Asia, the Middle East, and Africa, on the other.[5]

Those lines date from 1956. Since then, according to the data contained in Chapters II and IX, the dependence of the imperialist motherlands on the Third World has increased, and this is especially true of the United States (cf. Chap. X). At the same time, opposition to the imperialist system in the Third World has developed and spread. Wars of liberation against the vestiges of the colonial system in Portuguese Guinea, Angola, and Mozambique have broken out. Authentically revolutionary armed activity has sprung up in Laos, Thailand, and Burma, and the foundations for such activity are taking shape in various other countries of Southeast Asia. The anti-apartheid movement in South Africa is growing stronger. The ZAPU has armed itself in Zimbabwe (Rhodesia). In Latin America, the guerrillas, whose downfall has been announced fifty times over, are continually reappearing in new places and in new countries. El Che did not die in vain. The struggle is mounting in the hinterlands and in the cities. In the Middle East, faced with Israel's imperialism, the Palestinian people have been transformed from refugees into combatants. And, above all, the Cuban revolution has triumphed. It is building a genuine and legitimately ambitious socialism in America's backyard, while in the heart of the principal fortress of imperialism, Black Power, the vanguard of the Third World, has become an abscess swollen with terrible danger.

Of course, there have also been some defeats. Lumumba, Félix Moumié and Ben Barka were assassinated along with many others. Hybrid but unquestionably anti-imperialist regimes in Indonesia, Ghana and Mali were overthrown by remote-controlled imperialist-inspired operations. The democratic revolt in the Dominican Republic was smashed. But these momentarily defeated peoples are not lowering their arms. The blood of many hundreds of thousands of Indonesians was spilled, but the revolutionary movement was born again, enriched by the self-reproach of its martyrs.[6] And admirable examples show that the leading imperialist powers can be defeated in a direct and total confrontation. Almost eight years of cruel war permitted Algeria to break its colonial ties, and how many were there who believed in victory at the end of 1954? As for superimperialist America, it offers proof that the world's greatest power can succeed in conquering the moon at the same time that it is breaking its back in Vietnam.

I think I have adequately demonstrated in the preceding chapters that the domination and exploitation of the Third World were the basic material condition for the survival of imperialism. It is becoming more and more obvious, however, to the progressive political organizations of the Third World that the future of their countries depends, inescapably, on a complete break with imperialism and on political and economic emancipation through what can only be called socialism, however badly understood that concept often is. W. W. Rostow saw this clearly when he envisaged (I make no claims for the clarity of his terminology) that the peoples of the Third World might "become attached to the Communist bloc." In other words he was identifying anti-imperialist emancipation and the choice of socialism.

It is thunderingly obvious that in that half of the world quite mistakenly called the Third World, objectively revolutionary conditions exist and will be more and more of a factor as time goes on. The alienation of the populations of these countries goes well beyond anything known elsewhere. The people feel this alienation physically, nutritionally and in conditions that are often terrifying. The essence and the structures of their exploitation can also be exposed more concretely than elsewhere. And so the main contradiction of our time, in my opinion, is undoubtedly the contradiction of imperialism and the Third World. It does not eliminate the others—it even enhances them—but it supersedes them in importance.

Of course, in spite of the centers of struggle I have mentioned that are spread over three continents, subjective conditions are far from sufficient to allow us to expect that there will be a general revolutionary conflagration in the near future. The consciousness of the masses is still frequently at a crude level and incomplete. The thoughts and actions of many popular leaders are sometimes too superficially inspired by a certain irreplaceable revolutionary theory. And political divisions or feuds that are often sterile play a destructive role in some places.

Still, there is progress almost everywhere. Reformist and revisionist parties, in those places where they exist, are losing their momentum or they are shaken from within and without by the force of revolutionary currents. These new movements, these new centers of struggle springing up across the entire Third World are a fact cannot be denied. The extraordinary and victorious resistance in Vietnam has given people confidence. Support is now coming from the socialist countries that have rejected revisionism. And first among them is China, strengthened and revitalized by its great proletarian cultural revolution and looking like the giant of a tomorrow that soon will be dawning. And although the numerous coups in Africa and Latin America, in which apparently democratic governments have been overthrown by military or technico-military cliques, seem, in the short run, to accentuate the difficulties facing the movements of emancipation, if one takes the long view of these regimes, they no longer look like additions to imperialistic power, but, rather, like proofs of its weakness even in the face of precariously organized and not very cohesive popular opposition. These coups are signs of imperialism's inability to maintain its domination through governments based on a mere semblance of legality.

Imperialist economic and political world integration, which I have mentioned so often and which W. W. Rostow sees as the chief defense of the imperialist camp and, especially, of American superimperialism, was born at the end of the last war and at that time was directed against the "Communist bloc" and its leader, the Soviet Union. And so it remained for the duration of the Cold War. But then, at the same time that "peaceful coexistence" Soviet-style replaced the Cold War, unprecedented opposition to imperialism began to shake the Third World. The policy of integration and the agreements it produced remained in existence, but from that time on they have essentially been directed against the new enemy. It is very revealing that, in 1956, when Rostow made the statement I have quoted at length, the Communist bloc seemed to him, in a sense, like a fact of life to which one had to accommodate oneself, for better or worse, as long as it was not reinforced by Third World countries that had broken their ties with imperialism. The principal danger, in Rostow's eyes, that threatened the imperialist powers, including the United States, was "the evolution of the underdeveloped areas." And that was in 1956!

World imperialist integration is the result of the conjunction of two clusters of facts: a) on the economic level, it was dictated by the growing internationalization of production, trade, and capital movements and the accompanying activities of internationally based monopolies; b) on the political level, it became indispensable because of the geographic contraction of the imperialist market. First, the socialist states emerged, taking away one-third of the world's population. Then, a second phase began with the threat of still another contraction due to revolutions in the Third World, where imperialism more than ever acquires the basic and irreplaceable substance of its power. This threat is, ultimately, a matter of life or death for imperialism. It has its back to the wall this time. To put it in a nutshell, world integration represents imperialism's changeover from an offensive or victor's strategy to a defensive strategy. The word "containment," the name given to this strategy, means what it says. As a result, imperialist world integration, despite difficulties suffered, shocks received and certain contradictory appearances, can only grow stronger in the future: it is imperialism's leading means of defense. The supremacy of American superimperialism, from this point of view, seems to me unassailable, since all redistributions of power within the imperialist camp, except at the secondary level, have to be ruled out, first of all, of course, because of the economic reasons that I went into earlier, but, more fundamentally, because of political reasons. The "commitment to lead" that Rostow talks about was first assumed by the United

States on its own authority; it cannot now be taken away. Necessity has the force of law.

The main contradiction of our time is not as schematic in real life as I have defined it here. I have observed that rational anti-imperialist emancipation is finally tied up with opting for socialism. The example of Cuba is significant in this respect, since it began as an anti-imperialist revolution that was in no way Marxist or socialist, but rapidly changed (because of the objective effect of the opposition it met and also because of the political integrity of its leaders) into a Marxist and socialist revolution of a radical hue (which obviously does not mean that all comparable emancipation movements must, under all circumstances, necessarily evolve in the same way). If, then, an authentic and rational anti-imperialist struggle must, as a general rule, turn into equally authentic socialism, the peoples of the Third World who undertake such a struggle have as their natural allies, on the one hand, nations whose socialism is not open to question, and, on the other hand, the forces that struggle within the industrialized capitalist countries with a truly revolutionary outlook.

I am touching on a crucial point here. If those states are indisputably socialist, if those forces are revolutionary in more than words, their objective alliance with the radical and rational emancipation movements in the Third World also ought to be a subjective alliance. This is the acid test. Faced with imperialism, which is a worldwide system and, as such, is organized on a worldwide scale through integration, which enables it to coordinate its efforts and increase its ability to resist attack, how can states and organizations that claim to be loyal to Marxism not feel the subjective necessity of a worldwide anti-imperialist alliance directed toward the decisive struggles that are in progress or in preparation in the Third World? As Rossana Rossanda put it during the Italian Communist Party Congress in February, 1969 (where she was unfortunately part of a very small minority), it is essential "not to subordinate the acceleration of struggles on the international scene to the military and economic consolidation of the socialist states, but on the contrary to encourage the growth of liberation movements and revolutionary movements, and to subordinate . . . the policies of the socialist states to them." [7]

What is valid for the socialist states is clearly also valid for would-be revolutionary organizations and parties in the industrialized capitalist countries. For my own part, taking into account, among other things, how poorly these problems are generally understood at the present moment, I would gladly go a little further than Rossana Rossanda. Her use of the word "subordinate" is ambiguous and could be taken to mean an inclination to reduce Marxist states and parties to simple auxiliaries of the policies and actions of the Third World emancipation movements, which would be impossible. What ought to happen is that the necessity for a correlation of efforts inside and outside the Third World should be understood and agreed to, for such a correlation of efforts already exists.

Those who think that the contradictions inherent in the capitalist system actually constitute, now or in the near future, the principal potential for revolution (which would break out at that time in the imperialist mother countries), should recall that I rejected this hypothesis earlier and stressed that these contradictions did not seem to me to have matured sufficiently to open such a prospect all by themselves. I meant by that that their maturation could be accelerated by external factors. It is hardly even worth arguing the proposition that any serious or relatively extensive difficulties that imperialism might meet with in the Third World would have repercussions in one sector or another of the imperialist economy or in one or another of the mother countries—and vice versa. The ties of reciprocal dependence between the imperialist camp and the Third World, in a world where, generally speaking, economic life is always becoming more internationalized, mean that any serious shock felt in one place will inevitably be felt elsewhere. Even during a normal period, an eight-month strike by copper miners in the United States during 1967–1968 caused a considerable rise in the price of Third World copper, and a sharp drop when it ended. The prices of basic products from the Third World fluctuate erratically not only because of excess or insufficient production but also because of declines or jumps in demand by imperialist factories, etc. The ceaselessly growing interdependence of the two groups of countries creates an ever narrower correlation between the performances of increasingly wider economic areas. The industrialized capitalist world is not a closed field. And the same contradictions which are inherent to that system do not only develop within the imperialist camp but, because of the complexity of the modern world, they affect the entire imperialist sphere of influence. As a result, even those who argue for the preeminence of these internal contradictions cannot confine them to the political space marked out by the borders of the developed countries, where they are especially flagrant.

It is possible, then, to imagine quite legitimately that there exists in the industrialized countries a broad basis for potential agreement between organizations and parties that trace their lineage to Marx and Lenin, even when their analyses of the respective importance of the Third World and the imperialist mother countries at the present moment do not coincide at all points. Their essential common basis is that they all recognize that there are objective connections in all areas between the two halves of the imperialist world, and they also recognize that the seismic tremors that agitate the Third World, and will agitate it further in the future, are at least of very great importance, even if there are those who refuse to call it decisive.

From this point of view, it is politically intolerable to see that, in the programs of so many progressive and Marxist parties or organizations in Western Europe, the Third World only comes up in the last chapter, with other noble causes, as if to make up for an oversight. And to be more specific, how is one to explain the fact that Portugal has been able all these years to continue a classically colonialist armed defense of its domination in Angola, Guinea, and Mozambique, with what amounts to the economic and military assistance of its partners in OECD and the Atlantic Alliance, while not the slightest effort has been made in any of the countries belonging to those organizations to attack this example of imperialist solidarity? How can it not be understood that such efforts would also be useful to the development of the more specifically domestic struggles going on within the countries in question? And, of course, these struggles ought, inevitably, to produce some "fallout" of their own in the Third World, if they achieve some measure of success.

I do not intend to dictate a program of action to anyone, but simply to outline certain general positions that are indispensable because they are dictated by an analysis of the contemporary world and of imperialism today. My main goal is to initiate constructive reflection based on the facts brought to light in the preceding chapters. And I nourish the hope that such reflection will lead directly to this realization: that the worldwide system of imperialism ought to be opposed by a worldwide anti-imperialist front inspired by the theory of Marx and Lenin.

NOTES TO CHAPTER 11

1. *Op. cit.,* p. 108.
2. *"Le Nouvel Imperialisme," Les Temps Modernes,* August–September, 1964.
3. *Politico-Economic Problems. . . . ,* p. 238.
4. Cf. also the interesting study by Paul Sweezy, "Le Proletariat dans le monde d'aujourd'hui," *Tricontinental,* French edition, Maspero, no. 1, 1969.
5. Quoted in Magdoff, *op. cit.,* June 1968.
6. Cf. "Sudisman face à la trahison," in *Tricontinental,* French edition, no. 4, 1968.
7. As reported by *Le Monde,* 2-15-69. (This quotation, which has been repeated differently elsewhere, is probably not a verbatim record of what Rossanda said, but definitely conveys the substance of her remarks.)

LIBRARY OF DAVIDSON COLLEGE

Books on regular loan may be checked out for **two weeks.** Books mu be presented at the Circulation Desk in order to be renewed.

fine of **five cents** a day is charged after date due.

ecial books are subject to special regulations at the discretion of ¹ry staff.